CHINA'S ECONOMIC REFORM

STUDIES ON THE CHINESE ECONOMY

General Editors: Peter Nolan, Lecturer in Economics and Politics, University of Cambridge, and Fellow and Director of Studies in Economics, Jesus College, Cambridge, England; and Dong Fureng, Professor, Chinese Academy of Social Sciences, Beijing, China

This series analyses issues in China's current economic development, and sheds light upon that process by examining China's economic history. It contains a wide range of books on the Chinese economy past and present, and includes not only studies written by leading Western authorities, but also translations of the most important works on the Chinese economy produced within China. It intends to make a major contribution towards understanding this immensely important part of the world economy.

Published titles include:

Derong Chen
CHINESE FIRMS BETWEEN HIERARCHY AND MARKET

Du Runsheng (*edited by Thomas R. Gottschang*)
REFORM AND DEVELOPMENT IN RURAL CHINA

Qimiao Fan and Peter Nolan (*editors*)
CHINA'S ECONOMIC REFORMS

Christopher Findlay, Andrew Watson and Harry X. Wu (*editors*)
RURAL ENTERPRISES IN CHINA

Nicholas K. Menzies
FOREST AND LAND MANAGEMENT IN IMPERIAL CHINA

Ryōshin Minami
THE ECONOMIC DEVELOPMENT OF CHINA

Haiqun Yang
BANKING AND FINANCIAL CONTROL IN REFORMING PLANNED ECONOMIES

Malcolm Warner
THE MANAGEMENT OF HUMAN RESOURCES IN CHINESE INDUSTRY

China's Economic Reform

Shangquan Gao

Forewords by

Sir Alec Cairncross

and

Sir Edward Heath

First published in Great Britain 1996 by
MACMILLAN PRESS LTD
Houndmills, Basingstoke, Hampshire RG21 6XS
and London
Companies and representatives
throughout the world

A catalogue record for this book is available
from the British Library.

ISBN 0–333–61122–5

 First published in the United States of America 1996 by
ST. MARTIN'S PRESS, INC.,
Scholarly and Reference Division,
175 Fifth Avenue,
New York, N.Y. 10010

ISBN 0–312–12034–6

Library of Congress Cataloging-in-Publication Data
Gao, Shangquan.
China's economic reform / Shangquan Gao.
p.   cm. — (Studies on the Chinese economy)
Includes index.
ISBN 0–312–12034–6
1, China—Economic policy—1976–   I. Title.   II. Series.
HC427.92.K383   1996
338.951—dc20   93–38043
                                                        CIP

10   9   8   7   6   5   4   3   2   1
05   04   03   02   01   00   99   98   97   96

Printed in Great Britain by
Ipswich Book Co Ltd, Ipswich, Suffolk

Contents

Introduction

Reform and an open-door policy are the ways to make China powerful and prosperous. Since the adoption of these practices, China has achieved tremendous success and attracted worldwide attention, but it has also confronted difficulties and problems. According to a former foreign premier, 'China's reform is the greatest experiment in human economic history.' Why must China, a country with a population of 1.1 billion, carry out reform and open itself to the outside world? What progress can be achieved by doing so? What difficulties will confront the Chinese people as a consequence? Are there any lessons to be drawn from the experience? These are the kinds of question raised constantly by foreign friends. Professor Gao Shangquan provides comprehensive and systematic response in this, his latest authoritative work, *China's Economic Reform*.

The author of this book is a renowned Chinese economist who has been engaged in the research of reform theory and practice over a long period. As early as 1956 he pointed out with customary insight the defects of the highly centralised economic system, and proposed granting decision-making power to the enterprises (published in the *People's Daily* on 6 December 1956). He is now the vice Minister of the State Commission for Restructuring the Economic System, the president of China Reform and Development institute, the vice president of the Chinese Society of Industry, and the vice president of the Chinese Society of Urban Economy. He is also the vice board chairman of the Research Institute for Comprehensive Exploitation, and a professor Doctorate Supervisor at Beijing University. He participates directly in the planning and instigation of reform.

In this book Professor Gao Shangquan reviews and considers from the theoretical point of view the changes in China's economy and society during the course of reform, as well as assessing from a practical point of view the processes, difficulties and prospects of that reform. From the many data and illustrative examples provided in the book, the reader will readily grasp the fundamentals of China's economic policy, and will gain a vivid, true-to-life picture of the country's reform. In addition, some valuable statistical graphs and an appendix listing the major events of the ten-year economic reforms are included at the back of the book to help further the reader's understanding of China.

Foreword

The Rt Hon. Edward Heath, MBE, MP

With the Soviet Union in economic chaos and many countries in Eastern Europe discovering that the marketplace can be cold and uncomfortable, it is time to reevaluate the Chinese experience of reform. Professor Gao Shangquan gives us an opportunity to do so, not only with Chinese eyes, but through the mind of a minister in the Chinese government.

It is fashionable among pundits of the Hayek–Friedmann school of thought to assert an inflexible relationship between political freedom in the Western sense and economic progress. Few doubt that in the long run people whose minds are set free to unleash creative forces in commerce, industry and indeed agriculture will demand more liberty to speak and to act as they choose. Taiwan under the Kuomintang, Japan with its strict notions of social conformity, and indeed Singapore, all examplars of economic success, show how long a regulated social structure can coexist with economic liberalisation.

We foreigners can only hope that China will succeed in her drive to offer her citizens a decent standard of life – it is not so long ago that she was hard put to satisfy the more limited objective of offering them enough food to eat – and at the same time cope with the strains and tensions let loose by deep economic change. For much of my lifetime China has been ravaged by war and famine, sometimes caused by foreign aggression, sometimes convulsed by social movements that the political system could not contain.

The Chinese government has a narrow path to tread and a difficult pace to measure. To expose the entire economy suddenly to the forces of international competition would invite wholesale economic collapse. Not to open will foster continued backwardness. Failure to pursue economic reform will produce mounting discontent as the people's hopes for material prosperity evaporate. Too fast a pace risks inflation, economic instability and social disorder. Twenty years may bring forth riper fruit than 100 days.

Professor Gao charts the course of China's gradual reform over a decade with an insider's perspective, conscious of the immense problems of governing a nation of 1.1 billion. There can be no doubt of the success of the programme nor of the spectacular rise in incomes over

ix

vast tracts of the country, especially along the coast. This success is Deng Xiaoping's legacy to his country.

And in spite of occasional setbacks and political and human tragedies, there is a consistency in the direction of the reforms begun in 1978. When I first visited China in 1974, two years after my government restored full diplomatic relations with China, it was Vice Premier Deng Xiaoping who received me at the airport and accompanied me to my meetings in 1974 with Chairman Mao and Premier Zhou Enlai and again with Chairman Mao in 1975. Later, he fell temporarily from power. It would have been a bold man who at that time might dare to predict the seminal role he would play in the restoration of China's fortunes. As a new generation of leaders rises to power, his own position in history seems secure after a career marked by personal and political triumphs and periods of personal trauma and political wilderness. What a contrast with the career of Mao Zedong, which ended in tragedy for China and for himself.

The press, including the British press when its opinions are filtered through the kaleidoscope of Hong Kong, is apt to take a simplistic view of Chinese politics. In their vocabulary, decentralisation is good, centralisation bad, no matter whether the original decentralisation was misconceived, delegating power not to enterprises, but to lower tiers of government. Sometimes it is necessary to retrench in order to push ahead later on a sound basis. Ask businessmen what they think of the chaos created in raw material markets by ill-considered reforms; they welcome the restoration of orderly markets.

Nor is it surprising that the central government should sometimes have to make concessions to the poorer central and interior provinces, concerned as they fall farther behind the prosperous East. Given the acerbic debates on regional policy in Britain and the European Community, we need not regard this as anti-reform or a retrograde step, though it may not suit the interests of vocal Hong Kong magnates with investments in the Pearl River delta. The focus of development now moves to Shanghai and the Yangtze delta in an attempt to spread prosperity more widely across the country. Canton has made good use of the special treatment and priority it has received during the first decade of reform, and it is to be hoped that now Shanghai and subsequently other parts of China will in due course make the best of their opportunities.

Those who accuse the government of moving too slowly, in exposing enterprises to competition, reducing overmanning and permitting bankruptcy as a salutary reminder of the need for efficiency, may have a case. But for how long would the people of the Western democracies tolerate high unemployment in the absence of a system of social security? China is working towards the creation of such a system, but this cannot happen overnight.

Likewise analysts have accused the government of attempting to recollectivise agriculture because of its desire to establish cooperatives to provide agricultural services such as access to agricultural machinery and fertiliser to China's peasant smallholders. This is palpable nonsense and it is clear to any reasonable observer that in an intensively cultivated land a framework for cooperation among farmers is essential to the maintenance of irrigation and other services that each tiny unit cannot provide for itself.

Nor can a command economy be transformed at a moment's notice into one regulated by the market. The ideological acrobatics with which Chinese economists attempt to produce new rationale for the reconciliation or fusion of elements of planned and market economics may be regarded by Western friends with wry amusement, but the problems are real enough. In 1988 the attempt to introduce comprehensive reform sent inflation soaring and culminated in tragedy in June 1989. At the same time China's newly introduced panoply of macroeconomic management tools proved utterly ineffective. Attempts to cool down the economy while avoiding a hard landing did not succeed in controlling surging public investment and expenditure. Only after 4 June did the provinces appear sufficiently convinced of the central government's resolve to restore order in the economy to dust off the monetary and fiscal directives from Beijing that had been filed away and ignored. China's macroeconomic management system at that time appeared like a car with brakes that could be applied full on or not at all. Making systems of economic management designed for Europe and the United States work in the Chinese context is a major headache.

Friends of China can help her best by maintaining broad but not uncritical support and striving for a deeper understanding of this ancient culture and the political and economic structure of the nation. Professor Gao's book is a major contribution to this process.

Foreword

Sir Alec Cairncross

Few countries have changed so rapidly as China over the past dozen years. Some of the changes are visible to the naked eye in the sky-scrapers along the main streets, the dress of the pedestrians, the increase in motorised traffic, the improvement in shopping facilities, the revolution in the supply of consumer durables. Other changes can be seen in the statistics of GNP, investment and trade: GNP has more than doubled in a decade, investment has increased even faster and trade has expanded astronomically. But the more significant changes are those that underlie all these: the reforms in the economic system, the greater reliance on market forces, the opening to the rest of the world. Professor Gao Shangquan provides an invaluable guide to the Chinese experience of these changes.

Where China is heading is important to all of us. The momentum behind Chinese growth, and especially behind the growth of Chinese trade, is likely to be maintained. Already we have seen China grow to be one of the leading trading nations; and as industrial growth continues, it is only a matter of time until it is on a par with Japan. There will, however, be many difficult problems along the way.

One that has already arisen is the instability of the economy – an instability that foreign trade could aggravate. As the old methods of direct control are abandoned, new methods of regulating the pressure on the economy have to be devised. Neither fiscal policy nor monetary control is as yet capable of being used successfully for this purpose and expansion has taken place in bursts, with pauses in between, much like the experience of stop–go in Britain.

A second problem is the danger of imbalance between the light industry that has been making the running in recent years and the heavy industry and infrastructural investment that is indispensable to further growth. Expansion in the output of consumer goods puts pressure on the inputs of materials such as steel and heavy chemicals, on fuel and electric power, and on the transport system. All of these are highly capital-intensive and have in the past been financed by government, provincial and central, but especially the latter. In the last decade the central government has surrendered a large part of its share of national resources to provincial governments and enterprises and what it has surrendered has gone largely into light industry. At the same time household savings have grown rapidly, as in other parts of Asia, to form over 30 per cent of income; most of these savings have been deposited with the banks; and the banks in turn have been enabled to lend to industry and to some extent take the place of government in the finance of infrastructure. What is needed, however, is a supply of long-term finance through the issue of bonds and equity capital, and as yet the financial sector in China remains very underdeveloped.

A third problem is the growing disparity in wealth and living standards between the prosperous coastal areas and the more backward interior in various parts of the country. Similarly, there are large differences between the rural areas that ring the big cities and the more remote rural areas that have no adjacent markets with which to lever themselves up.

These are not problems for which an early answer can be found. The Chinese government has proceeded cautiously and has been much more skilful and realistic in its approach to reform than the regimes in the USSR and Eastern Europe. It has the great advantage of having begun with agriculture and securing a large increase in the food supply. It has also helped to breed enterprise and managerial experience by encouraging the development of foreign trade. The measures of reform have been thoroughly debated in advance and, as Professor Gao's survey brings out, they both conform to clear principles and have been introduced step by step in the light of experience.

1 From Planned Economy to Market Economy

It was determined at the Fourteenth Conference of the Communist Party of China that the goal of economic reform was to establish a new socialist market economy. The decision represented a great breakthrough in theoretical research on socialist economies.

WHY CHINA HAS TO BUILD UP A SOCIALIST MARKET ECONOMY

China's former highly centralized plan system served to impede productivity and thus required fundamental reform. The system came into being during the period of the first five-year plan and played an important role in socialist construction, especially in initiating industrialisation. A total of 156 major construction projects were fulfilled under the system, which had effectively concentrated the necessary manpower, materials and financial means for the purpose. With economic development, the growing complexity of the economic structure and people's increasing demands, however, the defects inherent in the system became more and more evident . Firstly, the state adopted too tight a control over enterprises, and the definition of administrative and management powers was rather vague, thus making the enterprises adjuncts of governmental agencies, with no autonomy. Secondly, China rejected the functions of commodity production, the laws of value and the market. Thirdly, egalitarianism existed in distribution, with everybody 'eating from the same big pot'. Finally, the unique ownership and economic structure seriously undermined productivity. Together these systemic defects severely dampened the creativity, initiative and enthusiasm of enterprises and their workers.

Even in the first five-year period these shortcomings had become evident. Enterprises at that time had no autonomy at all. It was reported that a certain enterprise in Shanghai intended to buy some electric fans during a hot summer. By the time the order had gone through the approval procedures, with eleven authorities stamping their seals, the summer had already passed. How could a system with such a high

1

level of centralisation meet the needs of modern economic development? At that time I was working in the No. 1 Ministry of Machinery Industry, and wrote an investigation report entitled 'The Enterprise Should Be Granted a Degree of Autonomy' (published in the *'People's Daily'*, 6 December 1956), stating my views on these defects. Some people disagreed with me, claiming that enterprises would become uncontrollable if granted autonomous power. It would, the critics stated, represent revisionism of the kind seen in former Yugoslavia. That is, they connected enterprise autonomy with the concept of revisionism. This clearly shows that the perception of the enterprise as an adjunct of government agencies was not only deeply rooted in the system but was instilled in people's minds at that time. Under such conditions it was impossible to give free rein to enterprises' and workers' enthusiasm, creativity and initiative. All that had been rigidly suppressed by the highly centralised system, administrative decrees and approval procedures at various levels.

Although various reforms had been instituted prior to the Third Session of the Eleventh Congress of the CPC they were mainly confined to the realm of power re-distribution among different agencies. Without substantial changes the system continued to move in a vicious circle: it was lifeless when controlled, but disorder occurred when it was de-controlled, prompting another round of control and decontrol, and so on. Only after the Third Session did we explore a way out of this predicament, namely to carry out fundamental reforms instead of merely amending the original system. As Deng Xiaoping stated, to develop productivity it first of all has to be emancipated. This meant abandoning the old system's constraints on productivity and fundamentally restructuring all those elements that were no longer appropriate to, or actively hindered the development of productivity.

Looking back on the reforms of the past fourteen years we can clearly see that, be it at the level of region, sector or enterprise, where market forces played a prominent role there was greater economic vitality and faster development. With regard to the regions, the Pearl River Delta enjoyed the quickest economic development in the country. Guangdong Province exceeded other areas by 3 per cent, whereas the Delta area recorded even faster development than the province as a whole – by 2–4 per cent. What is more, the area has averaged an annual 14–16 per cent growth since the beginning of reform. With a relatively strong economic foundation, the area even boasts having caught up with 'the four dragons'. In addition, Suzhou, Wuxi and Changzhou in the Yantyze River Delta have also witnessed rapid development. Among the reasons for the transformation of these areas one important factor is the significant role played by the market, which accounts for over 90 per cent of the total economy, and which encourages flexibility and productivity. In terms of sectors, once price control was lifted, commodities such as garments and farm produce underwent on increase both in production and variety. Take peanuts as an example. In the past just 0.5 Jin (equal to 250 grammes) was allowed per family for the Spring Festival. Now with price liberalisation people can buy peanuts at any time.

Finally, a group of enterprises boasting rapid development and high efficiency have come into being, among which there are state-owned, collective, foreign-funded, township and private operations. One feature common to them all is that they have taken the lead in market competition. Take the enterprise producing a tonic drink labelled 'Wahaha'. It used to be a school-run factory with a floor space of just ten square metres and 140 000 yuan worth of investment. It now has a turnover of 250 million yuan and 40 million yuan profit – much more than that achieved by most medium and large enterprises. What is the reason for their success? It is as simple as this: the enterprise does not rely on the state to allocate command-planned task nor on the supply of fixed-price materials, but instead on its adaptation to the market. It entered the market and achieved tremendous success by taking bold intiatives and grasping the opportunities available. From this we can see that the market mechanism is able to stimulate enterprises into creativity and thus realise their great potential. It has proved to have been correct to stress the market role, to undertake market-oriented reform and pursue the goal of a socialist market economy.

To resolve certain profound conflicts in economic development China must persevere with this market economy. Although the Chinese economy has now entered a stage of rapid development, structural adjustment is comparatively slow and efficiency rather low, representing a profound impediment to economic development. To resolve these problems China should no longer depend on the old method, but instead deepen the process of reform. In the past war was declared every year on superfluous construction, excess production and unnecessary imports, yet with little effect. The central reason for such failure is the systemic defect that fails to allocate resources in a rational way. Take mobile production as an example. There are over 120 auto plants and 620 assembly factories in the country. The reason for this situation is, on the one hand, that pricing is irrational, severely deviating from the law of value. Consequently whoever runs the auto project will earn enormous profits. On the other hand the enterprise is not responsible for its own profits and losses; instead investment and losses are covered by the state. I have discussed this issue with foreign experts and officials on many occasions. Japanese experts once told me that in Japan there was superfluous automobile production at the beginning, but mainly in the field of components, unlike in China where it is in assembly, that is, the production line. However, in the case of Japan production is solely an activity of the enterprise, which has to shoulder responsibility for its own profits and losses. This makes the enterprise extremely cautious in its decision making since it must take into account market demand and therefore make careful judgements. In China, however, enterprises act primarily out of consideration for state investment and to upgrade themselves in terms of scale. It follows that, without a substantial reform of the system, these deep-seated problems will remain.

The market economy is also a requirement of the open-door policy and entry into the world market. It has become increasingly apparent that the world economy is tending towards greater internationalisation, corporatisation and integration. According to World Bank statistics there are now 35 000 multinational corporations with assets of 1.6 trillion US dollars, whose volume of trade accounts for one third of the world total. Consequently they have become the main organisers of economic activity, as many trading activities are carried out wholly among themselves or between their parent and daughter companies.

China intends to modernise, to enter into the world market and to participate in international trade and competition. To this end the previous centralised system must be transformed into a market economy system. If China remains firmly within the embrace of the old system, it will never cross the threshold of the world market, let alone participate in its competition. It is analogous to the Olympic Games, which makes tournaments possible only under unified rules. At present China wishes to resume its status in GATT, which means abiding by the unified rules of world trade. In April 1993 I attended the International Seminar on Comparison of Economic Systems, sponsored by the United Nations with the participation of delegates from fourteen countries, including China, Vietnam, Laos, the Commonwealth of Independent States and some Eastern European and African countries. Nobody at the meeting considered that the centralised plan system was any good, or viable for the future. There was a consensus that the system is no longer suited to the development of productivity and thus needs to be changed. Of course ideas differed as to which direction such changes should go, since different countries may prefer different ways and methods. The delegates thought highly of China's economic reform and regarded it as a success for bringing about rapid economic development, strengthening national power and improving people's standard of living.

In a nutshell, it has been necessary and appropriate to advance the idea of a socialist market economy. Over a fourteen year period, first the material foundations were laid down, resulting in prodigious economic development, an enrichment of commodities and increased production capacity. Second, following public disputes over the issue of 'practice as the sole criterion for examining truth', the institution of reform and adoption of an open-door policy in the wake of the Third Session of the Eleventh Congress of the CPC, the people's commitment has greatly improved and the Party's basic lines have become instilled in their minds. Consequently the ideological basis for the practice of the socialist market economy has been established. Third, following the fourteen-year period of reform, the command-plan system has declined greatly and in its stead the guide plan and market regulation have played an increasing role. In industrial production, the command plan has accounted for only 11.6 per cent, while 70 per cent of enterprises' raw materials supply and product marketing has been accomplished through market regulation. Reform has enabled significant steps to be made towards the market economy in these years; in other words, it has blazed a new trail and provided necessary experience in the operational of the socialist market economy, which will in turn promote further economic development, deepen economic reform and establish the economy on a higher level.

THE SOCIALIST MARKET ECONOMY: A SIGNIFICANT BREAKTHROUGH IN THEORY AND PRACTICE

What is the market economy? And what is the socialist market economy? Ideas concerning this issue vary both at home and abroad. The topics are the subject of a great deal of discussion and theoretical exploration at present. According to my understanding, the definition of the market economy is meeting the objective needs of socialized production and an internationalized market, and conceiving the market as an economic operation and form of management for an optimized allocation of resources. The socialist market economy is a market economy within the context of the socialist system, effecting the operation of the market under socialist conditions.

The notion of the socialist market economy is a great breakthrough and development in comparison to the planned commodity economy.

It was clearly stated in the 'CPC Central Committee's Decision on Economic System Reform' in 1984 that the socialist economy is a planned commodity economy based on public ownership. From then onward, the commodity economy has assumed a legitimate status in the country and thereby found acceptance among party members. As is well known, consensus was achieved only after much difficulty, since some people would not accept the word 'profit', not to mention the existence of a commodity economy. It should be recognised that the major achievements of reform are attributable in great part to this guide-line. The commodity economy will change naturally into a market economy when fully developed; and in my view the socialist market economy will exist as a continuance and development of the planned commodity economy. By 'continuance' here, we mean that both commodity and market economies are indispensable, because fundamental to each is the notion that the division of labour in society and the means of production are distinct realms of interest. The market economy is the result of the development of the commodity economy at a certain stage. Lenin once pointed out that where there is a division of labour in society and also commodity production, there exists a 'market'. The market developed in keeping with the growth in society of the division of labour and commodity production. This indicates that the market is closely connected with division in the labour process and commodity production rather than with the social system per se. So the market is by no means specific to capitalism. By using the word 'development', we acknowledge that the idea of the socialist market economy has a precise and scientific basis in theory; it also enables us to concentrate our reforms on the defects in the old system and clarify their objectives in practice; and, finally, the term is one that is especially acceptable to the world as a description of our economic transition and therefore conveys a more favourable and positive status on our policy of opening up.

The essence of the socialist market economy is that public ownership forms its basis. Some people claim that the market economy is equivalent to privatisation and capitalisation, coupled with the ending of Communist Party leadership. I consider their arguments to be groundless. First, the market economy is the product of human civilisation rather than an outgrowth of capitalism. Comrade Deng Xiaoping has already made clear that the market economy does not equate with capitalism any more than the planned economy equates with socialism. Similar though they are in terms of operational method and mechanism, the two differ in essence. The socialist market economy is based on public ownership while the other is based on private ownership. Of course, the socialist market economy does not have public ownership as its sole component. In its development, the ownership structure will also undergo certain changes as the economic forms of different types of ownership overlap and play their own roles. But it goes without saying that public ownership must play a dominant role. As to the proportion occupied by other types of ownership, this should be settled in accordance with the most suitable structure for the development of productivity, or with the three criteria set by Comrade Deng – that it should promote the development of productivity, the strengthening of national power and improve people's standard of living. Second, in the light of domestic and international experience, the key factor in the success of public ownership is whether or not it can function under the pressure of market competition and maintain a flexible economic mechanism. In one of its publications, entitled 'Factors for the Success of Public-owned Industrial Enterprises', the World Bank cites data from *Fortune* concerning the 500 top enterprises in the world. Of these, 71 per cent are public enterprises whose assets, turnover, profits and employees account for 20 per cent of the total. The World Bank concludes that the main reason for their success is market pressure and the existence of a flexible mechanism. Public enterprises are well able to succeed in business; likewise private ones can fail. Ever since the reform, a number of state-owned enterprises in our country have shown their vitality and accomplished rapid development. As such, they represent convincing evidence for the argument. In conclusion, then, the market economy does not simply mean privatisation; it can succeed on the basis of public ownership as well.

THE BASIC VISION OF THE SOCIALIST MARKET ECONOMY

Establishing a modern enterprise system, making the enterprise integral to the market in a real sense.

First, all activities of the enterprise should centre on the market, thereby enabling the enterprise to benefit from the opportunities of the market and at the same time be an element in its operation.

Second, the separation of government and enterprise, and that of ownership and management rights, should be effected so as to rid the enterprise of its status as a government subsidiary and constitute it as a real entity responsible for its own management.

Third, the enterprise should establish profit as its main objective in business, thus assuming the responsibility for profits and losses and exercising independence.

Fourth, the enterprise should be exposed to fair competition in the market, and thereby undergo self-development and learn to survive through its own performance.

Establishing an open, unified and ordered market system so that all spheres of production can enter the market.

First, it is necessary to build up a modern market system with the commodity market as its foundation, the capital market as its hub and other markets connected with production playing ancillary roles. Since these latter markets are clearly underdeveloped, we should attach particular importance to the development of markets in capital, labour, technical expertise and real estate.

Second, it is important to accelerate the pace of reform and to set up a pricing mechanism based on market forces. Price is the core element of the market and the indicator and stabilising element of the market's operation. The fluctuation of prices reflects demand and supply in the market, by which the law of value is realized. The pricing mechanism should become increasingly market-oriented, eventually leading to the situation where the state regulates the market, the market decides the price and the price allocates resources. Aside from monopolised commodities, scarce resources and some public works, other commodities and the labour force should be free of price control, and instead should be priced by the market or by the enterprise.

Establishing a macroeconomic management system appropriate to the socialist market economy and to precipitate the transformation of governmental functions

To adopt the market economy is not to deprive the government of its functions and planning role in the economy, but rather to give greater scope in a more effective way to such functions and planning. The market economy is not a complete panacea; it has its own limitations and defects. Indeed, some states have increased government intervention in the economy since the Second World War in a bid to make up for the market's shortcomings and to correct certain defects. The purpose of such efforts is to effect an optimal allocation of resources and to maximise effectiveness. Take the case of Germany. The goals of macro-management in its social market economy are: (i) currency stability; (ii) full employment; (iii) stability in foreign exchange; (iv) proper economic growth. The government has played an active role in these four areas rather than opting to control enterprises. Japan and South Korea have also done well in this respect.

What is more, it is a crucial stage in the establishment of the socialist market economy to build up a macro-management system, with the functions of government transformed and its organisation simplified. But how will the government transform its functions and in what direction? In my opinion, it should first of all switch from exercising direct to indirect control; second, it should relinquish control over the micro-aspect in favour of a macro-approach; and third, it should cease the examination and approval of economic activities, projects and allocation of capital and materials, and adopt a programming, coordinating, supervising and servicing role by means of economic leverage. That is to say, we should leave to the market and enterprise those matters that they are best able to handle, leaving the government to manage affairs beyond their scope.

Building up a social security system fit for the socialist market economy

The socialist market economy should not merely aim to be effective, but should also strive to maintain fairness and justice in society. To this end it is necessary to speed up reform of the social security system to ensure the successful functioning of the reformed economic system. The introduction of an enterprise insurance system will guarantee the employees of failed enterprises daily necessities. In addition, reform of the systems of retirement pension, medical insurance and housing will also be undertaken.

Establishing market discipline and a legal framework appropriate to the socialist market system

One of the major tasks of the socialist market economy is to institute market discipline and to rationalise the legal and supervisory systems. Legislation to enable this must be introduced soon. Without a sound system of supervision in place, the enterprise, though actually suffering losses, can fake profits by fraudulent 'technical manipulation' and as a result may even win praise, despite the seriously harmful effects of such practices. Efficient operation of the socialist market economy depends upon the absence of unfair competition and the keeping of market discipline through various laws and regulations.

Deng has stressed the need to 'change our ideas'. By this he means that we should adopt new ways of thinking, not argue over whether one measure is to be attributed to 'socialism' or 'capitalism'. The most important criterion in evaluating the correctness of reform is whether it is helpful to the development of productivity, to the strengthening of national power and the improvement of people's standard of living. As there is nothing in our stock of experience to guide the present efforts to build a form of socialism with Chinese characteristics and on the basis of a socialist market economy, it is therefore necessary to innovate boldly and to experiment. Thus, by following the guidelines set by Comrade Deng, we should further deepen our reform process and blaze a new trail for the establishment of the socialist market economy.

2 The Achievements and Problems of China's Economic Reform

Over the past decade China has instituted a series of reforms in both rural and urban areas, involving everything from micro-economic mechanisms to macro-management systems, from internal rationalisation to the open-door policy extending from the economic base to the superstructure. The original economic structure has in large part been dismantled and a new structure is now taking shape. On the whole, reform has been a great success but it requires consolidation. The important task now facing those engaged in theoretical research into economic restructuring, as well as the officials responsible for its implementation, is to develop a clear-headed understanding of the present stage of reform and to study in a thoroughgoing way the characteristics of the crucial transition period so as to be able to propose further measures for deepening the overall reform process.

The major changes in economic structure effected through the implementation of reform and the open-door policy are as follows:

(1) Popularly owned enterprises have begun to transform themselves into independent commodity producers; and managers with the power of decision making in the original organisations are taking up positions within administrative organisations.

(2) Fully nationalised ownership has given way to various forms of shared interest with a majority public component.

(3) The mechanism of economic operation has begun to be transformed from that of mandatory allocation and distribution to a combination of planned economy and market regulation.

(4) The form of economic policy making has changed from the former centralised strategic command system, with its lack of distinction between the responsibilities of the state and the enterprises, to one involving a redefinition of governmental functions and the introduction of multi-level responsibility.

(5) The principle of social provision has begun to shift from the former egalitarian system – everyone 'eating from a big common pot' – to a variety of forms that operate on the basis of distribution according to contribution.

(6) The former principle of economic association based on a vertical division among government agencies has given way to a series of lateral relations.

(7) The style of economic management has been gradually transformed from a direct to an indirect practice.

(8) Employment policy and personnel management in the enterprises, based on the maintenance of a permanent workforce, and a system of commissioned cadres, has given way to the introduction of a competitive element, to the practice of open recruitment and to the optimum organisation of labour.

(9) China's economic relations with other countries are no longer determined by the long-standing closed-door policy, but follow an open style of economic activity that allows full participation in the system of international trade and cooperation.

In summary, China's economic structure has undergone a transition from a product economy to a new system founded on the commodity market.

The main architect of the reform and open-door policies was Deng Xiaoping, who applied Marxist dialectic and historical materialism in a concrete analysis of the gap between China and the developed countries. He proposed a comprehensive modernisation plan that visualised doubling the gross national product between 1980 and the end of the century, an improved standard of living for all, and catching up with the world's advanced countries by the middle of the next century. He also indicated the means whereby this trans-century task might be realised, initiating the general policies of reform and opening up to the outside world that will lead the people of China to create a new phase of socialist advance.

The Party and the government are exercising strong leadership of reform process. The major elements – both the fundamental steps and the experiments – are decided collectively by the Party Central Committee and the State Council, and are carried out by the Party committees and governments at all levels. Under such firm leadership, the process of reform and opening up is guaranteed to develop healthily along the socialist road. For these policies represent not the denial of socialism but its self-improvement. Through their introduction we have decisively regulated the productive forces and production relations; we have moderated the contradictions between the economic base and superstructure, and we have regulated relations between central government and the regions, between the state and enterprises, between the state, collectives and individuals, we have aroused initiative and creativeness in all sectors; and we have instilled vigour and vitality into the national economy. With all these achievements secure, our socialist foundation is greatly strengthened.

In the course of economic restructuring we have adhered to the principle of the public ownership of the means of production, and to the principle of distribution according to work in the field of provision. With regard to rural reforms, we adhered to the collective ownership of the land and of the basic means of production when we introduced the family contract system with remuneration linked to output. We have developed a system of cooperative agricultural servicing and other large-scale projects adapted to local conditions; these have greatly advanced the collective economy based on townships and village enterprises. According to the statistics the number of township and village enterprises engaged in industry, commerce, transportation and construction increased from 1.425 million in 1980 to 1.59 million in 1988, an increase of 11.6 per cent. The number of employees increased by 63.1 per cent, from 29.99 million to 48.93 million. The total receipts of village enterprises increased from 59.61 billion yuan to 423.13 billion yuan, a 6.1-fold increase. The ratio of the output value of village enterprises to the gross rural product increased from 42.9 per cent in 1985 to 54.5 per cent in 1988, which exceeded the ratio of the agriculture-based (crops and livestock) family contract sector where remuneration is linked to output.

With regard to urban reforms, attention has been focused on regulation of the relationship between state and enterprise; extension of the decision-making power of producers and management of the public-owned enterprises; increasing the responsibility of enterprises; recognition of the economic benefits of their relative independence; promoting the further development of enterprises toward self-management, self-development, and assumption of responsibility for their own profits and losses; encouraging the establishment of a specialised division of labour and forms of cooperation among publicly owned enterprises; pursuing lateral economic association and ensuring the optimum organisation of elements of production; and developing various kinds of integrated corporations and enterprise groups. All these measures help consolidate and develop the public-ownership economy.

Given the necessity of such a process of consolidation and strengthening, and in accordance with the characteristics of the first stage of socialism, the development of the individual economy, the private economy and 'three capitals' enterprises will be encouraged within the scope stipulated by the state. These economies are seen as useful supplements to the socialist public-ownership economy. The structure of ownership is currently changing from full public ownership to a variety of forms of ownership that maintain the public share as the principal part. The development of the above-mentioned economies does not challenge the foundation of our public-ownership economy. According to the statistics, of the total amount of fixed assets investment in the whole society, notwithstanding a drop in investment in public-ownership units from 81.5 per cent in 1981 to 76.9 per cent in 1988 (investment in units of popular ownership dropped from 69.5 per cent to 62.5 per cent, investment in units of collective ownership rose from 12 per cent to 14.4 per cent), public ownership still holds the majority interest. Private investment by both urban and rural residents rose from 18.5 per cent to 23.1 per cent, of which housing investment formed the principal part. In 1988, the combined value of the industrial output of popularly owned and collectively owned enterprises accounted for 93 per cent of the total value of national industrial output (the popularly owned enterprises accounted for 56.6 per cent, the collective ones, 36.4 per cent); thus public ownership retained the absolute dominant position. The output value of non-publicly-owned enterprises (including individual, private and 'three capitals' sectors) only accounted for 7 per cent. The combined turnover of popularly owned and collective enterprises accounted for 73.8 per cent of the total volume of retail sales (the popularly owned enterprises accounting for 39.5 per cent; the collective sector, 34.4 per cent); the turnover of individuals, both farmers and non-farmers, accounted for 25.8 per cent; Sino-foreign joint ventures and other sectors accounted for only 9.4 per cent.

In the sphere of distribution, we adhere to the principle of distribution according to work. Our reforms in this regard stress the transformation of egalitarianism and rejection of the principle of 'eating from a big common pot'. The focus is on the reform of the fixed-wage system operative in the enterprises. In some regions, and in some sectors of enterprises, various systems have been tried out – such as the bonus system, the floating wage system, the structural wage system, the responsibility-for-your-product (output value) wage system, the piecework system, and the responsibility for the total-amount of-your-wages system, and so on. Since 1987, we have been carrying out, countrywide, a kind of benefit-wage system which links enterprises' wages with the tax and profits turned over to the state. In 1989, we further improved the means of linking the total amount of wages of an enterprise to its economic performance. The state decided that enterprises' wages should be managed on different levels. The provinces, the autonomous regions, the municipalities, the cities with distinct plans, and the departments, were all required to link the total wages of the enterprises of each entire area or whole department to their economic performance. Within the scope of the state's authorised basic wage and the floating ratio (economic performance ± 1 per cent of the total amount of wages, generally ± 0.5–0.75 per cent), and according to the specific conditions that pertain, each area and department can adopt different methods of wage distribution in different enterprises. At the same time, certain forms of non-labour-based income distribution, such as bond interests, bond dividends and profits from private capital investment, emerged in society; however, these do not make up the principal part of our system of social distribution, accounting for only a very small percentage of staff and workers' income.

Reform has promoted the development of the productive forces, distinctly improved national economic strength and enhanced people's living conditions. During the ten-year period of reform we have aroused the enthusiasm of the mass of farmers, staff and workers, which made it possible for our economic development to enter a particularly vigorous period, leading to a rapid strengthening of national power. From 1953 to 1978 the average annual growth rate of the country's gross national product was 6.1 per cent, and in the ten years from 1978 to 1988 it reached 9.6 per cent, an increase of 3.5 per cent over that of the period before reform (1953–78), and 6.9 per cent higher than the world economic growth rate of 2.7 per cent over the same period. Per-capita national income from 1952 to 1978 increased from 104 yuan to 315 yuan, an increase of 211 yuan in a period of twenty-six years; in the ten years from 1978 to 1988 per-capita national income increased from 315 yuan to 1081 yuan, an increase of 766 yuan in ten years.

Investment in fixed assets and total accumulation over the ten years also increased sharply. From 1950 to 1978 the grand total of investment in fixed assets of popularly owned enterprises was 772.2 billion yuan; from 1979 to 1988 the grand total reached 1381.4 billion yuan – the latter ten-year investment representing an increase of 78.9 per cent over the previous twenty-nine-year period. Fixed-asset investment in 1950 was 1.134 billion yuan while in 1978 it was 66.872 billion yuan, in 1988, 276.276 billion yuan, and in 1989, 251 billion yuan. Total accumulation for the twenty-six years from 1952 to 1978 was 1202.9 billion yuan, while that of the ten years from 1979 to 1988 reached to 2088.3 billion yuan, an increase of 73.6 per cent over the preceding twenty-six-year period.

The major changes effecting the national economy over the ten-year reform are shown in Tables 2.1–2.4.

Table 2.1 Growth of the Chinese Economy, 1978–88

	1978	1987	1988	1978–88 Annual growth rate (%)	Growth rate of 1988 compared with 1987 (%)
Total population (million)	962.59	1080.7	1096.1	1.3	1.4
Labour force (million)	401.52	527.8	543.3	3.0	2.9
of which staff and workers	94.99	132.1	136.0	3.7	3.0
Gross domestic product (billion yuan)	684.6	2308.1	2925.9	11.2	15.3
Gross agricultural product	139.7	467.6	561.8	6.2	3.2
Gross industrial product	423.7	1381.3	1810.5	12.8	20.7
Light industrial product	182.6	665.6	895.0	14.9	22.6
Heavy industrial product	241.1	715.7	915.5	10.9	18.8
National income (billion yuan)	301.0	936.1	1153.3	9.3	11.5
Gross national product (billion yuan)	358.8	1135.1	1385.3	9.6	11.2
Revenue (billion yuan)	112.1	236.9	258.8	8.7	9.2
Expenditure (billion yuan)	111.1	244.9	266.8	9.2	9.0
Fixed assets investment (billion yuan)	66.9	229.8	269.5	14.9	17.3
Cargo turnover (billion ton/km)	982.9	2222.9	2349.5	9.1	5.7
Handling capacity of coastal ports (million ton)	198.3	373.0	412.7	7.6	12.7
Total volume of post and tele-communications services (billion yuan)	1.2	3.9	4.9	11.7	26.0

Total volume of retail sales (billion yuan)	155.9	582.0	744.0	16.9	27.8
Total volume of exports and imports (US$ billion)	20.6	82.7	102.8	17.4	24.4
Exports	9.8	39.4	47.5	17.2	20.5
Imports	10.9	43.2	55.3	17.6	27.9
Output of major products					
Cloth (billion metre)	11.0	17.3	17.6	4.8	1.8
Machine-made paper and cardboard (million ton)	4.4	11.4	11.0	9.7	−3.3
Coal (million ton)	618.0	928.0	950.0	4.4	2.0
Generated electricity (billion kw.hr)	256.6	497.3	539.0	7.7	8.4
Crude petroleum (million ton)	104.1	134.1	136.9	3.1	2.0
Steel (million ton)	31.8	56.3	59.2	6.4	5.2
Finished steel products (million ton)	22.1	43.7	47.0	7.8	7.1
Cement (million ton)	65.2	186.3	203.4	12.0	9.2
Grain (million ton)	304.8	402.0	394.1	2.6	−2.6
Cotton (million ton)	2.2	4.2	4.2	6.7	−2.1
Oils (million ton)	5.2	15.3	13.2	9.7	−13.6
Sugar (million ton)	23.8	55.5	61.9	10.0	11.5
Pork, beef, mutton (million ton)	8.6	19.9	21.9	9.9	10.5
Aquatic products (million ton)	4.7	9.6	10.6	8.6	11.1

Table 2.2   State's budgetary receipts and nation-wide extra-budgetary fund receipts (billion yuan)

	State budgetary receipts	Local extra-budgetary funds	Extra-budgetary funds of adminis-trative institutions	Extra-budgetary funds of state-owned enterprises and responsible institutions	Total extra-budgetary receipts	
					Yuan	Per cent
1978	112.112	3.109	6.341	25.261	34.711	31.0
1979	106.796	3.994	6.866	34.425	45.285	42.4
1980	104.222	4.085	7.444	44.211	55.740	53.5
1981	101.638	4.130	8.490	47.487	60.107	59.1
1982	108.394	4.527	10.115	65.632	80.274	74.1
1983	121.116	4.979	11.388	80.401	96.768	79.9
1984	146.705	5.523	14.252	99.073	118.848	81.0
1985	183.716	4.408	23.322	125.273	153.003	83.3
1986	218.452	4.320	29.421	139.989	173.730	79.5
1987	272.242	4.461	35.841	162.578	202.880	89.7

* After deduction of foreign loans.

Table 2.3   Changes in world ranking of output of Chinese major industrial and agricultural products

	1949		1980		1988	
	Output	Rank	Output	Rank	Output	Rank
Steel (million ton)	16	26	37.12	5	59.18	4
Coal (million ton)	32	9	620.00	3	947.00	1
Crude petroleum (million ton)	12	27	105.95	6	136.87	5
Generated electricity (billion kw.hr)	43	25	300.60	6	539.00	4
Grain (million ton)	11	2	320.56	1	355.46	1
Meat (million ton)	44	3	12.10	3	21.93	1
Cotton (million ton)	111	4	2.71	2	4.16	1

Reform has distinctly improved urban and rural living conditions. During the ten years of reform, ignoring price increases, farmers' per capita net income increased by an average 11.5 per cent, and urban residents' per capita income increased by an average 6.5 per cent per annum. Newly built housing space amounted to eight billion per square metres, and urban and rural savings increased from 21.1 billion yuan

Table 2.4 Total volume of exports and imports, 1950–88

	Total volume of exports and imports (Billion RMB)	Exports	Imports	Total volume of exports and imports (US$ billion)	Exports	Imports
1950	4.15	2.02	2.13	1.13	0.55	0.58
1952	6.46	2.71	3.75	1.94	0.82	1.12
1957	10.45	5.45	5.00	3.10	1.60	1.50
1962	8.09	4.71	3.38	2.66	1.49	1.17
1965	11.84	6.31	5.53	4.25	2.23	2.02
1970	11.29	5.68	5.61	4.59	2.26	2.33
1978	35.50	16.76	18.74	20.64	9.75	10.89
1979	45.46	21.17	24.29	29.33	13.66	15.67
1980	56.38	27.24	29.14	37.82	18.27	19.55
1981	73.53	36.76	36.77	44.02	22.01	22.01
1982	77.13	41.38	35.75	41.60	22.32	19.28
1983	86.01	43.83	42.18	43.61	22.23	21.39
1984	120.10	58.05	62.05	53.55	26.14	27.41
1985	206.67	80.89	125.78	69.60	27.35	42.25
1986	358.04	208.21	149.83	73.85	30.94	42.91
1987	308.42	147.00	161.42	82.65	39.44	43.21
1988	382.20	176.76	205.44	102.79	47.54	55.25
Total of the 1st 5-year Plan period	48.86	23.37	25.49	14.26	6.82	7.44
Total of the 2nd 5-year Plan period	57.81	30.33	27.48	17.66	9.08	8.58
Total of the 3rd 5-year Plan period	30.16	16.85	13.31	10.62	5.79	4.83
Total of the 4th 5-year Plan period	56.76	29.90	26.86	21.43	11.07	10.36
Total of the 5th 5-year Plan period	107.10	55.07	52.03	51.44	26.11	25.33
Total of the 6th 5-year Plan period	191.00	92.62	98.38	116.03	56.13	59.90
	563.44	260.91	302.53	252.39	120.05	132.34

in 1978 to 380.2 billion yuan at the end of 1988.

Table 2.5 shows the improvement in people's material circumstances during the ten years.

The ten-year reform proved a great success, yet inevitably there were mistakes. For instance, when we drew up the reform plan and began its implementation we lacked a thorough understanding of national conditions and strength; we were over-anxious for quick results. In the course of economic restructuring we overlooked a crucial detail: in placing an emphasis on stimulating the micro-level, we overlooked macro-regulation and control. The various reform measures therefore lacked key components, which prevented us achieving the expected results. Moreover, the economy and the regulatory system could not make up the ground. Therefore, we must assess our experience, uphold what is successful and correct what is faulty, and strive to make up for any insufficiency; only in this way can we advance confidently down the road of reform.

We now face a crucial stage in the process of improving the economic environment, regenerating the economic order and deepening reform. The chief characteristics of this stage can be summarised as follows.

(1) Friction between the new and old structures has increased during the transitional period.

Due to the coexistence of new and old systems, certain structural defects and management failings are unavoidable; a consequent increase in friction between the interested groups is to be expected. Such problems add to the difficulty of extending the process of reform. Currently the old structure is being converted into a new one, although in some respects it continues to function; for its part, the new structure is beginning to develop but has not yet established itself in the dominant position, nor have we yet built the new socialist commodity economy. Therefore, in those areas of overlap where the functions of both new and old structures are weak, some people are bound to avail themselves of the loopholes and indulge in illegal activities. In past years we have practised a two-tier pricing system for certain products that has played a positive role in stimulating production and increasing supply, but the negative effect of the policy was that it enabled some people to take advantage of the planned and non-planned prices by engaging in fraudulent buying and selling in order to extract exorbitant profits.

(2) The reform has now progressed beyond a dependence on individual

Table 2.5 Improvements in living standards

	1978	1980	1987	1989
Farmers' average per capita net income (sample survey) (yuan)	134	191	463	545
Staff and worker's average wages (yuan)	615	762	1459	1747
Per capita income in cities and towns (sample survey (yuan)	316	439	916	1119
Average per capita dwelling area (sample survey) (square metre)				
Urban	4.2	5.0	8.6	8.8
Rural	8.1	9.4	16.0	16.6
Urban and rural savings at end of year (billion yuan)	21.1	40.1	307.3	380.7
Average per capita deposit balance (yuan)	22.0	47.0	284.4	347.3
Number of TV sets per 100 population	0.3	0.9	10.7	13.2
Number of radios per 100 population	7.8	12.1	24.1	23.9
Daily newspaper circulation per 100 population	3.2	3.9	5.2	5.2
Per capita purchase of magazines and periodicals	4.8	5.8	8.2	8.2
Hospital beds per 10 000 persons	19.4	20.2	22.3	22.8
Physicians per 10 000 persons	10.8	11.7	13.8	14.8
Number of dependants per employed person	2.1	1.8	1.8	1.8
Retail trade, catering trade and service trade				
Number of networks (including individuals) per 10 000 population	13	20.5	111.6	115.4
Number of labourers (including self-employment) per 10 000 population	63	93.9	261.6	275.0

breakthroughs to a phase of extensive development, and overall reform is now required.

As regards the names of advancing reform, we have in previous years depended on isolated breakthroughs and gradual percolation from the lower to the upper levels. Now we are in need of complete programmes and across-the-board development plans to be transmitted from the upper levels to the lower. If reform is not programmatic, the positive and negative effects of a given measure will cancel each other out, and substantive development will be hard to sustain. For instance, it is impossible to deal with the issue of price in any simple way when setting about price reform. It is necessary to consider improving the pricing structure, to have a firm grasp of the objective demands of economic relations, to assess the limit of the state's financial burden, the capacity of enterprises to assimilate, as well as the masses' economic and psychological thresholds. What is more, we need a comprehensive reform wherein price restructuring acts as a mechanism, complementing and correcting the enterprises' own mechanisms and building up a market order. At the same time as we give priority to economic development, it is at once necessary to safeguard political stability and unity. Thus, although we are committed to creating a new economic mechanism through price reform, the difficulties and risks involved in this process must be reduced as much as possible. This undertaking is unquestionably a bold venture in social engineering; consequently skilful leadership and sensitive implementation are demanded.

(3) The difficulty of extending the process of reform increases the deeper the reform penetrates.

We assessed the reforms in terms of difficulty or ease of introduction; the course we then took was that of gradual progression from the easiest to the most advanced and from the least to the most far-reaching. For example, early reforms included the extension of enterprises' power to manage, reduction in the rate of taxation, and an end to the nonretention of profits – changes likely to bring tangible benefits to every member of society. Reform of the deeper levels, however, involves an overall regime of regulation that will unavoidably damage particular interests. For instance, we are intent on carrying forward, in a positive but cautious manner, reform of both prices and wages – reform that will certainly involve regulating of the conduct of much deeper levels. This is a more difficult and risky undertaking, but there is no way of avoiding it. The reason for the painful reversal in the reform programmes of some socialist countries can be found in this exacting issue of price. If we do not carry price reform forward in good time, the foundation of the new economic structure will not be solid, and we shall fail to hit our target of attaining the level of advancement of a medium-developed country by the middle of next century. As it stands at present, the risks and the opportunities for success are equal, and people are increasingly becoming interested in reform. However, the gap between people's expectations of the benefits to be gained from reform and the actual results is wide. This has led to disappointment and a lack of confidence. We must therefore actively canvass for reform and take the initiative to inform public opinion, thereby enabling people to gain a clear understanding of the state of reform and its achievements. We must also analyse in a practical and realistic way the difficulties and problems that exist, and try to gain an in-depth understanding in the drive for reform. Another problem that confronts us is how to mobilise the whole nation to carry forward the great task that confronts us.

(4) Reform is entering the stage wherein the old is being destroyed and the new established; the task of founding a commodity-based economic order is extremely demanding.

Reform is not only about destroying, but more importantly about constructing. In the first stage, we have shown sufficient courage to break the fetters of the old structure; now we must try harder and build a new commodity-based economy as part of the deepening process of reform. So long as we establish this new order and perfect the necessary laws, rules and regulations, the transition from the old to the new structure can be accomplished successfully, and the new structure assume the dominant position. At present, however, there is some disorder due to imperfections in the law and in the commodity-based economy. Illegal activities such as forcing up prices, hoarding and cornering, speculation, exploitation by middlemen, abuse of power by playing one's own game, graft and bribery, have seriously tarnished the image of both Party and government, corrupted social values and infringed the rights of the people. All such unlawful activities must be sternly punished in accordance with the law, and a new economic order based on the commodity must be established as soon as possible.

(5) Every effort must be made to improve the economic environment.

As regards the relationship between deepening the process of reform and improvement of the economic environment, the key problems are as follows: the excessive demand that has built up in recent years must be curbed; overheated economic growth must be slowed down; the high level of inflation must be reduced; popular panic at rising prices must be settled; a balance between total supply and total demand must be achieved. If these problems could only be resolved, a better economic environment might be created for reform. The alternative, to sit back and observe the sequence of rising wages and rising prices, would certainly mean missing the opportune time for reform and therefore delay the progress of change. For this reason, we must persist in simultaneously advancing reform, improving the economic environment and regenerating the economic order. It is necessary to adopt strong and decisive measures and deploy every possible means to push reform forward within an economic environment operating under fairly restrictive conditions.

The current crucial stage of reform is marked by the persistence of the following structural contradictions, successful resolution of which is vital for the continuation of our programme.

(1) The coexistence of economic imbalance and an uncoordinated structure.

At present, total demand outstrips total supply. In order to balance them, we must curtail demand on the one hand, and increase the supply of essential products on the other. But then we will face the problem of rising prices. To contain inflation it is necessary to restrict the speed of growth; this will in turn produce an increase in total supply. This is where the difficulty lies. Naturally, the present economic structure is better than the old one; however, it is not yet functioning in a rational manner. Take the industrial and agricultural sectors as examples: agriculture is weak and needs to be strengthened, while the industrial sector lacks energy and raw materials.

(2) The concurrence of price torsion and a tendency toward excessive price rises.

Because our price structure is irrational, it is hard to ease price torsion under conditions of rapidly rising prices.

(3) The coincidence of shortage of goods and materials and overstocking.

We have an overall shortage of goods and materials, and yet overstocking is a very serious problem. The value of stock throughout the country has reached almost 100 billion yuan. Goods and materials kept too long in stock have consumed a great deal of energy and materials, and held back a large proportion of funds. For instance, there is a shortage of steel products, but we have a stock in excess of 27 million tonnes 'sleeping' in warehouses. There is also a shortage of equipment, but we have heaps of idle equipment in stock. According to the statistics of some of the departments concerned, approximately 10 per cent (40 billion yuan worth) of the entire country's 400 billion yuan worth of equipment and fixed assets is lying idle, including unopened imported machinery and goods.

(4) The coincidence of shortage of funds and unused liquid assets.

Shortage of funds is a major problem, as it is with all developing countries. However, quite a sizable amount of money has been pigeon-holed and retained by some sectors. In fact, reciprocal loaning of funds should be allowed, to enable available liquid assets to flow between regions. The trouble is that some regions close their doors and will not allow the movement of their funds. This does not accord with the principles of the commodity economy, because the value of funds only appreciates after turnover; consequently, idle funds will perform poorly.

(5) The coexistence of egalitarianism and unfair distribution.

Egalitarianism was a major flow in the old structure, but now another kind of unfair distribution poses a problem. Egalitarianism certainly operates as a form of unfair distribution. Witness the striking unfairness of the inverted pay scales of workers by brain and manual workers: professors and college presidents are paid less than waiters. Tax levies have failed to regulate the situation adequately. Implementation of a policy of distribution according to work along with the development of a commodity economy will reverse and widen the income gap – between brain workers and manual workers, as well as between skilled and unskilled workers. There is a popular saying that encapsulates the current situation: 'the surgical scalpel is no better than the barber's razor, and the barber's razor is no better than a water-melon knife.' To make matters worse, due to the delay in establishing a macro-control system, some people are taking advantage of the loopholes that have arisen due to the coexistence of these two distribution systems in order to make exorbitant profits by devious means. We have yet to suppress these activities, which only exacerbate the situation.

(6) The concurrence of both labour shortage and surplus, and the presence of unoccupied and unqualified personnel.

According to studies, the level of labour employed surplus to requirements in enterprises accounts for some 15 per cent and is as high as 25 per cent in some trades. On the other hand, some enterprises are forced to hire temporary labour for jobs that are short-handed. This situation has produced a fictitious shortage of labour. What is more, temporary or casual labourers are entitled to receive higher pay than the regular workers get and a bonus; the total wage bill of an enterprise is thereby increased. The regular work force tend to make a comparison between their work and wages those of the temporary labourers; in this way a direct equation is made between high wages and poor workmanship. This creates a vicious circle that holds back the economic performance of enterprises. According to a survey of 200 enterprises in sixteen trades, carried out by a Shanghai research institute, the annual growth rate in casual recruitment has reached 9 per cent.

(7) The coincidence of excessive centralisation and excessive decentralisation.

The major flows in the old structure were excessive centralisation and over-rigid management. Since the implementation of reform, there has been a great change in this respect. The current problem lies in the fact that the power to manage, which central government has passed to the enterprises, has been held back by local government departments or by administrative bodies. Notwithstanding this, in some respects there has been excessive decentralisation in as much as the departments at all levels have failed to take control of these areas for which they have responsibility. Take foreign loans as an example. Since the country started to open up, everybody has wanted to take out loans from foreign countries, at high rates of interest and with attendant risks; the control of such borrowing has been neglected. It is clear that further studies must be undertaken on the appropriate balance between centralisation and decentralisation.

(8) The coexistence of competition and mutual dependence.

As competition in the world economy is keen, many countries adopt protectionist measures; but at the same time, interdependence among countries is increasing. All countries form part of an international economic structure, and all participate in the international division of labour, which obviously requires interdependence. The internationalisation of production and finance involves individual countries, but is ultimately a universal phenomenon. Take Japan as an example. Japanese businessmen produce in those places where production costs are lowest, and they sell in the places where prices are highest. There is no conception of Japan in their business policy – they have extended their business to the whole world. Japan's land prices have soared: the price of land in Tokyo is even higher than it is in New York. Under such conditions, it is not worthwhile, from the businessmen's point of view, to produce goods in their own country; they therefore transfer their funds to other countries. In the past, South Korea and Taiwan were the ideal places for such investment; however, since the rise in the value of their currencies, Japanese businessmen have felt it no longer worthwhile to base their production in these places, and have sought to transfer their funds elsewhere.

We must be aware that, despite the improvement in our investment environment, competition is keen, and we are now more dependent on others than before. The extent of our dependence on foreign trade accounts for 28.1 per cent of GDP, exports accounting for 12.45 per cent, imports accounting for 14.7 per cent. In the context of opening up to the outside world and our increased dependence on foreign trade, adaptation to the world market may produce unexpected set-backs, which will in turn render policy making more difficult.

The aforementioned problems need to be resolved in a thoroughgoing manner in this crucial stage of reform, but this is a far from easy to do.

Some further considerations on the process of deepening reform

(1) Our commitment to the course of reform must remain firm, but its implementation and administration must be rational and take no risks. It is important that people fully understand the gradual nature and complexity of reform.

The process of reform is a long and developing one involving both short-term and long-term variables. The short-term variables include reducing the number of mandatory plans and regulating certain distribution relations. The long-term variables include the growth and consolidation of the market, as well as improving the quality of cadres. These latter variables restrict the course of development of the overall restructuring project.

Reform is aimed at developing those productive forces which act as a brake on reform. The development of the productive forces requires as low pace of change in production relations. Therefore, we must look anew at the protracted nature of the reform process, and accept the limited nature of short-term reform targets.

The doctrine of the first stage of socialism insists on the necessity and urgency of reform, but it also stresses the distinction that exists between the course of reform and the formation of a new system. It makes clear that the intended results of reform cannot be achieved within a short period. Consequently it is not advisable to have an unduly short-term target because it can only be a limited one.

We must take the development of a commodity economy to be the goal of the first stage of socialism. In this stage, the commodity economy is embryonic and the productive forces are unbalanced and at a low level of development. What we face is a shortage economy with a pattern of conditional resources, and our cadres and masses lack both knowledge of the workings of a commodity economy and the experience to manage it. Therefore a considerable amount of time is needed to effect the transition to modern socialist commodity economy.

The same applies to future construction: nothing will be gained by our being impatient for quick results. We have learned the lessons of overhasty attempts at socialist transformation. Reform is a gradual process; it is not possible to accomplish everything at once. There is certain logic behind the transition from quantitative to qualitative change. An artificially imposed qualitative change will not bring success. It has taken about five years to gain universal acceptance of the rural reforms that began with the experimental household contract system with remuneration linked to output. Much more time will be required for the more complicated urban reforms. Reform, then, is a protracted and complicated business, but it is important to proceed resolutely, with full confidence that the goal of improved economic conditions can be attained.

(2) Promoting the stability and development of the economy during the course of reform.

The experience of recent years has shown that overheated growth and inflation are likely to inhibit the success of reform measures. We need urgently to address the following issues as part of the effort to promote stability and sound economic development: how to prevent the overheated growth of economy; how to reduce excessive demand; how to regulate the speed of economic development; how to check inflation; how to cut back severely on the issuing of paper money and the scale of loans; how to promote in a coordinated fashion the interests of reform, economic stability and further development.

(3) It is essential to grasp the centrality of the reform of enterprises to the promotion of improved economic performance.

The key to the wider reform process is to improve the economic performance of the enterprises. Consequently, the plans to transform the economic environment and overhaul the economic order must accord with the enterprises' leading role.

Reform of the enterprises must be combined with industrial restructuring and directed at improving economic performance. The aim is to increase the dynamism of the enterprises. However, macroeconomic performance will only improve under the guidance of rational industrial policies. It is not necessary to stimulate all enterprises; those that have no part to play in the industrial policy should be eliminated.

Over the past ten years of reform, the economic benefits have gradually accrued, but they are far from satisfactory given the demands made, and are considerably below the world level. A Japanese bank director made a comparative study of the economic performance of China and Japan. According to his estimates, China's consumption of cement was 2.3 times higher than Japan's; its energy consumption, 1.6 times higher and yet its steel consumption was only 90 per cent of Japan's. China's GNP, lowered, was only one quarter of Japan's. From 1975 to 1987 world consumption of steel products increased by 100 million tons, of which China accounted for 45 million tons while Japan accounted for only 8 million tons. It is worth reflecting upon the considerable disparity between the two countries.

The manager of Shijiazhuang Plastic Products Manufacture was the first to propose a regime of full-time work, which has now been introduced throughout the country. He had observed the difference between foreign enterprises and ours in the same trade and, certain that this was the best way forward, proposed a reform of working hours. Before reform, the effective length of the working day was about two hours, and the output of the factory with more than 800 staff and workers was only equivalent to that of a Japanese factory with around 100 employees. It took 123 days to effect the turnover of funds, compared to only 30 days for the same trade in Japan. The machinery operated at 50 per cent capacity in this factory, that of as opposed to a capacity as high as 99 per cent in Japan. Since the introduction of full-time work and other reforms into this factory, the economic benefits from improved performance have been considerable.

Experience shows that the reform of enterprises, alongside an overall strategy for the introduction of other measures, will guarantee the continuity and stability of the wider reform policy, and also directly benefit the enterprises, which are able to plan and develop in accordance with the long-term programme. On the other hand, successful reform of enterprises will also promote the stability and development of the national economy, and serve to create a better all-round economic environment. We should therefore concentrate on this sector, and especially on the need for the large and medium-sized state-owned enterprises to transform their system of management. Extension and growth of the market should be promoted in the wake of the progress of such reform. For the creation of a healthy market environment is the goal of this process of regulation and control, this linking of macroeconomic restructuring to reform of the enterprises.

Internal reform of the enterprises must undertake the separation of ownership and management authority, thereby producing an operation that is both self-motivating and self-regulating, combining responsibility, power and benefits. Only in this way can self-management and the exercise of sole responsibility for profits and losses be practised under the macro-control system. In recent years, experiments have been carried out at selected enterprises in some regions into the working of different management techniques, such as the contract-out system, leasing, the annexation or association of enterprises, the optimum organisation of labour, and the stock system. These experiments have proved a great success, and we have gained valuable experience.

We should continue to improve and develop the contracted managerial responsibility system. The main requirements are to set up a competition mechanism, a risk mechanism and a self-regulating mechanism, and to implement the Enterprise Law and the Insolvency Law. We must, without hesitation, introduce those measures, such as the system of overall responsibility, the inviting of competitive bids, the optimum organisation of labour, and the annexation of enterprises, that have contributed to the improvement of the economic environment and general economic efficiency. Measures such as the stock system and the separation of taxes and profits may be practicable from a long-term point of view but should not be introduced under current conditions; instead they should form the basis of an experiment at selected enterprises. Owing to the undeveloped state of the commodity economy, we lack experience in operating the stock system on the basis of public ownership. It would therefore be unwise to proceed too quickly down this road; it is better that we advance experimentally, step by step.

(4) Price reform should not be isolated from other reforms, but should be considered integral to the comprehensive reform of social conditions.

Price reform plays an important part in the process of economic restructuring. It will play a positive role in industrial regeneration, in stimulating enterprises, in reducing financial deficits, in implementation of the open-door policy and in checking the growth of unhealthy tendencies. The wider reform programme will fail if there is no price reform and no regulation of price relations. Nevertheless, this has proved a difficult task in China as it has in other countries. Price reform is not a panacea. We will not solve everything by its introduction, but must link it closely to other reforms. Only by combining price reform with improvement of the economic environment, with reform of the enterprises, with market growth and macro-management, and by linking financial policy, monetary policy and income-distribution policy, can the desired results be achieved.

Price reform will go ahead not only on the basis of the need for development of a commodity economy, but will also be guided by the ability of society – both enterprises and the mass of people – to absorb price rises. Without considering wider social and economic factors, a rigid price reform would definitely lead to economic chaos and the alternate rising of prices and wages, and ultimately to restoration of the old price relations.

(5) Improvement of the economic environment is needed mainly to bring inflation under control.

In recent years, excessive capital construction, the overexpansion of production, increased social consumption, the outstripping of total demand by total supply, and the unconstrained issuing of paper money, inevitably caused inflation, a condition under which it is impossible to solve any problems. Inflation is a worldwide phenomenon. Different countries have adopted different measures to bring it under control. Postwar Japan, for example, has experienced three periods of inflation in the past forty-three years: the period of postwar restoration (1945–49); the period of rapid development (1960–65); and latterly a period of composite inflation caused by both external and internal factors.

Japan's production level in September 1945 had dropped to one tenth of the prewar level owing to destruction caused by the war and the serious shortage of materials. In order to restore the economy rapidly the government issued a huge number of deficit bonds; these caused the depressed prices to skyrocket, and they remained high for some time. Tokyo's wholesale price index doubled in the six-month period after the war.

At the beginning of 1949, the economic consultant working under General MacArthur (the Commander of the Occupation Army in Japan), Joseph Dodge, the governor of American Detroit Bank, introduced a deflationary policy in Japan that was called 'Dodge's Line'. Dodge maintained that genuine stability and economic development should be established on the basis of solving all the problems through financial means. The government, which had opened the floodgates, was obliged to close them again. To bring inflation under control requires striking at the root of the problem. The outstanding tension within Japan's economy, then, was the simultaneous presence of excessive consumption and an insufficiency of supply. Therefore it was not possible to increase the state's financial deficits by expanding production.

Japan practised a kind of weighted industrial policy, which proved to be effective. A list of key industries was drawn up according to priority of investment. Enterprises in category A were to enjoy a full investment; enterprises in category B received only limited funds for restoring production, and therefore a restriction was placed on the deployment of new productive forces; no funds were provided for enterprises in category C.

Japan's deflationary strategy and weighted industrial policy achieved striking success. First, in macro terms the government effectively controlled inflated demand, which immediately dropped sharply. The contradictory relation between demand and supply in certain materials resolved itself. Then prices stabilised, the gap between official and black-market prices narrowed, the number of items subject to rationing decreased too. Comparing figures for the end of 1950 with those for the end of 1949, the number of products remaining under price control had undergone a drop of 80 per cent, and the level of subsistence had fallen by 75 per cent, so the way was paved for Japan's commodity economy to emerge from the former controlled economy. Second, in micro terms, enterprises were forced to adopt rational management techniques. The deflationary policy and the reduction in demand had undoubtedly created a harsh external environment for Japan's enterprises, but it was to be a turning point in improving their competitive capacity. Those enterprises that had been used to the postwar controlled economy were exposed to the harsh competition of a market economy and were forced to rationalise their operation. For instance the production of rolling stock experienced a sharp reduction in government demand, cutting the number of employees by as much as 25 per cent; cuts in certain sectors of industry and mining were as high as 10 per cent. The growth rate of nominal wages in the various trades was 159 per cent in 1948, but down to 14 per cent in 1949. At the same time, the quality of production improved and unit consumption dropped. These improvements laid the foundation for economic restructuring.

By 1980, South Korea was in a serious economic crisis, with an inflation rate as high as 40 per cent. An anti-inflation plan was devised, the main aims of which were: (i) to stabilise prices; (ii) to ensure that the market mechanism played its role; (iii) to encourage balanced economic growth. The results were impressive: the inflation rate dropped to 4.7 per cent in only a year, and the economic growth rate showed no sign of falling. The key to this success was the comprehensive application of monetary, financial and income-distribution policies, as well as foreign-trade and foreign-exchange policies and a campaign of public propaganda and education. First of all, the government restricted the money market and controlled the circulation of currency; this caused a decrease in the growth of internal credit from 40.6 per cent in 1980 to 13.1 per cent in 1984. Second, they tightened financial expenditure; indeed, in 1984 all government expenditure was frozen, which reduced the size of the public administration financial deficit from an internal output value of 4.5 per cent in 1980 to 1 per cent in 1985.

Third, the policy of regulating income distribution put an end to the situation where nominal wages constantly outstripped labour productivity, and greatly enhanced the competitiveness of the country's products in the world market. Fourth, the government stimulated exports by devaluing the currency and restructuring taxation. Lastly, they launched a propaganda drive to coincide with the measures to stabilize the economy, and won over both the people and the opposition political parties to their policy. But it is important to understand that a package of measures was deployed, as well as a flexible approach to regulation, in carrying out the policy. For instance, when the economy took a turn for the better in 1982, they slackened monetary policy in order to prevent the tight money market restricting economic growth; the result was an 11.9 per cent rise in the growth rate the following year. However, the country's financial policy has always been tight in order to provide the necessary funds for productive construction.

(6) The strengthening of macro-control, reducing demand and increasing the supply of essential products are the keys to checking inflation.

In recent years, our investment in fixed assets has undergone too rapid an increase, an expansion that exceeds national capacity. In the three years from 1986 to 1988, the total of such investment increased annually by 18.8 per cent on average; the average annual increase was 16.4 per cent in the nationalised sector, and 23.3 per cent in the collective and individual investment sector. The rate of increase in all cases exceeded the growth rate of national income. The total value of social fixed-assets investment exceeded 360 billion yuan in 1988. The proportion of non-production investment in that year accounted for 37.1 per cent of total construction investment capital.

Overexpansion of investment and its irrational structure are the major causes of inflation. First, 40 per cent of total fixed-assets investment has been transferred directly or indirectly to consumption funds. This has served to sharpen the contradictions. Second, they have resulted in seriously unbalanced bank credits and the issuing of more paper money. Third, they have interfered with the regulation of the industrial sector. And, finally, there have been too many unnecessary or unwise investments in construction and imports. For instance, we have imported sixteen ring-pull can lines for the whole country, production equipment that cost us several hundred million US dollars. However, as the best hotels and restaurants abroad no longer serve canned drinks, we have therefore followed an obsolete fashion! Likewise, a number of small cotton mills, woollen mills, breweries and tobacco plants were established in some regions without any consideration of the economic conditions and benefits. All such activities intensified the short supply of energy, raw materials and transportation.

We must control the consumption of funds in order to check inflation. From 1983 to 1987, the average annual wage increase was 10.1 per cent – excluding the additional cash earned by some 30 per cent of staff and workers. Consumption continued to increase progressively at an average of 21.2 per cent annually. The total wage bill for staff and workers in 1988 was 150.9 billion yuan, an increase of 21.2 per cent over the same period the previous year; the bonus portion accounted for 44.6 per cent more than the previous year. The groups' total corporate consumption had outstripped the total budget for construction investment capital. The following particulars relating to purchasing power must be noted. First, the range of commodities available for purchase has steadily grown, and the quality of commodities has likewise improved. The main commodities the groups purchased in the 1950s and 1960s were appliances for the office and protective equipment. This has now extended to almost every sort of commodity, including articles for daily use. Second, in terms of resources, most administrative units and enterprises have expended extra-budgetary funds. Third, there is the issue of the sharp increase in food prices. Since 1984 the cost of food purchasing increased progressively by 50 per cent annually, which in 1984 accounted for 2.7 per cent of the groups' total purchasing budget, rising to 5.6 per cent in 1987 – a more than two-fold increase. What is more, people in administrative units and enterprises have been using public money for personal pleasure. Extravagance and waste have become very serious. We must therefore reduce the scale of investment and the groups' purchasing power, cutting down especially on unnecessary non-productive and superfluous projects, and placing restrictions on the purchase of extravagant commodities. It will be necessary to adopt such measures in order to check inflation and to deepen reform.

However, the difficulties we now face are not as serious as those of the 1960s, and we are starting from more solid foundations than before. During the ten-year reform, our economy has developed rapidly, our national economic strength has improved, and people's living conditions have been greatly enhanced; in particular there is no longer a problem of providing adequate food and clothing for all. Almost everybody has the feeling that their standard of living has risen. We overcame the difficulties in the 1960s; there is no reason why we should not overcome the current difficulties.

3 China's Open-Door Policy

The structural reforms and the open-door policy will have a direct bearing on the success or failure of China's project of socialist construction. Implementation of the open-door policy is a fundamental process for the country that demands persistence over a long period; it is a strategic measure aimed at speeding up our socialist modernisation.

OPENING UP TO THE OUTSIDE WORLD IS PART OF AN INEXORABLE TREND OF SOCIAL DEVELOPMENT

In the wake of the initial expansion of commodity production and exchange, the development of economic links between countries boomed. According to Marx, owing to the application of machine and steam power, the scale of the division of labour makes large industries break away from their domestic base and rely entirely on the world market, international exchanges and the international division of labour. That is, socialised mass production makes it necessary for a country to step beyond its boundaries and develop economic contacts with other countries. As Marx and Engels had pointed out earlier, the bourgeoisie internationalised the production and consumption of all countries when they opened up to the world market. Policies of regional and national self-sufficiency and consequent isolationism gave way to those of mutual reliance and contact in all fields between all nationalities. Over the past century, historical experience has shown that economic problems exceed national boundaries. It makes no sense to perceive as separate spheres what are in fact international relations of production and consumption. It is necessary to take a world-wide perspective in order to solve the problems that arise in international economic relations.

After the October Revolution, Lenin stated that the socialist countries should maintain normal commercial contacts with the capitalist countries, and make bold use of foreign capital to accelerate the process of socialist construction. By the end of 1931, the Soviet Union had made such use of foreign capital to the tune of 1.4 billion roubles. In the years 1929–32, the machinery they bought from abroad was alone worth 2.35 billion roubles, which made them then the leading machinery importer. By 1932, the Soviet Union had engaged twenty thousand foreign specialists and skilled workers. During the 1930s and 1940s, two thirds of the country's large-scale enterprises were being assisted by the United States and its technology, and one third by Germany, France, Britain and Italy. These enterprises laid the foundation of Soviet industrialisation.

In recent decades, especially since World War II, production has increasingly become internationalised; this has also been the inexorable trend in social development. The adoption of an open-door policy has been the pattern for every country: the fundamental step in economic development. Since the end of World War II, as a consequence of their international interests, capitalist countries such as the United States, Federal Germany and Japan have greatly developed their economic relations with other countries, which has resulted in rapid economic development. In the 1970s the United States set up a number of domestic free-trade zones in order to develop foreign economic and technological trade. According to the available data, American investment in foreign countries in 1986 reached US$1068 billion; at the same time, they absorbed foreign capital totalling more than US$1331 billion as investment in their country. Recently they have further relaxed restrictions on foreign investment. They import tens of thousands of items of new technology each year from abroad, and engage tens of thousands of foreign specialists at huge salaries.

Japan is a country which exports a large amount of capital; its investment spreads all over the world. At the same time, it adopts a flexible policy on the utilisation of overseas funds. In 1957 it imported US$7 million of foreign capital. By 1981, this figure had increased to more than US$890 million. Japan has created a miracle of postwar economic development in the capitalist world by adopting a policy of combining imported capital with full use of imported technology and other assets, and innovation. Some developing countries – in particular Singapore, South Korea and Brazil – have in recent decades made full use of the advantageous international conditions to foster international economic and technological trade, and thereby bring about rapid development of their economies. By the end of 1982, Singapore had imported foreign capital to a value of US$9.65 billion, 34 per cent of which was American capital, 16.6 per cent Japanese, 16.3 per cent British, and the remainder Dutch, German and Swiss. This imported capital has established Singapore as a competitive centre for assembly, manufacture and selling. It enjoys a supply of raw materials, capital, technology and access to overseas markets. The country's per-capita GDP reached US$5240 in 1982, second only to Japan in Asia.

Nowadays, productive capacity and advanced technology are being ever more rapidly developed. In spite of the complexity and delicacy involved in international relations, generally speaking economic and technological contacts are close. Because if a country shuts itself off from reciprocal international relations, it cannot achieve modernisation. The reasons are as follows:

First, the economy of every country has its strengths and weaknesses. Modern production requires various resources and the deployment of advanced technology; however, no country possesses all the resources it needs. Moreover, owing to the different economic conditions that exist, in terms of technology, manpower and material resources, it is inevitable that the cost of labour and the labour-time invested in a product will differ. The best economic results are obtainable by a country through access to the world market, where it is possible to make the most of one's advantages and be less concerned with the disadvantages. Even an economically developed and technologically advanced country like the United States is attentive to the international division of labour and the value of international cooperation. The USA-made Boeing 747 airliner is produced cooperately by 1500 large-scale enterprises and 15 000 medium- and small-scale plants in six countries. The spare parts used by the Ford Motor Company are produced in Spain, Italy, Britain, Japan and Brazil, and are assembled in America, Britain and Germany.

Second, if a country can make good use of foreign capital, and is able to import technology and skilled workers, it will certainly avoid setbacks, save time, and start from a more advanced position. At the present time, there are huge deposits of idle funds, millions of advanced technology components and patents, some two million specialists, and an information capacity of four billion information units per day in the world ready for use. These represent an accumulation of tremendous resources and wealth created jointly by the whole of mankind. Whoever deploys these resources will be guaranteed great economic success. According to some sources, Japan spent US$6 billion in the period 1950–70 on importing and developing technological patents. If she had relied on her own research and invention for these patents, the direct and indirect expenditure on research, experiment and design alone would have cost US$180–200 billion, more than thirty times what was paid, and much more time would have been required. Time is wealth, time is advantage!

A new worldwide technological revolution is in progress. It presents a new opportunity and challenge to the course of our economic development. We must therefore further extend the open-door policy and encourage the growth of international economic and technological trade, but only on the basis of Marxist principles.

THE OPEN-DOOR POLICY HAS USHERED IN A DIVERSITY OF INITIATIVES

(1) Guangdong and Fujian provinces have been implementing 'the special policy and flexible measures' for external economic work. In July 1979, the Party's Central Committee and the State Council undertook an assessment of the advantageous conditions existing in Guangdong and Fujian provinces: their close proximity to Hong Kong and Macao with their large native Chinese populations, the presence of good transportation facilities, and wealth of natural resources. The decision was then taken that these two provinces should follow a special policy and adopt favourable measures for overseas trade and economic activity. They were required to take sole responsibility for their own finances and to share out a portion of the surplus foreign exchange they earned from their export trade. They were granted greater decision-making power in dealing with foreign trade. In this way, they could use their local know-how to full advantage and take the opportunity to spearhead reform and accelerate economic development. This represented an important step toward an open-door policy.

(2) We have set up a number of 'special economic zones'. On 26 August 1980, the Standing Committee of the Fifth National People's Congress ratified the regulations of Guangdong special economic zone, which were then promulgated and put into force. Shenzhen, Zhuhai and Shantou special economic zones were successively set up and developed. Xiamen special economic zone was also established.

A special economic zone differs in function from an overseas export processing zone. It is an extensive economic zone centred on industry linked to trade, and which undertakes the simultaneous development of other business activities. It also differs from the special administrative regions to be established in line with the one nation, two systems policy when Hong Kong and Macao are returned to us. The special economic zone is a region where a special economic policy and a economic management system operate. It is under the same political rule as the rest of the country: a regime of people's democratic dictatorship under the leadership of the Communist Party of China, which follows the four cardinal principles and is committed to the construction of socialist material and spiritual civilisations. Foreign businessmen who run factories or engage in other activities in the special economic zones must abide by China's constitution and laws. The direction of investment, the scale and the location of such enterprises are subject to the approval of the Chinese departments concerned. The main differences between the special economic zones and the country's interior are as follows:

First, the special economic zones attract and utilise foreign funds as their main means of economic development. Their economic structure permits the simultaneous existence of various economic sectors, granting priority to foreign-funded enterprises, on the condition that they are compatible with a continuing socialist orientation. There are numerous joint ventures with joint investments and joint managements, foreign-funded enterprises, a number of popularly or collectively owned enterprises, and also private enterprises.

Second, the special economic zones give priority to market regulation in their economic activities and allow it full scope under the guidance of the state plan. The state grants the special economic zones greater decision-making and project-approval powers for their economic activities.

Third, the special economic zones give priority to selling their products in the world markets, and make efforts to develop export-oriented economies.

Fourth, the foreign entrepreneurs who invest in the special economic zones enjoy favourable rates of taxation, such as apply to enterprise income tax.

Lastly, we have simplified the zones' exit and entry formalities in order to create a convenient environment for foreign traders to come here to invest or to carry out business negotiations.

(3) Hainan Island operates certain policies in common with the special economic zones. In line with their objectives, the party's Central Committee and the State Council granted the Island more decision-making power in October 1984. Those whose stay in Hainan will not exceed fifteen days may go through entry formalities at Haikou or Sanya Port in Hainan Province. Foreign businessmen and their dependents resident in Hainan are granted multi-entry visas. Natives of Hong Kong, Macao and Taiwan, as well as overseas Chinese, will enjoy even simpler and more convenient exit and entry formalities.

(4) We are opening up more coastal cities to world. The Party's Central

Committee and the State Council also decided in April 1984 to open fourteen more coastal cities to the outside world. They are: Tianjin, Shanghai, Dalian, Qinhuangdao, Yantai, Qingdao, Lianyungang, Nantong, Ningbo, Wenzhou, Fuzhou, Guangzhou, Zhanjiang and Beihai. This represented another significant step forward. These are the most economically developed cities in our country, with higher levels of scientific and technological expertise and better transport facilities. They have experience in developing overseas economic links and trade, as well as creating cooperative economic networks. Moreover, some of these cities are industrial centres. Accelerating the process of technological innovation in the industrial enterprises in these cities will be the key to realizing the goal of modernisation.

These coastal cities were opened up even wider in some respects. First, we gave them greater decision-making power in their dealings with foreign contacts so as to strengthen their capacity to develop international economic and technological cooperation. Second, we created attractive business conditions by giving foreign investors preferential treatment that was only slightly inferior to that on offer in the special economic zones. Third, coastal cities with the right conditions were permitted to set up economic and technological development districts that pursued policies similar to those in the special economic zones, thereby creating the right 'microclimate' for better investment opportunities. These measures provided foreign traders with centres in which to concentrate their investment and introduce advanced technology and scientific research and projects, as well as to develop new products and set up new enterprises. At the same time, these measures were intended to bring innovation to the old enterprises and produce an economic boom in the respective hinterlands.

(5) We introduced a number of 'open coastal economic areas'. The Party's Central Committee and the State Council made a further decision in February 1985 to open up Changjiang Delta, Zhujiang Delta and the triangle region of southern Fujian including Xiamen, Zhangzhou and Quanzhou as open coastal economic areas. These territories are located by the sea; they have good transportation facilities, a temperate climate, a greater range of products, and unrestricted communication. They offer the most advantageous conditions for foreign economic and technological trade. There are thirteen cities, forty-six counties and two district counties within the three areas. In March 1988, the State Council further decided to expand the scope of these coastal areas, and designated several more territories to share this status. These include

Liaodong Peninsula, Shandong Peninsula, some cities and counties in the Circular Bohai Region, as well as the counties governed by the open coastal cities. The open coastal economic areas now include two cities and twelve counties in Hebei Province, seven cities and sixteen counties in Liaoning Province, seven cities and forty counties in Jiangsu Province, five cities and thirty counties in Zhejiang Province, four cities and twenty-eight counties in Fujian Province, three cities and twenty-seven counties in Shandong Province, thirteen cities and thirty-nine counties in Guangdong Province, one city and five counties in Guangxi Autonomous Region, ten counties in Shanghai, and five counties in Tianjin.

The main policies operating in the open coastal economic areas are as follows:

First, the productive and scientific projects under foreign investment, whether they are run by the city authorities, by the district outside the city boundaries, or by authorised satellite cities in the provinces, enjoy preferential treatment similar to that of the open coastal cities. Those direct-foreign-investment projects – agriculture, forestry, animal husbandry, aquaculture and processing – based in the countryside and open areas with the aim of developing an export trade also enjoy the above-mentioned treatment so as to realise the potential of foreign-exchange-earning agriculture in these areas.

Second, the people's governments of the cities and the key counties in the open coastal economic areas have been granted an appropriately expanded decision-making power for their engagement in foreign economic activities. And the export restrictions on certain local products have also been relaxed.

Third, for the purposes of quarantining imported animals and plants, the local governments of Guangdong, Fujian, Zhejiang and Jiangsu provinces have the choice of one or two off-shore islands or river sand bars. These quarantine zones permit experimental farms to be set up to undertake crop trials and animal breeding, the benefits of which can be shared with other regions when experiments meet with success.

Ten years' experience of open-door policy have enabled us to establish a varied structure, with numerous levels of activity, key locations, and an integrated system of locations and spheres – such as operates in the special economic zones, the open coastal cities, the open coastal economic areas, and in the interior. We have now established advanced open coastal zones from the south to the north, including two municipalities directly under the control of central government, twenty-five municipalities directly under the control of provincial governments, and sixty-seven counties, with a total population of around 150 million.

This innovation will play a significant role in adapting to the transfer of world economic attention to the Pacific Rim area, and in accelerating our process of modernisation.

THE MAJOR RESULTS OF THE OPEN-DOOR POLICY

(1) The policy has actively promoted development of the productive forces and the economy in general. Take Guangdong and Fujian as examples. Before the introduction of the policy, the industrial and agricultural growth rate of these two provinces was slower than that of the national average. Now, production in these regions has increased. The standard of living has improved, and the domestic economy has taken on a new look. The value of gross industrial and agricultural output in Hainan Province in 1987 reached 5.07 billion yuan – higher by a factor of 1.5 than that of the period before the new policy. Per-capita income in the rural economy doubled. The value of gross industrial and agricultural output for 1988 in the four special economic zones amounted to 15.7 billion yuan – a fifteen-fold increase on that for 1979, before the establishment of the special zones. Shenzhen used to be a small border town with weak industry, the value of its gross industrial output for 1980 totalled only 51.21 million yuan. But now it has become a special export-oriented comprehensive economic zone with industry as the dominant factor; the value of its gross industrial output for 1988 reached 9.09 billion yuan, its annual exports amounted to 4.75 billion yuan, its per-capita output value reached 5492 yuan. The value of gross industrial and agricultural output for the fourteen open coastal cities reached 270.2 billion yuan in 1987, 58.7 per cent higher than in 1983. The value of gross industrial and agricultural output in the open coastal economic areas in 1986 had grown 50 per cent since 1984. In sixteen cities (counties) the value of gross industrial and agricultural output reached more than 2 billion yuan, accounting for 37 per cent of the total output of the forty-nine cities (counties) in the open coastal economic areas. There has been further development in these areas since 1987.

(2) The investment environment has improved. Since the introduction of the policy, energy has been concentrated throughout the country on infrastructural development – energy resources, communications systems, ports and municipal works – thereby enabling rapid improvement of the investment environment. There are now air-transportation facilities in twenty cities out of twenty-seven in the open coastal

areas. Fifty-four 10 000-ton dead-weight berths have been newly built or expanded. The railway from Nanning to Beihai has been extended to Qinzhou, and both the viaduct and bridges on the rail route from Shenzhen to Nantou are now operational. The capacity of the telephone systems in the four special economic zones and fourteen coastal cities have been greatly enhanced. Domestic telephone systems featuring automatic or semi-automatic long-distant calls are in public use in the fourteen open coastal cities. International direct dialling is available in the cities of Tianjin, Shanghai, Fuzhou, Xiamen, Shenzhen and Zhuhai. Telecommunications are in general greatly improved. Numerous industrial factory buildings, commercial buildings, guesthouses, hotels, tourist facilities, as well as large municipal complexes, have been constructed in the special economic zones, and in the economic and technological development zones and cities. As a consequence, the cities have taken on a new look.

(3) The policy has promoted a dramatic increase in the use of foreign funds. By the end of 1988, we had signed a total of 16 377 projects with foreign businessmen throughout the country. These were worth US$78.5 billion, of which US$31.96 billion was in direct foreign investment. More than seven thousand foreign-funded enterprises are already in operation, 80 per cent of which are distributed over the open coastal areas. Four special economic zones had signed 1262 foreign-invested projects by 1988, worth US$1.2 billion, of which US$624 million was actually utilised. The fourteen open coastal areas signed up more than 1500 foreign-invested projects within three years; the total joint investment is US$3.55 billion, the funds received totalled US$860 million. In 1988, the number of foreign-invested projects has doubled in Shanghai, Fujian and Tianjin. Those signed by Shandong exceeded the total of the previous 1–9 years. We have also taken important steps to improve the quality of exported commodities, and to increase the proportion of luxury products. The proportion of industrial goods exported from the coastal areas rose from 61 per cent in 1987 to 68 per cent in 1988.

(4) Our technological progress has been made possible by the importation of advanced technology and equipment. The fourteen open coastal cities have imported some 5000 units of high-technology plant at a cost of US$3.45 billion. More than 3900 units have already been set up and put into production, improving to varying degrees half of our popularly-owned enterprises. Through technological innovation, then, production speeds have increased, the conditions in numerous industrial enterprises using outmoded equipment and producing dated prod-

ucts have been transformed; advanced technology has been imported; and new products have been developed, some of which have filled the gaps in certain fields.

(5) The policy has enhanced the foreign-exchange-earning capacity of the export trade, and has promoted the development of an export-oriented economy. The volume of exports of the fourteen coastal provinces and cities reached US$27.4 billion last year, which accounted for 68 per cent of total exports. In 1988, the volume of exports of the five special economic zones, Shenzhen, Zhuhai, Shantou, Xiamen and Hainan, reached US$3.08 billion in 1988, 47 per cent up on 1987. Since the introduction of the policy, the rate of increase in the volume of exports in the fourteen open coastal cities and three open coastal economic areas has exceeded the value of gross industrial and agricultural output.

(6) The policy has strengthened lateral economic links and promoted the economic development of the country's interior. The key cities of the open coastal areas are the 'windows' through which the hinterlands deal with international economic contacts; they also act as centres for two-way business traffic and thereby serve to strengthen economic contacts between the areas and localities throughout the country. Lateral links provide not only significant support for the export-oriented economic development conducted by the areas, but also act as important conduits outward. In addition to the enterprises in the special economic zones and the open economic and technological areas that are run by parent enterprises elsewhere in the country, various forms of lateral economic association have also taken shape. According to statistics, the open coastal areas have signed more than ten thousand economic contracts with the country's interior. Such lateral economic association has strengthened the capacity of the interior to earn foreign exchange, by exporting raw materials and primary products via the open coastal areas. The linkage has also promoted the economic development of the interior by means of imported advanced technology and management experience transferred from the open coastal areas.

We will continue to implement the open-door policy. To this end, the following issues must be confronted.

(1) The relationship between self-reliance and the open-door policy. China is a socialist country with a population of 1.1 billion. If we are to achieve modernisation, we must maintain our independence and retain the initiative, as well as continuing a policy of self-reliance. We must not depend on foreign economies, nor rely on any form of

exploitation, but instead trust in our own strength and the people's hard work and ability in order to develop our national economy. We must make full use of our own natural resources, capital and productive capacity, and give every encouragement to our superior socialist system to develop the socialist economy. But it is important not to set self-reliance against opening up: self-reliance must not be interpreted as a closed door policy. It is impossible to resolve all our economic and technological problems by our own efforts. To isolate ourselves from the world would be a display of ignorance and narrow mindedness.

We aim to strengthen our capacity for self-reliance and to promote the development of our national economy by expanding international economic and technological trade. In other words, self-reliance and opening up will be mutually sustaining. We must strive to manufacture whatever machinery we can by ourselves. We must also make better use of our idle funds. But this does not mean it is desirable to depend upon ourselves for everything. The key to gaining substantial economic benefits from a lower consumption of labour is to make use of the international division of labour and to develop international economic relations. It is therefore permissible to import machinery and equipment that is not required on a large scale and which if we manufactured it ourselves would cost too much. In this way we avoid the labour and time involved in research, design and manufacture, and yet are able to proceed from the most technologically advanced starting point. Making use of international trade in order to import advanced technology is therefore a shortcut to a more developed national economy. Even developed countries do this, not only those like ours that are rather backward in terms of scientific and technological know-how. For instance, the former West Germany imported from us generator technology involving carbon and oxygen; the United States adopted our technique for growing hybrid rice and imported computer components from Asia. Even our computer software has entered the American market. These choices were made after careful consideration of the options.

(2) The utilisation of foreign funds and the establishment of joint ventures and exclusively foreign-invested enterprises.

Some worry that the open-door policy may lead to capitalism. Some want to know whether it counts as exploitation when foreign capitalists profit from joint ventures or from enterprises exclusively funded by their own investment. 'If it is exploitation', they ask, 'then why do we, a socialist country, allow them to invest in and run enterprises in our country?' The response is that in fact our use of foreign funds and our willingness to allow foreign interests to invest in and run enterprises here are based on principles of equality and mutual benefit. We cannot expect foreign businessmen to have pity on us and to give us something for nothing. For our part, we do not allow them to gain excessive profits through illegal means; rather, we enable them to make legal profits in pursuit of normal economic activities in an environment that attracts them to invest here.

Lenin wondered whether it was right to invite foreign capitalists to go to Russia after the Soviet regime had driven away Russian landlords and capitalists, but decided it was right! Lenin repeatedly suggested in his discussion of the lease system that foreign capitalists should be allowed to gain a certain amount of profit. He held that it was essential to pay foreign capitalists in order to obtain Western advanced technology and equipment, and to secure the foundation of a developing socialist economy. Conditions in the Soviet Union were bad then, but the government boldly introduced the lease system as detailed in Lenin's policy in order to improve people's standard of living. They had some 200 leased enterprises, and the foreign funds they used amounted to tens of millions of roubles. We enjoy much better conditions than those existing in Lenin's day. Our aim in allowing the existence of joint ventures, cooperative enterprises and foreign-run enterprises is to attract foreign funds and to import advanced technological equipment. Certainly, foreign businessmen take a risk in investing and running factories in our country, but they benefit from our payment for the imported advanced technology and equipment.

Sino–foreign joint ventures are jointly managed enterprises set up in accordance with China's needs, with Chinese participation, and within the jurisdiction of China and the leadership of the Chinese government. The means of production of our share are owned by our socialist country or by collectives. Workers participate in labour and management in a controlling capacity; they are not the labour commodities of capitalism.

The setting up of foreign ventures exclusively with their own investment is an effective form of attracting foreign funds that has been widely adopted in the world; it is permitted in explicit terms in our constitution. Foreign businessmen must employ advanced technology and scientific know-how in their enterprises in order to make profit and strengthen their competitive capacity; we benefit by getting hold of this advanced technology and management experience. Allowing the establishment of foreign enterprises in China will increase our receipt of foreign currency, and will encourage the development of public works and related undertakings in some cities, promote the development of other areas, and increase employment as well as train people for professions. The staff of the joint ventures and foreign enterprises are members of the working class and hold power in the country – their well-being is protected by the state; the foreign traders' profits are gained under the state's supervision and within the limits permitted by law and policy. We have to pay for the training we need to carry out our socialist modernisation; we allow foreign businessmen a reasonable profit in exchange for advanced technology and management experience as well as for the time we save. We pay a supplement for gaining time; this is a kind of mutual benefit. All these arrangements are beneficial to the development of our national economy and to the goal of socialist modernisation. Therefore, they will not lead to the restoration of capitalism but, rather, are a necessary and valuable complement to the course of socialist economic construction.

Introduction of the open-door policy and establishment of the special economic zones and economic and technological development areas were significant steps intended to speed up the development of our socialist economy, whilst protecting our sovereignty. These reforms are very different from the opening up of trading ports and the establishment of concessions in old China. These latter grew gradually during the course of imperialist aggression after the Opium War, and formed the basis of the political, economic and cultural aggression that was committed against us. The traitorous governments of the Qing Dynasty sought power and wealth by betraying our country; at the imperialists' beck and call, they granted them extraterritorial rights in some areas. However, today's special economic zones and the economic and technological development areas are our sovereign territories; foreign traders do not enjoy extraterritoriality, but must abide by our laws, decrees and regulations. The trading ports and concessions of old China enslaved us; the new economic zones and development areas will make us prosperous and strong by importing advanced technology and extending the scope of international economic trade.

(3) Making use of foreign management experience.

Establishment of a vigorous socialist economic system with Chinese characteristics must be based on fundamental Marxist principles in the light of China's real situation. We must depend on our own historical experience, but we must also take advantage of the management experience gained by others, including that of the developed capitalist countries.

Some Chinese hold that, as we are a socialist country, we may learn from the advanced technology of the capitalist countries but it is not acceptable to learn from their management experience. This viewpoint shows a lack of analysis. We should, on the contrary, conduct a scientific and practical study into their experience of managing mass production. It is true that some capitalist management techniques and methods are peculiar to the capitalist process of production, and are therefore connected with the exploitation of labour; we will certainly not adopt these measures. However, certain of their management techniques, while they did develop from the capitalist mode of production, are not peculiar to the capitalist production process and play no part in the exploitation of labour. Such techniques, which reflect a common feature of socialised mass production, represent a common fund of human experience in the field of production. They are not restricted to capitalism and hence destined to be eliminated; rather, such methods of management will receive a new lease of life under socialism. According to Marx, labour involving many individuals requires someone to coordinate and unify the process, but management techniques are distinct from the social system and it is therefore inappropriate to lump them together.

After the October Revolution, Lenin repeatedly stated that it was necessary for the building of socialism to make full use of the management expertise and the cultural and technological advances of capitalists. He suggested the following formula. Be ready to absorb good things from foreign countries, because the Soviet regime plus the Prussian railway management system plus American technology and trust organisations plus American national education and so on equals socialism. As we know, capitalist countries have developed over several hundred years, during which time they have accumulated valuable experience in management and production. As Lenin said, the realisation of socialism depends on a socialist regime and socialist administrative organisation with the latest and the most progressive aspect of capitalism. It would therefore be stupid and ignorant to reject the advanced scientific technology and scientific management methods of the capitalist countries. To refuse to learn from them displays a destructive and primitive attitude.

In 1956 Mao coined the slogan 'Learn from foreign countries'. He considered it important to recognise that all nations have their own merits, be this in politics, economics, science, technology, literature or art, and that learning from others' successes can yield positive results. Let us take an example. The Furi Television Company is a Sino-Japanese joint venture; they have imported an integrated operation involving both plant and management expertise. In 1984 they produced 34 000 television sets, the value of their gross industrial output reached 400 million yuan, labour productivity of the whole work force amounted to 40 000 yuan, working hours without stoppage in the black-and-white television and colour television sections have stabilised at 10 000 and 20 000 hours respectively. These four indices rank highest in the trade country-wide. Learning from foreign countries, including socialist countries, does not mean copying their methods and practices indiscriminately, but rather incorporating them into our own practices in order to create an economic system and management methods specific to China. Of course, we must reject and resist firmly those features of the capitalist system that are reprehensible and inimical to our own.

(4) The dual benefit of the open-door policy.

There are two strands to our open-door policy: opening up to the outside world, and opening up to other provinces, areas and regions. The policy is designed to enhance the value of mutual cooperation and marketing opportunities to enable economic rejuvenation. The Resolution of the Party's Central Committee on Reform of the Economic System states the policy clearly: 'According to the principles of maximising our strengths and avoiding weakness, and of promoting diverse forms of mutual benefit and common development, we will energetically promote lateral economic ties, the rational exchange of capital, equipment, technology and skilled personnel.' All regions, departments and enterprises must reach out and open up to each other; there must be unity and cooperation in all areas of the economy. In particular, the regions which are lagging behind must open up to the advanced areas, and vice versa. From 1987–8 the nationwide effort in economic and technological cooperation achieved impressive results, and a new dynamism became evident. According to official statistics, more than 50 thousand cooperative projects have been established in the country; the value of materials supplied reached more than 26 billion yuan; the funds in circulation amounted to more than 20 billion yuan – all these factors have actively promoted development of the local economy. Wuhan, the so-called 'thoroughfare to nine provinces', and the cities of Shashi, Jingmen, Xianning and Xiaogan have set up The Jiang-Han Plains Economic and Technological Cooperative Association; they have successively signed up around a thousand cooperative projects, some of which have made substantial progress. There are now 101 economic and technological cooperative regions and urban groups established in various areas, forty-nine of them transprovincial or transregional cooperative associations. They include the Shanghai Economic Region, the Quintet Economic Zone, which includes four provinces and one city in southwest China, Zhujiang Delta Economic Zone, Circular Bohai Gulf Economic Region and the Southern Economic Regions of Liaoning Province. The experience of such associations is that the policy of opening up internally and strengthening lateral economic ties and co-operation are essential to the success of socialised mass production and the development of productive capacity and represent inexorable trends in our socialist economic development.

ADAPTING STRUCTURAL REFORM OF FOREIGN TRADE TO THE OPEN-DOOR

The structural reform of foreign trade was introduced in 1979. The key problems it set out to resolve were: the overlap of responsibility between administration and enterprise, inflexible monopolistic control, the disjunction between production and marketing, centralised income and expenditure, an over elaborate import and export tariff combined with complicated approval procedures.

(1) We have transferred management power to the lower levels and aroused the enthusiasm of localities and enterprises.

In order to arouse the enthusiasm of localities and industrial departments for developing foreign trade, we gave them greater power of management over it. We also established a principle of classifying export commodities whereby the different commodities were managed by different organisations. The specialist companies under the Ministry of Foreign Economic Relations and Trade took charge of the following export commodities: the few mass commodities of vital strategic importance to the national economy and the people's livelihood; commodities subject to fierce competition in the world markets; and commodities with special requirements of processing, organisation, essential fittings and transportation. All other commodities were made available to the local companies and the foreign-trade companies of the industrial departments. The twenty-nine provinces, autonomous regions, municipalities and the cities of Guangzhou, Dalian, Wuhan, Xi'an, Shenyang, Harbin, Chongqing, Qingdao and Hainan Island, and the special administrative areas with autonomy subsequently opened up ports for foreign-trade, engaged in export and import business, for which they had full responsibility.

At the same time, the state authorised the establishment of twenty-five or so general export and import companies under the jurisdiction of the industrial departments for specialised trades, including metallurgy, non-ferrous metals, electronics, shipping, petrochemicals and agricultural machinery. These companies were permitted to export directly a proportion of their products. The state also granted self-management power to those large- and medium-scale enterprises that possessed better production equipment and machinery and had experience of producing export commodities and the capacity for self-management. Some 1400 companies and enterprises are now authorised to engage in foreign trade.

The ending of monopoly control by the foreign-trade departments has served to arouse the enthusiasm of localities and industrial departments for developing foreign trade. Reform of the management system has therefore played an instrumental role in the development of our foreign trade. It is worth noting that during the 1980s, when we faced an unpropitious international trading environment experiencing restricted growth in world trade and the return of trade protectionism, our export trade still showed a considerable increase. The volume of exports rose from US\$9.75 billion in 1978 to US\$47.54 billion in 1985, an increase by a factor of 3.87, which greatly exceeded the growth rate in industrial and agricultural production during the same period.

(2) We have experimented in selected locations with a combination of manufacturing and trade and a combination of technology and trade.

In order to solve the problems of poor quality and obsolescent design in our export commodities due to the disjunction between manufacturing and trade and the absence of linkage between production and marketing, we launched a trial reform in selected places with various combinations of manufacturing and trade and of technology and trade; these included joint operation of manufacturing and trade, joint operation of productive enterprises, the integration of production and marketing, and the self-management of productive enterprises.

There are two models of joint operation of manufacturing and trade. In the first, the foreign-trade companies and their counterparts in industry share office space and conduct the following operations jointly: production planning, negotiation with foreign traders, organisation of overseas delegations for the purposes of inspection and fact-finding and marketing. In the second model the foreign-trade companies grant the industrial departments favourable prices for export commodities, who in turn reduce the cost of industrial production to the foreign-trade companies.

The joint operation of productive enterprises means establishing enterprises as complete business entities with integrated foreign trade companies that deal directly with their export trade. The main foreign-trade companies based on this model are the China Wire and Cable Joint Export Company, China Electric Equipment Joint Export Company, China Bearing Joint Export Company, and China Grinding Tools and Abrasives Joint Export Company.

The integration of production and marketing means, in effect, the operation of an association combining industry, commerce, trade, production, supply and marketing. The China Silk Company and the China General Shipping Company, established in February and May of 1982 respectively, are enterprises of this nature.

The self-management of productive enterprises is a trial that is running in the large- and medium-scale state-owned enterprises, such as The Capital Iron and Steel Plant, The Anshan Iron and Steel Plant, and The Shanghai Machine Tool Plant. At the same time, we have been experimenting with the model in a few small-scale collective enterprises, such as the Beijing Silk Flower Factory.

(3) With the aim of continuing in partnership and collaboration with our foreign counterparts, we have introduced a two-tier system for the management and administration of foreign trade.

Depending on the type and category of export and import commodity, the central government and the local foreign-trade administrative organisations share responsibility for the following functions: examination and verification of export and import contracts, the issuing of export and imports permits, allocation of quotas and supervising the coordination of the system. This measure has transformed the previous management system based on the concentration of administrative jurisdiction for foreign trade in the hands of the central government.

The localities have more administrative power to deal with export trade. The central government organisations are only in charge of a few important and internationally competitive commodities, while the local administrative organisations take charge of the bulk of commodities with permits authorised by the Ministry of Foreign Economic Relations and Trade. The standards of examination and approval for the permit are rigorously enforced. Permits are issued to those who hold signed export contracts. In other words, whoever holds a signed export contract may apply for a permit; the issuing department then examines the contract item by item. The scope of the examination includes the letter of credit and the export price of the commodities.

The permit may be rejected when the contract is at variance with regulations. We are also working to improve the system of import permits and textiles quotas.

The transfer of control of foreign trade to the lower levels has enabled more and more productive enterprises to participate directly in the intense competition in world markets. This has played an important role in enhancing the technological level of production and increasing the labour productivity of the enterprises. The gulf between industry and trade and between production and marketing has also started to narrow.

(4) We have reformed the system of allocating foreign exchange and closed the gap between the earners of foreign exchange and its users.

The most essential component of the reform in this regard is the retention by the localities and enterprises of a portion of the foreign exchange they earn. The main elements of this system are as follows. Depending on the policies in force, the localities may retain for their own use a proportionate amount of the foreign exchange earned by their export trade. However, the localities must give half of this share to the enterprises that produce the export commodities to enable them to import necessary technology, equipment, raw materials and other resources or to send inspection delegations abroad. The localities must use their share to import the necessary materials for important local projects and public works. When necessary, the enterprises may vary the apportionment of these funds under the supervision of the local government and the foreign-exchange administrative departments. Moreover, in order to implement the macro-industrial policy, the state has increased the proportion of foreign exchange that is to be earmarked for machinery and electrical equipment – products requiring considerable concentrations of capital investment in technology for their manufacture. The system of retaining a portion of foreign exchange has proved popular with those localities and productive enterprises that benefit. In 1988 we adjusted the system, allowing localities and enterprises to retain a greater proportion of foreign exchange. We also opened up foreign-exchange-regulating markets throughout the country. We cancelled the quota system in favour of one that permitted the localities and enterprises to buy and sell freely their portion of foreign exchange in the regulating centres at market prices. These reform measures have successfully closed the gap between the earners and users of foreign exchange, and have played a positive role in expanding the export trade market.

(5) We have reformed the foreign-trade planning system and intro-

duced a market mechanism. We have substituted a system of combined mandatory and advisory planning for the former system of exclusively mandatory planning. This reform has laid the foundation of a planned commodity economy in the field of foreign trade.

(6) The comprehensive application of various economic levers has begun to build an embryonic form of macro-regulating system for foreign trade. This has promoted a shift in the macro-management of foreign trade from direct administration to indirect economic control. More importantly, we have introduced an incentive policy in connection with foreign-exchange earning at the heart of those enterprises engaged in foreign trade. We have also carried out successive trials into the operation of a contract that involves responsibility for economic targets, enterprise funds, a system of retaining a portion of profits, a fund-retaining system intended to reduce the portion of loss and increase the portion of profit, and a contract granting overall responsibility for management. These experiments have transformed the means of controlling foreign-trade enterprises, and produced enhanced economic benefits. We have also looked into the ways of keeping separate accounts, running businesses, independently, and allocating sole responsibility for profit and loss.

The reform of the foreign-trade system in recent years has been a transition period from the old to the new. Although we have achieved considerable success through the reforms a number of problems nevertheless remain to be solved.

First, the contradiction that exists between the rigid planning of export and import assignment and financial soft-budget restrictions must be resolved. Although in recent years we have introduced significant changes to the system of planning foreign trade and to the financial system, the monopoly system of responsibility for profit and loss has not been thoroughly transformed. This cannot but affect the development of foreign trade in terms of both scale and speed. And it also threatens the early establishment of a new foreign-trade system.

Second, we failed to implement the macro-management of foreign trade when management authority was transferred to the lower levels. The administration still plays a leading role in this macro-management. The overlap of responsibility between administration and enterprises is still widespread. What is more, the legal framework and certain economic factors relating to macro-management have still to be perfected. Sometimes things happen like this – the enterprises went so far to compete with each other by cutting prices that the result was a failure to realise any profit. This represents a political and economic loss to the country.

Third, most foreign-trade enterprises have not yet become independently managed economic entities with responsibility for their own profit and loss. Control over foreign trade has been mostly transferred to local government and industrial departments and has yet to be devolved to productive and foreign-trade enterprises themselves (with the exception of a few large- and medium-scale enterprises). As a consequence, many enterprises still lack motivation and vigour. Most are still unable to compete in the world market directly. The problem of combining industry and trade has not yet been adequately solved. The conflict between the central authorities and the localities, or an alliance of localities, as to which should liaise directly with our foreign counterparts remains to be resolved. The problem of overlapping control of commodities among localities also requires resolution.

Fourth, the policies of distributing the benefits of foreign trade differentially between areas, retaining a portion of foreign exchange and continuing price subsidies, make it hard to establish the competitive mechanism that is essential for a stable growth of foreign trade. A prerequisite for such a mechanism is a roughly equal trading environment for all enterprises, which means that a socialist market system must be established. The price index, an important feature of the market system, will be distorted if a fair, competitive environment does not exist. The enterprises will be hard pressed to orientate themselves and sustain competitiveness under such circumstances. In recent years, during the process of reform when the market system is still in the stage of growth and development, it has been difficult to avoid indiscriminate competition among the enterprises and regions.

4 China's Rural Economic Restructuring

The restructuring of China's rural economy began in December 1976, immediately following the third plenary session of the Eleventh Central Committee of the CCP. In the first ten-year period of reform, our rural areas underwent a tremendous transformation, the outstanding success of which attracted worldwide attention. Reform has brought about the conversion of the country's natural rural economy of self-sufficiency to a system based on the commodity, and thereby opened the way to rural modernisation. The primary aims of reform were (i) to develop a socialist commodity economy; (ii) to promote the modernisation of agriculture; (iii) to increase the wealth and prosperity of rural areas. In practice, the ten-year period of reform witnessed the following measures, aimed at making good the weaknesses of the old structure: reorganisation of the people's communes; separation of government administration and enterprise management; establishment of a dual-level system of management based on household contract; regulation of industry with the aim of developing a diversity of enterprises; reform of the circulation system; cultivation of a market; encouragement of a variety of flexible economic associations; deployment of mechanisms of price, taxation, credit and the law to regulate the operation of the rural economy and thereby accelerate the process of founding a new system based on a commodity economy.

DRAWBACKS OF THE FORMER RURAL ECONOMIC STRUCTURE AND THE STARTING POINTS OF REFORM

(1) For a long time the state has exerted rigorous and rigidly centralised control of agricultural management. Exacerbated by the influence of the 'left deviation', a number of problems developed in the structure of the rural economy which served to dampen the peasants' enthusiasm, adversely affect the successful functioning of the emergent cooperative economy, and hinder the development of the rural economy. The following stand as striking examples of this process.

The highly centralised style of management deprived the peasants of decision-making power. The people's communes practised a system whereby government administration was merged with commune management, thus composing a level of state organisation with political power at the grassroot level combined with collective rural economic organisation. In addition to this blurring of functions, the tendency was to operate a 'large and public' system – the largest size of commune with the highest degree of public ownership. With regard to the overcentralisation of management, this even extended to the setting of a regular time for the peasants to begin work in the fields – signalled by a whistle blown by the production team leader. What is more, the peasants were regularly criticised as 'capitalist tails' for the fact of their tilling family plots and engaging in other family enterprises on the side. Under such conditions, the development of agriculture in accordance with natural law and the demands of a commodity economy were out of the question. Moreover, egalitarianism and the system of eating from a big common pot had seriously violated the principle of distribution according to work.

The slogan and practice of 'taking grain as the key', resulting in unbalanced production, as well as instructions relating to the planting of all crops, formed part of a mandatory plan. The production teams and peasants had no power of decision-making. This seriously impeded the development of the agricultural economy as well as restricting the development of ancillary enterprises, for only a slight increase in the output of grain.

The economic structure lacked vitality. Overcentralisation and imbalance in the economy dominated the rural areas for a long time, ensuring that most labour was expended on the fields. Further, the long-standing practice of centralised purchasing and assigned sales dampened the peasants' enthusiasm, restricting development of the rural commodity economy and depressing the level of peasant income.

(2) In the ten-year period from 1966 to 1976, the annual allocation to peasants under the system of collective distribution remained at about 60 yuan per capita. The allocation in 1976 amounted to only 62.8 yuan per capita, of which 23.7 per cent (14.9 yuan) was paid in cash. In 1978, two years after the end of the 'cultural revolution', per-capita allocation was still as low as 74.7 yuan. With respect to the allocation of the grain ration in the same year, 22.7 per cent of the members of the people's commune received a per-capita grain ration under 180 kg. of which half received under 150 kg. That is, each peasant was re-

stricted to a ration of less than 0.5 kg. of grain a day. At this time there were one hundred million peasants badly off with not enough to eat and without adequate clothing. This situation was in urgent need of change.

THE UNIVERSAL PRACTICE OF THE CONTRACTED RESPONSIBILITY SYSTEM WITH REMUNERATION LINKED TO OUTPUT

The period since 1979 has witnessed a transformation, in most parts of the country, in the nature of the production-related contract system of agriculture. Based successively on the group, the labourer and the household, work was subsequently to be contracted in most cases directly to household units, each of which assumed full responsibility for its own production level and management. The contract responsibility system is a form of agricultural production that monitors producers' results – both gross output and value – and pays remuneration for the labour accordingly. This kind of system adapts to the characteristics of farm production and is advantageous in preventing the producers laying undue stress on quantity at the expense of quality – as tends to be the case with other forms of responsibility system – as well as serving to raise labour productivity.

During the period of farm cooperatives in the 1950s, the system was organised around production groups; this was readily accepted by the peasants and therefore was rapidly popularised. By the early summer of 1978, 41.7 per cent of production teams in Guangdong Province operated this kind of responsibility system. By the winter of the same year, the proportion of such production teams was 61.6 per cent in Anhui Province, 57.6 per cent in Sichuan Province, 52 per cent in Guizhou Province, and around 25 in the suburban districts of Beijing. This, then, was at this time the predominant form of farm production. Although the group responsibility system was egalitarian in respect of allocation between the work groups, within them, however, traditional management practices and allocation principles operated. The majority of peasants tended to lose motivation and become dependent on others as a direct result. This led, in turn, to cadres issuing arbitrary and impractical directives. Therefore, in some places, the system was changed to a labourer contract system and then to a household contract system; finally work was contracted directly to households. Here the peasant households contract production quotas from the production brigade.

The produce handed in earns 'work points' in accordance with output. The accumulated work points subsequently determine the household units total allocation. An overfulfilled quota results in an additional award of 'work points'.

What work contracted to households meant in practice was that, after the peasant households had paid tax, sold a fixed amount of farm produce to the state, and dedicated a portion of the fruits of their labour to the collectives, they were free to dispose of any remaining produce at their discretion. This system established clear and precise responsibilities, and resulted in more direct benefits; it was a simple and convenient way of working that was welcomed by the peasants. It took the peasant household not only as a production unit but also as a management unit. As such, it was much more likely to arouse peasants' enthusiasm and to encourage them to play their full role.

The transformation of China's agricultural system from a group to a double contract system produced great change in the rural areas. The household system had been practised as early as 1956, the late period of cooperativisation, in some regions, but it was soon prohibited by official order as a 'capitalistic system'. It was not until the third plenary session of the Eleventh Central Committee of the CCP that, as a result of practical and realistic reappraisal free of dogma, the production-related household system, so popular with the peasant, was put forward again. The results since 1979 have been surprising. Peasants in some backward provinces such as Anhui, Henan and Shandong, had for a long time depended on resold grain for their meals, loans for production, and relief to enable them to live. The practice of the double contract responsibility system put an end to these three dependences, and improved the peasants' living conditions in only a year. As a consequence, in both the backward and poor and the richer areas, the system was adopted and put into practice. This kind of set-up – a combination of decentralised peasant-household and centralised management – has extensive adaptability; it can function well with manual labour as the principle part, or adapt to the requirements of developing the productive forces during the course of agricultural modernisation. At the beginning of 1983 93 per cent of the country's production brigades operated the double contract responsibility system, most of them on the principle of work contracted to households.

As a result of this universal practice, the disadvantages of unduly centralised management and egalitarian distribution in the people's commune system were entirely overcome. The collectives still discharge those management functions that are beyond the capability of single households, and provide services to the peasant households for their production and management roles. They also have responsibility for the management of collective lands and assisting the state to ascertain targets and supervise the achievement of assigned production tasks. The peasant households have become the main element of rural production undertakings. They possess every kind of means of production except land. They engage in production independently and deal directly with the market. They are the basic production units and management units in the countryside. The acquisition of decision-making power by the mass of peasants has established favourable conditions for the development of our rural socialist commodity economy.

For the sake of stabilising the initiative of the mass of peasants toward developing production, the Party and the government have repeatedly stressed the need for continuity in the practice of peasant household management. In order to encourage the peasants to invest in land so as to cultivate soil fertility and practise intensive management, it is permissible to extend the land-contract period beyond fifteen years; at the same time, contracted lands may be transferred for payment. Various forms of social support may also be called upon when the peasants are in need. As with the regulation of the structure of the rural industries, a number of problems arose in the management of land. During the initial stage of transition to the household contract system, some regions adopted a measure of contracting out the arable land on the basis of average household size. However, the drawback of cutting the land into small pieces quickly became apparent. To solve this problem, the Party and the government suggested that, where conditions permit, the arable lands should be concentrated in the hands of farming experts so as gradually to produce farming on a proper scale, to improve the economic performance, and to perfect the household management system. Quite a number of regions have achieved these ends, and won initial success. By the end of 1987 94 per cent of villages and 93 per cent of grain lands in the Shunyi county of Beijing had accomplished the proper scale of farming. In Yinxian County of Zhejiang Province there are 157 family contract farms of 30 mu each (1 mu = 0.1647 acre). Also a number of considerable sized family farms or associated farms have come into being in Changjiang Delta, Suzhou, Wuxi, Changzhou and in some economic developed zones.

REFORM OF THE PEOPLE'S COMMUNE SYSTEM

The people's commune system, with its combined functions of government administration and commune management, was not adapted to the household contract system. The peasants have been freed from the centralized management of the production brigade and have become independent commodity producers; it follows that they should receive aid and be managed in a new way that accords with the objective requirements of economic development. In line with the developing commodity economy, it is necessary to adopt a system of proper economic management to coordinate the various kinds of rural economic organisation. If the collective economic organisations were to remain in an administratively subordinate position and lacked the autonomy befitting their status as independent commodity producers, it would be hard to mobilise the initiative and flexibility of both the rural organisations and peasant households. The lack of separation between government administration and enterprise management also served to weaken the functioning of grass roots organs of political power, rendering their mediatory and problem-solving role problematic. This made economic development and social progress difficult. It follows, therefore, that we must carry out a total reform of the management operative in the people's commune system.

In the early spring of 1979 experimental reform began at a number of selected places. In December 1982, the fifth plenary session of the Fifth National People's Congress passed a new constitution, in which the structure of political power at the village level was redefined. The functions and powers exercised by the village people's commune were transferred to the village government, thereby restricting the commune to its role as part of the collective rural economy. In this way, the task of separating government administration from commune management was achieved throughout the country: by the end of 1984, 99 per cent of the people's communes had complied, creating some ninety-one thousand village (town) governments and ninety-two and a half thousand village committees. The details of the reform were as follows:

(1) The establishment of towns and town governments came within the jurisdiction of the people's commune (in cases where the scope of this jurisdiction was too wide, it could be reduced); this was in place of the function of exercising grassroots political power in the rural areas. The commune was thus to be developed as a cooperative economic organisation at the township level.

(2) The establishment of villages was to be the responsibility of the former production brigades, as was the formation of village committees, the new grassroots organisations of self-government. The village committees took charge of local public affairs and welfare, mediated disputes between people, undertook the servicing role and coordinated work for local production. The former production brigades were thus transformed into cooperative economic organisations at the village level.

(3) Village groups were to be established either in place of the former production teams or on the basis of natural villages. The production teams were to cease to exist, with the exception of those established on a more popular or collective basis. The new cooperative economic organisations and the village committees were to take charge of production management and the job of coordinating between organisations.

REFORM OF THE SYSTEM OF BUYING AND SELLING FARM PRODUCE AND THE SYSTEM OF SUPPLY AND MARKETING

For a long period of time the sale of agricultural produce was effected either by centralised or assigned purchasing – as part of the mandatory state plan – or by negotiated purchasing. With the advent of reform, these facilities underwent considerable change. The centralised purchasing and marketing of grain, edible oils and cotton – so-called planned purchasing and supply – was changed in 1986 to a system of contracted order purchasing. In assigned purchasing the peasants had to sell a certain amount to the state via trade organisations at planned prices. Once the peasants had fulfilled this obligation, they could sell the remaining produce in the markets. In 1983, the state began to phase out assigned purchasing. Currently we practise negotiated purchasing and selling of all agricultural products except certain popular vegetables, the purchasing of which is assigned within a price range. Another exception is that of live pigs, which are subject to negotiated purchase but under guidelines laid down by the state. Negotiated purchasing means that the state purchases farm produce at prices that have been agreed between the state and the peasants in negotiations. Most produce is now purchased in this way.

Our cooperative supply and marketing system was developed step by step in the late 1950s. It was established on the basis of the peasants' voluntary participation, and was supported by the state. But the cooperative system oriented itself more and more toward the state-owned enterprises; this was especially the case during the 1970s. What began as a system run by local people developed gradually into one run by officials. In 1982, the Party's Central Committee and the State Council determined to restructure the supply and marketing mechanisms: to restore their cooperative nature based on mass, democratic and flexible principles, and to ensure that they were run not by officials but by the people. This reform has achieved gratifying results after a six-year effort. The money invested in shares by the cooperative members increased from 360 million yuan in 1982 to more than 3 billion yuan in 1988; the cooperative has its own reserves of more than 40 billion yuan; and the reassertion of collective ownership has been successful. Presently, one hundred thousand peasant members hold leading posts in cooperative management organisations at all levels, participating directly or indirectly in policymakings and supervision. The peasant members therefore exercise the central role.

TEN YEARS OF AGRARIAN REFORM

Reform has brought about an impressive degree of change to the rural areas. First, people have gained a better sense of what a commodity economy is about. Hundreds of millions of peasants have freed themselves from the fetters of the small-scale peasant economy which has existed for hundreds of thousands of years, and turned in the direction of the market and committed themselves to developing a competitive commodity economy. Second, reform has increased the peasants' productivity. In a short period of five or six years we have become self-sufficient in grain, and thereby solved the problem of providing people with sufficient food that has plagued us for several decades. The annual per-capita consumption of food grain in 1984 reached 400 kg. Third, the structure of the rural economy enjoys a greater degree of coordination: as reforms have taken hold, so has the scope of proper regulation expanded. Agricultural policy has developed from grain-centred production to combined grain and cash crops. The output value of cash crops in 1988 accounted for 18.4 per cent of total crops planted – an increase of 6.5 per cent on the figure for 1978. However, in the same period, the proportion of grain, in terms of output value, decreased to 58.2 per cent of the 1978 total. Agriculture, in addition, oriented itself toward the overall development of forestry, animal husbandry, fishery and related sidelines. The output value of these latter activities accounted for 44.1 per cent of the total in 1988, an increase of 20.8 per cent on that of 1978. The agrarian economy, in short, underwent a comprehensive reorganisation in all spheres – cultivation, agro-industry, construction, transportation and marketing. Fourth, rural reforms accelerated the pace of urbanisation of villages. In the course of these changes in rural enterprises and economic centres, the rural population dropped from 82 per cent (1978) to 48.7 per cent (1988) of the country's total; in the same period, the farming labour force dropped from 70.7 per cent to 59.5 per cent of the country's total. Approximately ninety million peasants switched from farm labouring to non-farm labouring.

Gross agrarian output value was 1207.8 billion yuan in 1988, 2.7 times higher than that of 1979, accounting for 40 per cent of gross national output value compared with 29.8 per cent in 1978. Non-agricultural output value, including agro-industry, marketing, construction, transportation and services, accounted for 31.4 per cent of gross agrarian output value in 1978, increasing to 53.5 per cent by 1988. The proportion of agricultural output value has thus dropped from 68.6 per cent to 46.5 per cent. As part of this growth in the agro-industry and marketing sectors, a number of new small market towns were established.

At the same time, the (more or less) self-sufficient agrarian economy has been transformed into a larger-scale commodity economy. Business in the commodity markets is brisker than it has ever been. The rate of return on agro-industrial and agricultural products increased from 45.2 per cent in 1978 to 58.3 per cent in 1988. A multi-channel rural trading network has taken shape, involving the establishment of collective specialist markets, trade warehouses and wholesale markets. Around ten million peasants have entered the new market system. Some seventy thousand urban and rural free markets have been set up, mainly to serve farmers; the volume of their business had reached 155.7 billion yuan by 1988, a 4.7-fold increase since 1978 in absolute terms.

Over this ten-year period, peasant income steadily increased: from 133 yuan per capita in 1978 to 544 yuan in 1988, 3.1-fold increase (1.6-fold not taking into account price changes). The proportion of cash income has risen from 30 per cent to 83 per cent, while expenditure on commodities has increased from 39 per cent to 70 per cent. In this ten-year period, the total area of new living space created in rural areas amounted to 6 billion square metres; also average dwelling space increased from 8.1 square metres to 16 square metres. Total deposits rose ten-fold during this time. Peasants in some regions are set to become wealthy.

The ten-year period of reform strengthened the vitality of the rural economy; the need to 'dress warmly and eat one's fill' is now a thing of the past for the one billion peasants. Nevertheless, fluctuating grain and cotton output in the four consecutive years after 1984 presented agricultural development with a difficult situation. The contracted purchasing prices of grain and cotton were on the low side, the cost of production rose steeply, and the 'scissors differential' between the costs of industrial products and the costs of agricultural products widened again: all these factors affected the peasants' productivity. During this period, both the state and the peasant collectives cut back on investment in agriculture, especially grain production. As a consequence, agricultural installations were vulnerable to breakdown, irrigation works fell into disrepair, the capacity to fight natural disasters was weakened, and the ecological environment degenerated – all these factors served to delay agricultural development.

THE DEEPENING OF AGRICULTURAL REFORM AND ENSURING STABLE RURAL ECONOMIC DEVELOPMENT

Deepening rural economic reform is a very arduous task, especially given the convergence of urban and rural reforms, a development that has both created favourable circumstances and a host of difficulties. So far as the external environment is concerned, the price structure has not yet been ironed out: for example, too many restrictions militate against further regulation of agricultural prices; agro-industrial goods are in short supply, and prices have skyrocketed; the markets are open, yet they suffer from an insufficiently stable connection between producers and markets, that is, production is not geared to marketing; although rural reforms have developed apace, other reforms have not adapted sufficiently to their requirements. With regard to internal factors, there are a number of outstanding problems; for instance, although the peasants' decision-making power has expanded, the contracts and service provided leave something to be desired; the pattern of small-scale diversified production runs counter to the demands of agricultural specialisation, marketing and the demands of modernisation; the product market is taking shape, yet the funds are not available and technological markets not developed; the different elements of production are not optimally organised; the task of developing grain and non-staple food production is great, yet the benefits of producing grain and vegetables and of raising pigs are small – the peasants have lost interest in such production; although there exists great potential in the rural enterprises and scope for rapid development, macro-management remains inflexible.

In view of the above-mentioned difficulties, it is clear that the reforms should concentrate on the following: raising the level of agricultural production; working continuously to improve the contract responsibility system; developing an appropriate scale of farming; deploying scientific technology to the full in the development of the rural economy; accelerating the circulation of rural commodities; tying reform closely to development; regulating the industrial structure; paying close attention to grain production; developing agro-industry; promoting the development of the productive forces and forcing the pace of modernisation in rural areas. Let us consider some of these areas more closely.

(1) Strengthening the socialised system of servicing and raising land productivity.

We must strengthen all elements of the socialised servicing system, building on existing foundations to improve quality of the service to the peasant households and to maximise the system's own economic performance. In particular, the sector responsible for agricultural machinery must be improved. What is needed is an integrated servicing system, with sectors responsible for supply, production, processing and sales; the main components of the system would be village small businesses or processing plants. A socialised servicing organisation would need a cooperative effort on the part of the state, collectives, cooperatives, associations and specialised households.

As well as the need for development and improvement, it is vital to perfect the land contract outlining the rights and duties of both parties. These must be clearly stated so as to encourage the contractors to farm the limited land effectively and to raise the productivity of the land steadily.

(2) Developing the appropriate scale of voluntary peasant farming.

Farming on a sufficiently large agricultural scale is necessary for the development of a rural commodity economy, and is an important factor in stabilising grain production and preventing the dispersion of land – vital to the orientation of agricultural modernisation. The proper scale of agricultural enterprise should be steadily encouraged, in the light of local conditions and on the principle of voluntary peasant undertaking. The scheme should be tried out in selected locations, with priority given to commodity-grain production. When conditions permit, the scheme can be expanded.

(3) Persevering with industrial restructuring, in order to further develop the rural economy.

By improving the system of agriculture and expanding grain production, the production of non-staple foodstuffs should also be greatly enhanced. In accordance with industrial policy, rural enterprises should be regulated, developed and upgraded. In the meantime, the export-oriented, foreign-exchange-earning sector of the agricultural economy should be developed too, according to local conditions.

(4) Further reforming the system of commodity circulation by encouraging peasant participation.

As far as the agricultural interior is concerned, we should first establish an effective purchasing contract system for the staple foods sector. The key to success is recognition of the interests of both states and peasantry – to respect the peasants' right to decision-making power.

Second, the farm produce that is excluded from the purchasing contract should be made available through a diversity of channels. The point here is to help peasants participate in the circulation process. Third, cooperatives and peasant households that produce a number of different commodities but in small quantities may jointly organise a new type of economic association that cuts across the usual trade, regional and ownership definitions. Responsible collectively for supply, production and sales, the participants of the associations will share both the profits and the risk in accordance with their contract.

5 China's Enterprise Reform

IMPROVING THE VITALITY OF ENTERPRISES

Why is reform of enterprises central to the overall process of economic restructuring? First, the enterprises, especially the large-scale ones, play a very important role. The purposes of reform are to establish a socialist economic system that possesses vigour and vitality, and to promote the development of the productive forces. Enterprises are the primary socio-economic units, and form the basis of the developing productive forces. The multitude of large- and medium-scale enterprises provide about 80 per cent of the total financial revenue of the country. As such, they represent our hope for the future. If we are able to arouse the enthusiasm of the enterprises and those who work in them, and turn them into real producers and managers, we will be well on the way to developing a planned commodity economy, and the entire urban economy will be revitalised.

Second, in 1979 we began to expand the decision-making power of the enterprises; we subsequently laid down new regulations concerning the relations between the state and the enterprises, and between the enterprises and their employees. The main elements of the reform were: to simplify administration; to grant the enterprises decision-making power; to reduce taxes and lessen mandatory planning; to replace the system whereby profits are made over to the state with one based on taxation, with the enterprises retaining a proportion of profits after tax; and to practise the system of 'more pay for more work'. There is no doubt that these reforms aroused the initial enthusiasm of the enterprises and their employees. However, the effects of the various reforms were not balanced. In many of the enterprises under public ownership, especially the large- or medium-scale ones, the capacity for self-development has been weak, the economic benefits few, and the function of independent commodity producers and managers not yet operational. Third, revitalisation of the enterprises must involve the regulation of economic relations at all levels; it demands the coordination of reforms in planning, finance and pricing. Indeed, it is essential to have an overall strategic plan of reform covering all sectors in order for the enterprises to play the leading role.

EXPANSION OF THE DECISION-MAKING POWER OF ENTERPRISES

In the past few years, the State Council has promulgated thirteen documents and ninety-seven provisions on the expansion of the enterprises' decision-making power, stipulating clearly that the enterprises, as relatively independent commodity producers and managers, should assume particular responsibilities within certain guidelines, and enjoy a number of benefits the effect of which has been to remove their subordinate relation to government. The enterprises now possess the following decision-making powers:

(1) Power to plan production.

Before implementation of the reform, the publicly owned enterprises were bound to abide by the government's mandatory plans in the fields of production and trade. The enterprises were not entitled to regulate their own product mix and production plans in accordance with the demand in the markets. Following several years of reform, the enterprises responsible for carrying out the state's mandatory plans may now draw up their own production plans, involving new products and developed in accordance with their own actual capacity; however, the prerequisite is that they fulfil the government's order.

(2) The purchasing and marketing power of the products.

In the past, the state-run industrial enterprises were not allowed to purchase the raw materials they required in the markets; nor could they purchase directly from the point of production. Instead they had to depend on state allocation. Enterprises were not allowed to sell their products freely in the markets; they were obliged to submit to the system of centralised purchasing, coordinated by the materials departments or commercial wholesale organisations of the government. The commodities traded by the commercial enterprises were not allowed to be purchased from the markets or to be ordered directly from the factories; rather, they had to be sold wholesale from one level to another – from the first to the second, and then to the third level of wholesale station. Reform has broken the fetters of this outmoded practice. Now industrial enterprises may purchase the raw materials they require directly from the markets or from the point of production. Their products, after fulfilment of the state's plan, may go directly to the markets for sale, or may be sold on a commission basis by trust companies or commercial centres. Commercial enterprises may directly go to the factories to order the commodities they choose. Enterprises are allowed to sell each other's products on a commission basis. They also have a certain power to dispose of unsaleable commodities.

(3) Power to fix prices.

When the state centralised the control of prices, the enterprises had no power to fix the prices of their own products. Consequently the prices of the products could not reflect their cost and quality; nor could they reflect the status of supply and demand in the markets. The enterprises could not regulate their products mix and their trading policy according to price signals. The result was an incapacity to force down the prices of 'long-line products' (goods in plentiful supply) and raise those of 'short-line products' (goods in short supply). Some enterprises became overstocked with unsaleable products; they thus had no alternative but to increase production, resulting in a waste of both materials and labour with no hope of reimbursement. This not only held up the flow of funds but also increased the state's financial burden.

In the course of reform, the state narrowed the range of price control, and gave the enterprises greater power to fix prices. The enterprises may now freely fix the prices of their own products in accordance with cost and the condition of supply and demand in the markets. They may also undertake the purchase and marketing of those products that are produced with raw materials obtained at negotiated prices. With certain products, the enterprises may float prices up and down within the range stipulated by the state. Commercial enterprises are allowed to adopt a flexible price-fixing policy with regard to the purchasing or marketing of regulated goods in the markets. Thus those commodities not subject to state price control are allowed a relative degree of latitude in terms of regional, seasonal, wholesale and retail, as well as quality, differentials.

(4) The right to utilise funds.

Before the reforms, the state exercised rigid centralised control over the income and expenditure of the enterprises. All profits went directly to the state, which then allocated funds to the enterprises for their expenditure. The enterprises therefore had no funds at their disposal. Since the reforms, the proportion of profits retained by the enterprises has been increased annually. Retained profits are divided into several funds: production development, new products development, welfare, bonus, and reserve. At the same time, the method of allocating funds for depreciation was changed: whereas previously a sum for depreciation had to be handed in to the state, now an allowance is budgeted for by the enterprises.

(5) The allocation of wages and bonuses.

For a long period of time the wages of staff and workers were directly controlled by the state, including differentials and the size and type of bonuses paid. The negative effects arising from the system whereby the enterprises ate from 'the state's common pot' and the staff and workers ate from 'the enterprises' common pot' were very serious. Since the introduction of reform, the enterprises' right to allocate wages and bonuses has been extended, and the egalitarian principle and the form of 'eating from the common pot' have been reassessed. Now the state only stipulates the range of increase permissible for annual wage rises, and determines the scope for promotion within the enterprises, thereby allowing the latter to introduce whatever measures they see fit regarding the form of wages and bonuses. Presently, most enterprises link wages and bonuses directly to quotas and profits. Generally speaking, wages and bonuses are allowed to be raised in the range 0.3% to 0.7% per 1 per cent increase in profit. In the event that the total wage and bonus bill of the enterprise exceeds the limits stipulated by the state, taxes are levied to claw back the excess.

(6) The right to develop lateral economic associations.

Before the introduction of reform, due to the fact that our enterprises were under the jurisdiction of the various bodies that composed the departments of central and local government, permission to forge cooperative links was only granted to enterprises within the same levels of given departments. The capital, technology and qualified personnel of the enterprises were not allowed to circulate between different trades, regions or, indeed, enterprises with different ownership. Now, however, enterprises have the right to establish associations across these former demarcations, thereby permitting the exchange of capital and technology, cooperation in production matters and a flow of qualified personnel.

(7) The right to control employment.

In the past, enterprise labourers were allocated directly by the labour departments. Following reform of the labour recruitment system, enterprises now have the right to recruit labourers openly dependent upon the requirements of the work in production. They may also determine the level of skill or qualification demanded by a particular line of work. In the past, factory directors and enterprise managers were appointed by the responsible departments. Now, with the exception of the large-scale enterprises, the managers of which are still nominated by the responsible departments and elected by the staff and workers, the heads of general medium- and small-scale enterprises are appointed in one of the following ways: through direct election by the workers (or through the workers' congress); through an invitation to an external candidate to apply for the job; through competitive interview of applicants from the jobs market. In the past, factory directors could not appoint middle-level cadres (the administrative offices), nor dismiss workers guilty of violating the codes of discipline. Now, they have these powers.

POPULARISING THE SYSTEM OF CONTRACTED MANAGERIAL RESPONSIBILITY AND IMPROVING THE MANAGERIAL MECHANISM

As was the case with the enterprises' decision-making power, the system of economic responsibility was established gradually. The system is intended to enhance economic performance, by practising efficient management of the economically beneficial relationship between the state, the enterprises, and the staff and workers. In 1980, we began a trial that gave economic responsibility to the enterprises; since then we have worked to improve the system. In the first half of 1987, the contracted managerial responsibility system was introduced and quickly became popularised. By the end of 1988, 93 per cent of industrial enterprises were operating the system, including among them 95 per cent of the large- and medium-scale operations. The contracted period was generally between three and five years.

The contracted managerial responsibility system is based on the theory that ownership and management should be separated. The degrees of responsibility and authority held by the state and by the enterprises are defined by contract. The fundamental principles underpinning the system are: an agreement guaranteeing that profits are made over to the state; retention by the enterprises of any surplus; a commitment by the enterprises to make up any shortfall in income. There are a number of variants of this system, as follows:

(1) Two guarantees, with profit-linked wages. The first guarantee is that profits will be turned over to the state, and that enterprises will make up the shortfall when contracted quotas are not fulfilled. The second guarantee is a commitment to technological reform. Wages are linked directly to economic performance and benefits.

(2) A contract that links the progressive increase in profits to an incremental scale of payment to the state. Once the enterprise has paid

its product taxes (or value-based duty) on the basis of agreed profit-linked terms, it must also pay to the state a rising scale of profits for each financial year.

(3) A contract that links profits to turnover and stipulates the percentage of the surplus to be retained and

(4) A contract based on quotas. The terms of the contract differ to suit the conditions of different kinds of enterprises. In some cases, the surplus (or loss) will be retained (or absorbed) by the enterprises, in others allotted in accordance with the proportions stated in the contract.

(5) Trade-specific contracts. This system is practised in the following sectors: petroleum, coal, metallurgy, non-ferrous metals, railways, post and communications, the chemical industry, and civil aviation. It is intended to promote the successful development of specific industries, although the emergence of monopolies remains a danger.

(6) The managerial responsibility system. The enterprises are obliged to pay income tax at 55 per cent on their basic profits. The rate is reduced to 30 per cent for surplus profits. Whereas the state receives 70 per cent and the enterprise 30 per cent of basic profits, these proportions are reversed for all surplus profit.

The contracted managerial responsibility system has recently seen two new developments. The first is the introduction of competition through a system of inviting tenders for contract. The aim in inviting tenders for contract is to engage the services of outstanding managers for the enterprises, and thereby to optimize the terms of the contract. An element of competition goes a long way toward improving the contract system and instilling vitality into the enterprises. In 1988, approximately 30 per cent of all managerial contractors were engaged through competitive tender; the proportion in Jilin Province was as high as 65 per cent. The introduction of this system in turn promoted reform of personnel management in the enterprises, and changed the way negotiations over the terms of contracts are conducted, and thereby instilled a greater sense of responsibility in enterprise managers.

The second development has been the introduction of an element of shared risk. The managers and employees of the enterprises contribute a certain amount toward a contracted mortgage fund and thereby share the risk carried by the managerial contract to which they work. If an enterprise falls short of the profit stipulated in its contract, the mortgage fund will be used to make good the difference. In 1988, 25 per cent of all contracted enterprises practised this system of risk-sharing involving the entire work force; the proportion in some regions is as high as 80 per cent. In addition to its important function in the system of contracted managerial responsibility, such risk-sharing also represents valuable testing of a mechanism that can help enterprises assume sole responsibility for their own profits and losses.

The system of contracted managerial responsibility is the practical choice in the present economic conditions for the practice of enterprise reform. It adapts well to China's national conditions and style of management, and combines rights, responsibility and benefits; it has therefore been universally accepted by the regions and enterprises.

Since the system of contracted managerial responsibility was popularised throughout the country, the enterprises have overcome difficulties arising from the external environment, and have deepened the set of comprehensive internal reforms, arousing the enthusiasm of the staff and workers. Thus the system played an important role in stabilising and developing the economy. One major achievement has been a steady increase in the state's financial revenue. In 1988, state income from taxes and profits increased by 36.9 billion yuan – a sum equivalent to the total enterprise increase in the period 1980 to 1986. In 1988, the contract system helped the state-run industrial enterprises achieve profits and taxes of 155.8 billion yuan, an increase of 17.4 per cent on the previous year, notwithstanding difficult trading conditions – a reduction in income and increased expenditure on raw materials and electricity, the non-staple food subsidy, and a rising rate of interest on bank loans. Among these contracted enterprises, 9024 were large and medium scale. This sector saw profits and taxes increase by 20.8 per cent over the previous year; the turnover period of the circulating fund was reduced from 104 days to the present 97 days; labour productivity was improved by 9.3 per cent.

It is time that the relationships – involving responsibility, authority and benefits – between the state, enterprises and staff and workers are set out in the form of a contract that is so stringent as to put enterprises under considerable pressure; nevertheless the degree of motivation thereby produced is impressive. Enhanced decision-making power has strengthened enterprises' capacity for self-restraint, investment and development, and enabled them to take responsibility for their own profits and losses. The system of contracted responsibility has also helped the enterprises tap their hitherto untried resources, to develop production, to cater to the needs of the market, to regulate the product mix, and to strive to improve product quality and economic performance.

The system has also facilitated the state's administrative control over the enterprises and accelerated the programme of comprehensive internal reform.

Among the problems encountered in the course of popularising the contract system were the following. First, the contracted terms were too low in some enterprises, with the result that the rising scale of profit to be given over to the state left the enterprise with a large surplus, or that the larger part of the profit was allowed to be retained rather than benefiting the state. Second, some enterprises, especially the medium-scale and small ones, that had short-term contracts and inferior managers, paid little attention to the delayed effect of development within the enterprises. Third, some enterprises failed to impose strict control over consumption and instead permitted rapid increases. What is more, they had set aside a high budget for bonuses and welfare within the retained-profits fund; this consequently squeezed the production development fund. Fourth, the managers of some enterprises, especially the smaller operations, paid themselves a salary higher than that stipulated in the contract provisions. This naturally affected relations between the managers and the staff and workers, and dampened the workers' enthusiasm. Fifth, some enterprises practised a policy of relying on the contract instead of on management, which resulted in neglect of necessary internal management tasks. These problems are expected to be resolved in the course of further improving the contract system.

GENERAL RESTRUCTURING OF ENTERPRISE MANAGEMENT

(1) At the beginning of reform in 1979, certain enterprises restructured their entire management system, granting the factory manager effective control, and placing the system under the authority of the workers' congress or the factory management commission. By 1984, in the light of this experience, the Party's Central Committee and the State Council formally moved that the experiment be extended to all publicly owned industrial enterprises. In October of that year, the Third Plenary Session of the Twelfth Central Committee of the CPC duly passed a Resolution on the Restructuring of the Economic System. This proposed that, because modern enterprises entail a complex division of labour, the need for continuity in production, sophisticated technology, and a complicated cooperative relationship, it was necessary to establish a unified and highly effective system of production and

management. It concluded that only a system that gives overall responsibility to the factory manager can meet these requirements. It was thus resolved that six cities – Beijing, Tianjin, Shanghai, Shenyang, Dalian and Changzhou – should adopt the system. In the meantime, other cities throughout the country had also joined the experiment. By September 1986, on the basis of this extensive trial, the Central Committee and State Council formally promulgated three documents detailing provisions for the publicly owned industrial enterprises to follow; consequently, the system of the new managerial responsibility was assured. In order further to strengthen the system, a supplementary notice was issued, requesting enterprises to restructure in line with these provisions. The notice additionally designated the factory manager as both the head of factory and the legal representative of the enterprise; as such he holds the key position and takes full responsibility for the enterprise. The State Economic Commission, the Organisation Department of the Central Committee of the CPC and the All-China Federation of Trade Unions jointly convened a working conference in August 1987 asking for implementation of the provisions and popularisation of the new system. This served to accelerate the process. By the end of December 1987 440 000 publicly owned enterprises were practising the system.

(2) The benefits of restructuring.

The system has cemented the responsibility and authority of the factory manager. He represents the body of staff and workers in terms of their relation to society and the state. He also has decision-making power, control of labour and personnel matters, authority over the production process, and the deployment of funds.

The blending of distinctions between the Party and government administration has been ended. By ceding overall responsibility for the enterprises to the factory managers, enterprise-based Party committees can concentrate their efforts on improving the Party's work in the ideological and political realms, and helping to ensure implementation of the Party's line and the successful functioning of the enterprise sector. A number of Party committees produced valuable work in the field of ideological education, as an accompaniment to the new measures, as a result of which staff and workers have adopted a new, constructive outlook. Topics for discussion at workers' congresses have changed as a consequence, and employees are now encouraged to pay close attention to policy decisions and management targets.

The new system has resulted in a considerable improvement at all levels of enterprise management. Target fulfilment has, in many cases, been achieved due to the establishment of proper systems of management projection and a network of economic responsibility. It is likely that further rights will be granted by the state to allow the enterprises to push through reform in the areas of personnel management, the system of labour, and distribution. This considerable advance notwithstanding, a number of problems remain unresolved. For example, how will the operation of the new system accord with a strengthening of Party control leadership over the enterprises, and with the consolidation and extension of democratic management? How can the political and ideological work of the Party organisations in the enterprises be harnessed to that of the administration and trade union at the point of production? Only if we can arouse the enthusiasm of everybody can we make big strides both in reform and in socialist construction.

THE MERGING OF ENTERPRISES

(1) The merging of enterprises represents an inexorable trend in the development of a commodity economy.

Mergers are not a phenomenon specific to capitalism, but rather an objective requirement of economic development. In capitalist countries such merging takes place on the basis of private ownership, whereas ours is a development of public ownership involving the introduction of competition and the principle of survival of the fittest. In this way we mean to realize the optimum organisation of productive capacity and to achieve rationalisation of the enterprise sector.

In the long course of development of our economy there have been several hard nuts to crack. We have not yet found a way round many of these problems. First, the economic benefits have been few in a system that has seen too many loss makers. In 1989 16 per cent of enterprises failed to make a profit; the total loss was as great as 13.6 billion yuan. Second, the structure of both industry and enterprise are organised on irrational grounds. It is difficult to regulate the deployment of buildings and to optimise functional capacity. Third, there exists both a surplus of idle capital and, in other words, a deficiency. It is estimated that one third of existing capital has an idle or semi-idle status; on the other hand, enterprises in need of development have insufficient funds. We have tried certain administrative measures, such as closing down some enterprises, but with little effect. We thus concluded that the best way to solve the problem was to merge a number of enterprises, and to establish an effective mechanism to free up capital reserves.

(2) The forms of merger and their growth.

The merging of enterprises has been carried through alongside the development of the contract system and expansion of the network of economic associations. According to incomplete statistics covering twenty-seven provinces, autonomous regions, metropolises and cities, each with separate plans, by the end of 1988 a total of 3424 enterprises had been merged into 2856 enterprises. The forms of merger are chiefly as follows:

First, merger in the form of incurring obligation. The accounts and the capital of both parties are merged. The debts and current losses of the mergees are incurred, serviced and made up by the merged unit. The property rights of the mergees similarly transfer. To date, 73 per cent of the publicly owned enterprises that merged have adopted this form.

Second, merger by purchase. Payment is made for the property of the merging enterprises so as to combine the assets into a single organisation. Some 19 per cent of enterprises have adopted this kind of merger, including eight pairs of enterprises in Chongqing, where the purchasers paid 4 million yuan for assets valued at 3 million yuan and more than 50 mu of production space.

Third, merger by majority control of shares. An enterprise gains control of sufficient shares of the mergee to force a merger.

Fourth, merger by transfer. Two publicly owned enterprises agree on a merger; the assets and accounts are then transferred voluntarily by both parties.

A pattern of mergers can be clearly seen: (i) the trend started with a small number of enterprises in a few cities, but is now spreading rapidly; (ii) what started as a process of consolidation between two enterprises subsequently developed to include compound mergers – several enterprises becoming one; (iii) a pattern of mergers within the same regions or trades has changed to one that includes cross-regional and inter-trade amalgamation; (iv) what began as a simple exercise in loss elimination became in due course a self-conscious movement intent on rationalising the economic structure; (v) a process of experiment and exploration gradually standardised its practices.

Eight cities in all have established enabling measures to encourage the transfer of markets and premises, and to make the merger of enterprises common practice. In this regard, the state also promulgated a document, Interim Regulations on the Merger of Enterprises, in order to promote the smooth and healthy development of mergers.

(3) Preliminary results arising from the merging of enterprises.

Mergers are an effective way to achieve the right combination of reform and development and to meet the demands of economic restructuring. First, the optimum organisation of production has helped to advance integrated economic performance. Merger between enterprises effectively creates the conditions that encourage the flow of asset reserves and maximise productive potential, and thereby contributes greatly toward economic reorganisation. The redeployment of asset reserves among enterprises does not increase total demand; instead it increases supply by making effective use of existing assets, and therefore helps balance total supply and total demand. For example, in the five years since the merger movement began, Baoding City has transferred 37.39 million yuan of fixed assets; this represents one quarter of the city's reserved assets. In 1987, the original value of hundred-yuan fixed assets of publicly owned Baoding industrial enterprises had achieved profits and taxes amounting to 27.2 per cent above the average level achieved by 382 cities.

Second, competition, through practice of the survival of the fittest, helps regulate the economy in a rational way. As a result of mergers, unwanted products will be eliminated in time, and popular, high-quality products rapidly take their place. (For example, according to Nanjing's survey of twenty-five merged enterprises, eighteen unsaleable products were eliminated, while eleven new, saleable products were developed.) The enterprise groups or blocs are based on large- and medium-scale enterprises with popular product lines. In that way optimum group strength is achieved. Take the Changsha Motor Electric Appliance Plant, the country's leading producer of motorised appliances. It is the product of thirteen successive mergers, through which it established an inter-regional, inter-departmental and cross-trade joint venture responsible for the production of ten big-selling quality products, involving specialised production techniques. In 1988 the group sold 400 000 units, compared with 200 000 before the mergers – a doubling of output.

As a result of the merging of enterprise, the industrial sector was rationalised and regulated. Mergers are launched in accordance with general industrial policy and regional economic development strategies. Take Baoding City as an example. In recent years, by means of mergers, the four key developing trades – textiles and clothing, paper-making and printing, foodstuffs and fodder, and mechanical and electrical products – boasted total assets of 25.99 million yuan; 17.457 million yuan of reserved assets was redeployed to maximal effect in order to ensure the realisation of industrial policy.

Third, the rationalisation process, whereby superior enterprises absorb and strengthen the inferior ones, has improved the overall quality of enterprises. In the process of merging, the entire culture of the successful organisations, including management practices, codes of conduct and traditional ways of working formed over a long period of time, is transferred to the less effective of the enterprises, thereby injecting them with new energy. The experience in every region was that merged enterprises were not content simply to amalgamate their assets and accounts, integrate organisational structures, centralise the deployment of fixed assets and personnel, but were focusing on the transmission of successful enterprise culture in order to improve overall quality.

Fourth, the burden has been removed from the failing enterprises, reducing the state's financial burden and lessening the likelihood of social instability. Since the mergers began, 57 per cent of enterprises have turned losses into gains, and secured the livelihood of staff and workers in the process. For example, the second Flarky Textile Plant declared a loss for several consecutive years; their debt amounted to 9.4 million yuan; the employee absentee rate was high. Just before the plant was merged, some seven hundred workers petitioned the city government, complaining that they had received no pay for half a year. Following merger, production was resumed and a number of workers were re-employed (others were engaged elsewhere). The profits that year hit 1.05 million yuan; the workers received their pay and a bonus, and their livelihood was secured.

THE DEVELOPMENT OF ENTERPRISE GROUPS

The development of China's enterprise groups is still at an early stage. There are four types of group, characterised by the type of internal link between member enterprises.

The first group is linked by funding arrangements. The means of establishing a single, unified fund common to a number of enterprises is achieved either by the merging of enterprises or by practising a share system. This kind of enterprise group does not add up to much, but it represents the developing trend. The Capital Iron and Steel Complex, for example, successively merged sixteen enterprises; the group now includes groups such as the Iron and Steel Plant, the Mechanical Engineering Plant, the Construction Plant, the Electronics Plant and the General Corporation of Development. Shenzhen Saige Group is another example, this time based principally in the electronics industry. It has 158 member enterprises, 21 of which are subordinate ventures wholly responsible for their own investment, and 59 of which are based on investment in shares. The total assets of this group amount to 1.07 billion yuan. They are organised around a board of shareholders and a board of directors, and are seeking to become a stock-based company. The China Merchants Group, for its part, has 350 enterprises engaged in shipping, industry, banking, real estate, foreign trade and travel.

The second group is founded on productive technological cooperation in the manufacture of leading products. For example, the Second Motor Vehicle Manufacturing Group has 201 member enterprises and institutions distributed across twenty-four provinces and cities, and under the authority of fourteen departments. With Dongfeng (East Wind) Automobile series at the centre, the group consists of a specialised cooperative network. Fourteen member enterprises and institutions between them produce the chassis and the car body; 64 are engaged in the production of cars for special use; one conducts scientific and technological research; 62 provide maintenance fittings, and so on.

The third group shares responsibility for technological development. This group is centred on scientific and technological institutions connected with production enterprise, such as the Keli High Tech Group that is led by the research institutes of the Chinese Academy of Science and associated with twenty-five scientific research, production and marketing units. Among these, there are twelve research and design institutes, with scientific and technical personnel accounting for one third of the total staff; they have a heavy responsibility for tackling many key problems arising in the seventh five-year plan. Products from five categories of this group meet advanced domestic standards. Some groups are based on production enterprises that work closely with scientific research units. An example is the Changjiang Computer Group, which works with eight units including the Shanghai Electric Computer Plant and forty-eight scientific research institutes, universities and companies. There are twelve thousand scientific and technical personnel among the 410 000 staff. This kind of group makes up the technology-based industry which is able to feed the results of technological research directly into the productive forces.

The fourth group deals with entire planned programmes. This kind of group is advantageous in opening up international markets. Examples are the three corporations that produce electrical power equipment Shanghai, Harbin and (Eastern) Dongfang. Their work includes the supply of electrical machinery plant, boilers, steam turbines, in liaison with scientific research units which undertake the design, manufacture and supply, the instalment and testing, and after-sale service. The Luoyang Mining Machinery Corporation, Xi'an Electrical Power Machinery Manufacture Corporation, and Northeast Power Transmission Corporation are examples of this type of groups.

According to statistics in thirty-six provinces, autonomous regions, municipalities and cities operating separate plans, 1630 enterprise groups have been approved by the relevant governmental departments and been registered in the Administration Bureau for Industry and Commerce. With regard to the trade distribution of such groups, the machinery trade has developed most rapidly, there being 282 groups, accounting for 17 per cent of the total; light industry comes next, with 164 groups, 10 per cent of the total textiles account for 8 per cent; electronic groups, 5 per cent. With regard to regional distribution, the coastal areas have developed most rapidly; for example, Guangdong has 240 groups; Shanghai, 163; Jiangsu, 109; and Shandong, 81.

(2) The role of enterprise groups in construction and reform.

The establishment of enterprise groups is a new development that has shown great promise. First, development of enterprise groups will help regulate the economy. It will do so in two ways. One, regulation of the economy depends not only on a policy inclined toward new and increasing investment, but also on the rational flow of reserved assets. Experience has shown that if reserved assets fail to flow, the policy of increasing investment will be greatly weakened. To develop enterprise groups either by merger or by strengthening key players in the sector, or by issuing or gaining control of shares in order to strengthen the groups, can all effectively advance the rational flow of reserved assets so as to strengthen the effect of economic regulation. Two, regulation of the enterprise structure may in turn produce regulation of the industrial structure, especially in terms of the product mix, which is so vital to the entire economy. The development of enterprise groups not only enables enhancement of specialised production facilities; it also helps the formation of economies of scale.

Second, development of enterprise groups may raise the efficiency and flexibility of macro-control. To strengthen macro-control is both an important end it itself and an important means of improving the economic environment and rationalising the economic order. Some current economic activities are out of control following the decentralisation of enterprises, in particular most of the medium- and small-scale enterprises, which have each dispersed activities. To organise the medium- and small-scale enterprises into a group, with the key large-scale ones at the core, can effectively counter the tendency towards dispersion and disorder and centralise enterprise organisation. Only by doing this, can direct or indirect state regulation improve efficiency and increase flexibility.

Third, development of enterprise groups may break through regional limitations to develop specialised production and produce economies of scale. A specialised division of labour will centralise production of certain common components and produce them in large quantities, an important measure to effect an economy of scale. Certain groups, in particular those with trans-regional interests, may promote the development of specialised cooperation across the whole country, so as to centralise production and enable more enterprises to achieve economies of scale. This will enhance economic performance as a whole. For example, since the Jiefang and Dongfeng motor enterprise groups were formed, centred on No. 1 and No. 2 Automobile Manufacturing Plants respectively, the disorganised and repetitive system of producing the medium-sized truck has been abandoned in favour of specialised co-operation and full deployment of available assets. Guangzhou City has organized a Wanbao Electrical Appliance Group by merging four plants manufacturing household electrical appliances formerly engaged in dispersed production, in order to achieve a production capacity of one million refrigerators. This group is now one of the eight largest refrigerator manufacturers in the world. It has opened up international markets by virture of its inherent superiority, and an export output value that accounts for 28 per cent of its total output value.

Fourth, development of enterprise groups will enhance the ratio of assets available. To combine the assets of individual enterprises into group assets can, on the one hand, utilise idle or semi-idle assets; on the other hand, because each member of the group contributes to its collective strength, and a greater range of assets is thereby brought into play, production capacity can be expanded and effective supply increased. This not only has the practical effect of improving the economic environment, but also has long-term significance for economic development.

Fifth, development of enterprise-groups should enhance China's competitive standing in world markets. Under conditions of such strong competition, our products will not hold their position in world markets if we depend solely on individual enterprises. By relying instead on the superiority of integrated enterprise groups, we can become a national force able to compete with powerful international interests.

(3) Development of the enterprise groups.

A number of new trends become manifest during the development of the enterprise groups. These were as follows.

The pooling of production technology resources has developed toward sharing of capital expenditure. The Dongfeng and Jiefang Motor Vehicle Groups, the Shenzhen Saige Group, the Shanghai Baoshan Iron and Steel Complex and the Capital Iron and Steel Complex have taken this road. The sharing of capital resources takes a number of forms: (i) The group corporation and the member enterprises invest reciprocally and hold each other's shares, as was done by the No. 2 Motor Vehicle Group and twenty-five member enterprises. (ii) A new enterprise is established with the newly invested capital in the form of a stock system. For example, funds for the newly established Baoshan Iron and Steel Associated Corporation (Group) were collected by forty-five units at 100 thousand yuan a share. The investment units included key consumers, and institutions responsible for materials, finance, transportations, foreign trades and scientific research. The group deployed the collected funds on steel, intensively processed in the iron and steel plants of Shanghai, Nanjing and Jiaxing, thereby both enhancing the economic benefits and meeting the needs of consumers. (iii) The integration of capital was achieved by means of merging enterprises.

The enterprise groups put their considerable manufacturing expertise into the development and marketing of new products. They can now concentrate on gathering information for joint use, a task performed by qualified personnel backed up by funds and technology. They can also explore possibilities for new products, and put them quickly into production. They can also establish their own marketing networks at home and abroad.

Some groups are tending toward development of international corporations. Shenzhen Saige Group, for example, has established cooperative relations with more than one hundred firms in various regions and countries – the Hong Kong Shenzhen Saige Corporation has set up branches in the United States, Japan, Canada and Kenya.

The internal management system of the groups has changed from the factory system to a corporate style. Some groups have formed a management framework based on three administrative levels, with the corporation as the investment centre. Decisions on long-term development and the utilisation of funds are generally taken by finance corporations. The administrative institutions or branches in the main undertake the business activities and are responsible for profits. The major tasks of the factories are to improve the quality of products and to reduce production costs. This kind of management system has helped solve the groups' internal problems arising from the combination of centralised and decentralised powers. The Capital Iron and Steel Complex and the Shenzhen Shaige Group are adopting this system; the No. 2 Motor Vehicle Manufacturer will follow suit.

THE SHARE SYSTEM

(1) The purpose behind its introduction.

The share system is integral to the development of a commodity economy, and is the fundamental form of enterprise ownership adapted to large-scale socialised production. The experiments in operating a share system in the publicly owned enterprises is a significant step toward deepening enterprise reform. The main purposes of the experiment are:

- To ask owners to take full responsibility for the operation of public enterprises and to enhance their operational efficiency.
- To promote the separation of ownership and management authority in order to produce the capacity for independent management, self-promotion and self-restraint, as well as for assuming sole responsibility for the firms' profits and losses.
- To enable the rational deployment and optimum organisation of the factors of production so as to enhance the performance of the publicly owned enterprises.
- To absorb idle funds in order to transform consumption into production and correct the balance between supply and demand.
- To take over and control enterprise shares and to coordinate lateral associations so as to produce economies of scale.

The following principles must guide the experiment:

- A commitment to majority public ownership and the safeguarding of national property. It is impermissible to convert public property into private property, or covertly to embezzle national property, or to seek high returns from the shares system, causing inflation in consumption funds.
- Within the parameters of China's national conditions, the share system will be tried out first in a number of prepared enterprises, thereby avoiding a headlong rush into mass introduction.

- The buying of shares must be voluntary, the rights of shareholders must be equal, and the benefits and risks must both be accepted.
- The aim is to carry through industrial policy and to promote the optimum product mix, and the best structures for the industry and the enterprises.

(2) The form of the experiment.

Since 1984, Beijing Tianqiao Department Store has led the way in experimenting with the share system. A few enterprises in Shanghai and Guangzhou have also issued shares internally for staff and workers to buy. At the present moment, thousands of enterprises are trying out the share system. This advance is closely related to the development of the commodity economy. Due to an insufficiently developed commodity economy, and imperfect markets for production factors, a lot of joint-stock enterprises are only in embryonic form. Their characteristics are as follows:

- Those enterprises that are trying out the share system are in the main small-scale and based on collective ownership, but also includes smaller-scale publicly owned enterprises. According to data collected by Liaoning Province, for examples of the enterprises involved in the experiment, 85 per cent were collectively owned, and only 15 per cent publicly owned.
- Most shares are held by the enterprises' own staff and workers, rather than issued openly. One of three systems in the enterprises tends to operate. Some enterprises have converted mortgage funds into shares; some have their employees buy shares for cash; some have transformed balanced-premium funds into shares. At present fewer than sixty enterprises are genuinely issuing share certificates openly to the whole society.
- In terms of overall share rights, the state holds more shares than others. In the current experimental enterprises, the state's shareholding amounts to some 60–70 per cent of the total, which gives the state absolute control; individuals, for their part, hold very few shares. Take Shanghai Vacuum Valve Stock Company as an example. The total value of their shares amounts to 200 million yuan, of which the state holding is 140 million yuan, accounting for 70 per cent of the total; the value of institutional shares amounts to 15 million yuan, accounting for 7.5 per cent, while the value of individual shareholding accounts for 8.5 per cent at 17 million yuan.

(3) The development of experimental stock enterprises.

Judging by the situation of the experiment of share system in the enterprises in each region, the patterns are generally as follows:

The enterprises hold each others' shares, thereby forming joint-stock enterprises. In the process of forming lateral economic associations and redefining property rights, some enterprises bought shares with fixed assets such as factory buildings and installations evaluated in monetary terms, while others invested in enterprises by using their reserved funds or, in some cases, with technology, patents and trade marks. This kind of share system should be actively developed, because it is advantageous to promote such lateral economic associations – advantageous to the development of enterprise groups, in promoting the rational flow of production factors, in optimizing the industrial structure and product mix as well as the shape of the enterprises themselves. What is more, it does not generally involve a change of ownership.

The enterprises first collected funds from their own staff and workers, and then transformed themselves into joint-stock corporations. In this way – with the participation of shareholding employees – the development of the corporations remained closely connected to the employees' interests. This in turn meant that employees had to be concerned with both production and transaction activities – adding to the strength of the enterprises. The system also encouraged the authorities to pay close attention to the relationship between the economic benefits of the enterprises and the interests of employees. Employees' income should be linked to development in production and the needs of the given enterprise. The state's interest must not be sacrificed to increases in employees' income, resulting in excessive consumption.

The enterprises openly issued share certificates in order to collect funds from society to expand the programme of enterprise construction and establish new enterprises. Some concentrated on financial bodies; others combined with other large-scale enterprises to buy shares, and then issued share certificates to society at large. Sometimes share certificates were issued by commercial and industrial firms in order to collect funds from society to enable the development of production.

The workers collected funds to buy the shares and then set up joint-stock corporations. This kind of corporation was mainly to be found in the collective economy, especially in township enterprises. Some enterprises were established by means of workers' investment in both cash and in kind – such as the provision of production tools. Bonuses from the shares were to be distributed in accordance with the shareholding. Some existing enterprises recruited workers on the basis of their investments or employed them on terms that involved them buying shares. Such joint-stock corporations are, in effect, a cooperative economy.

(4) The arguments in favour of a share system.

In general, there are two points of contention. First, does the share system belong to capitalism or to socialism? Some people hold that the share system has developed from capitalism and private ownership, and is a form of financial organisation as well as a system of enterprise organisation. However, it is not the case that shares are a phenomenon peculiar to capitalism; socialism is quite able to make use of this system for its own ends. Many people maintain that there are clear advantages to practising the share system. These are (i) Ownership will be specified and personalised, and the interests of state, enterprises and individuals can be linked in such a way that the situation in the publicly owned enterprises whereby everyone is the owner and yet nobody assumes responsibility is ended. (ii) A set of agreed practices will be established between the owners, managers and producers of the enterprises in order to rationalise working procedures. (iii) The fact that employees hold shares should arouse their enthusiasm and interest in the trading activities of the enterprises. (iv) The practice of the share system enables the collection of idle capital funds from society, leading to lateral flow and rational utilisation of capital. (v) The shareholders' acceptance of the risk involved will serve to restrain the development of excessive demand for investment.

Others, however, object to the practice of a share system on the following grounds. (i) They hold that the share system will lead to private ownership, and that distribution will be dependent upon investment, resulting in polarisation. (ii) These people hold that the share system cannot solve the problem of rationalisation in the conduct of the enterprises, and could even lead to the opposite effect. (iii) They hold that socialism will not be able to apply the capitalist share system in order to collect capital.

Second, will the 'enterprise share' form part of the share structure? There are a number of ways of looking at this question. Some hold that the 'enterprise share' is a product of our particular national conditions, and that it is wrong to do away with it just because it does not exist in capitalist countries. Since the implementation of reform, and especially since the introduction of the contract system in the enterprises, profits have been retained for investment and transformed into fixed assets and a supplementary circulating fund; in addition, further fixed assets are formed by means of after-tax loan payments. All these fixed assets make up the capital fund of the enterprises, and the capital fund is practically the same as the 'enterprise share'. The shareholder should be the Workers Property Commission elected by the Workers Congress. The Commission is the legal agent of the group, which has the right to budget these capital funds. Some people believe that when enterprises close down, the proprietary rights to these capital funds should go to the state. Therefore the existence of the 'enterprise share' benefits a system that combines the contract system with a share system, and serves to create enthusiasm among managers and employees of the enterprises; this in turn strengthens the case for the enterprises assuming sole responsibility for their own profits and losses.

The other point of view, however, is that the proprietary rights of the enterprises' reserves should belong to the state, and the enterprises should only have the rules of budgeting and spending. They hold that it is not right for these reserves to be assigned to the enterprises. Therefore the state-run enterprises have no proprietary rights over property; nor is there any 'enterprise share'. The 'enterprise share', it is maintained, introduces a lot of problems, such as how to define rationally the size of an enterprise's reserves; who will represent the 'enterprise share'; who will enjoy bonuses from the 'enterprise share'. These problems remain to be studied by the theoreticians, and the comrades of related departments and enterprises.

THE EXPERIMENTAL SEPARATION OF TAXES AND PROFITS

(1) The nature of the experiment.

The reform involving the separation of taxes and profits, after-tax loan repayments and after-tax contracts was proposed in the latter half on 1987. The major strands of the experimental reform programme were: (i) to reduce the rate of income tax and to enforce the income tax system; (ii) to annul the regulations governing repayment of fixed-asset investment loans before declaring tax-deductible profits; (iii) to annul the current regulatory taxes applying to state-run enterprises; (iv) Enterprise contracts governing declared after-tax profits.

Chongqing City was the first to experiment with the separation of taxes and profits in 1988. Yiyang City in Hunan Province and Xiamen City in Fujian Province followed in the same year. Shanghai for its part selected five large and medium-scale publicly owned enterprises, including Siyang Boilers Plant, Zhengtai Rubber Plant, Analytical

Appliances Plant, Jingang Tools Factory, and the Essence and Perfume Corporation to try out the reform.

Chongqing has had 616 enterprises engaged in a programme of separating taxes and profits. This represents 59 per cent of total budgeted enterprises in the city, of which 228 were industrial enterprises (44 per cent of the sector's total) and 273 commercial grain enterprises (41.8 per cent of the sector's total); non-industrial enterprises totalled 115. A total of 257 were large and medium-scale – 84.5 per cent of the total. The percentages in Chongqing city itself are, respectively 65.9 per cent, 82 per cent; and 50 per cent. In Yiyang City twenty-five enterprises engaged in the experiment, accounting for 67.5 per cent of the state-run industrial enterprises of the city. In Xiamen a total of sixty-seven enterprises are engaged in the reform.

(2) Preliminary results from the experimental separation of taxes and profits.

Judging by the experience of the regions that participated in the experiments, the results were striking. According to data compiled by Chongqing, the 228 industrial enterprises increased their total output value by 8.6 per cent over the previous year, marketing receipts increased by 27 per cent, the marketing taxes by 16.65 per cent, and profits by 57.94 per cent. The profits actually banked increased by 51.27 per cent, retained profits by 44.85 per cent, and the repayment of loans increased by 66.3 per cent. The twenty-five experimental enterprises in Yiyang City paid income tax of 5.553 million yuan in 1988, a 28.8 per cent increase over the previous year; profits totalled 26.376 million yuan, an increase of 25.1 per cent; retained profits increased by 52.7 per cent. Xiamen's budgeted state-run industrial enterprises achieved an increase of 7.71 per cent in their output value in 1988, with marketing receipts up by 33.91 per cent, and profits by 22.08 per cent; total profits and taxes turned over to the state increased by 10.41 per cent, and retained profits were 3.4 times higher. The data in Table 6.1 show the growth of output value in five Shanghai enterprises in 1987–88 following changes in production method and operation.

Preliminary results from the experiment areas follow: (1) Taxation has been standardised and rationalised nationally. Before the experiment began the nominal tax rate for the enterprises was 55 per cent, (the five rates were in fact 43 per cent, 44 per cent, 50 per cent, 51 per cent and 55 per cent). For the trial the tax rate for all enterprises was fixed at 35 per cent, and the nominal rate was the same as the actual rate so as to restrict tax revenue. In 1988, although the profits

Table 6.1　Growth of output value in five Shanghai enterprises (million yuan)

Item	1988	1987	(88)–(87)	Increase rate (%)
Total industrial output value	786.195	745.226	40.969	5.5
Marketing receipts	915.889	772.592	143.297	18.5
Marketing tax	126.955	104.824	22.131	22.0
Profits achieved	134.619	146.783	−12.164	−8.0
Loan repayment	30.026	25.743	4.280	16.7
Funds drawn	–	0.950	−0.950	−100.0
Profit tax	134.610	120.082	14.537	12.1
Income tax	47.143	66.061	−18.918	−28.6
Regulating tax	–	22.859	−22.859	−100.0
Potential fund	6.550	4.665	1.887	40.0
Property holding fees	12.862	–	12.862	–
Net retained profits by enterprises	37.132	25.483	11.649	45.7

of the five enterprises dropped 8 per cent, profits eligible for taxation were 12.1 per cent higher. (2) Distribution of after-tax profits across differing enterprises has been equalised in order to enable fair comparison. Before the experiment, 100 yuan profits would have meant payment of 55 yuan in income tax, 18 yuan in regulating tax and 4 yuan in development fund, leaving only 23 yuan as retained profits, which allowed only 16 yuan for production. Under the terms of the experiment, the income tax for 100 yuan profits was set at only 35 yuan, with 11 yuan going to the development fund; the remainder, after repayment of loans could be used by the enterprises at their own discretion. Thus the distribution of after-tax profits drew level with that of other kinds of enterprise. (3) Loan repayments will now be made after tax, and enterprises can decide on their own investment orientation. This will increase the risk and responsibility carried by enterprises, which will benefit investment and restrict inflation. The experimental enterprises have all, to different degrees, reduced their investment programmes and scale of operations. This will strengthen the investment mechanism of the enterprises and help establish and improve self-control and responsibility.

The separation of taxes and profits, the repayment of loans after tax, and the new contract system are changes in the enterprise management system that will help to establish standardised procedures and perfect the management mechanism of the enterprises, improve the vitality and the self-control of the enterprises, and arouse enthusiasm as well as enhance economic performance. What is more, the separation of taxes and profits will also improve the state's mechanism of macro-control, and condense the scale of investment.

(3) The separation of taxes and profits is a long-term strategy.

The separation of taxes and profits has a significant role to play in the improvement of the distribution relationship between the state and the enterprises, in clarifying the state's socialist economic administrative function and that of the owners, in forcibly restricting tax revenue, standardising taxation procedures, and enabling equal competition. However, owing to the great differences in the scale and performance of different enterprises, it seems that the regions and the enterprises are finding it hard to accept voluntarily the separation of taxes and profits. To compare the programme of separating taxes and profits with the contract system, the former has ensured the stable increase in the state's financial revenues, and restricted the investment conducts of the enterprises. However, the scale of after-tax contracts has been smaller, and the incentive mechanism relatively weakened. In order to be successful, the separation of taxes and profits would have to be introduced comprehensively. Under our current conditions, both the financial system of the enterprises, and the market system are imperfect, and the prices levels distorted; therefore the lever of tax revenue is not able to play its normal role. In outline, major problems are as follows.

The enterprises have a weak tolerance to the separation of taxes and profits. Take Chongqing as an example. A total of 463 enterprises out of the 616 participating in the experiment (75 per cent) were contracted to paying after-tax profits. A total of 78 enterprises (13 per cent) declared no contracted profits, and 75 enterprises (12 per cent) whose contracted profits put them in deficit, which meant that the enterprises could not pledge the minimum retained profit and loan repayment after tax. In other words, of the experimental enterprises, 25 per cent were unable to honour their after-tax contracts, and 12 per cent could not even repay their after-tax loans. In Chongqing, only 44 per cent of the budgeted industrial enterprises were in fact able to put into effect the separation of taxes and profits. The remaining 56 per cent made only small profits, some even declaring losses. It is therefore difficult for them to practise the separation of taxes and profits.

Although the separation of taxes and profits stipulated a cut in income tax, at the same time pre-tax loan repayment had given way to after-tax repayment, placing a heavier burden than before on the enterprises. In addition to income tax, the enterprises still have to pay the development fund and regulating fund, which are based on the receipts they gain. Compared with enterprises in other countries, this represents a heavy burden in taxation.

The conception of retained profits was changed, the calculated bases for all taxes were raised, including that of income tax, development fund, and budgeted regulation fund. This has weakened the capacity for internal loan repayment and transformation. Comparing the situation with that before the practice of the separation system, and with those enterprises not yet practising the system, unfair and irrational conditions exist.

After tax loan-repayment has effected significant technological transformations in the enterprises. Following the latest financial and taxation measures, the enterprises possess limited financial resources. The tax burden accounts for half of the net receipts of the enterprises. In addition they pay income tax, are contracted to handing-over a proportion of profits and development funds, – in total, between 70 per cent and 80 per cent of net receipts must be turned over. Insufficient financial resources make it impossible for the enterprises to undertake long-term programmes involving large-scale investment and militate against the infrastructure deriving direct economic benefits, or key technological reforms being instituted. Instead, only short-term programmes, with direct and quick economic result, are practised.

The above-mentioned problems show that the separation of taxes and profits will take a long time to effect; we should not be over anxious for quick results.

STRENGTHENING THE ENTREPRENEURIAL SECTOR AND ENSURING THE VITALITY OF ENTERPRISES

If we want our enterprises to be relatively independent commodity producers, and to have the capacity for self-development and self-control, we must not only create the right external conditions but also work to build a first-rate entrepreneurial sector so as to encourage the transformation of the enterprises' internal mechanisms. Taking a long-term perspective, if there are politicians and theorists but no practitioners and entrepreneurs, the nation will suffer. It is of utmost importance for the development of the society and the accomplishment of the four modernisations that the creative spirit of entrepreneurs be engaged.

From the point of view of reform, factory managers in key positions have a strong bearing on the management of an enterprise. Therefore, if we want to stimulate the enterprises, we must let the factory managers play a full role. In addition, a macro-environment with the separate powers of ownership and management must be produced in order to utilise the growth of the entrepreneurial sector.

Competition is a law of the commodity economy. Opportunity and risk coexist in all its forms. Our entrepreneurs must foster a spirit of competition and try to minimise risk. They must also grasp any opportunity to carry forward existing plans. We are clearly able to see, in both the foreign and domestic contexts, that well-known entrepreneurs have achieved their success under circumstances of competition and risk. Aiccoca's autobiography shows that he, a world-famous American entrepreneur, is perhaps the outstanding example in this respect.

Along with the continuous deepening and development of the economic system, we must be strict in our demands that entrepreneurs possess knowledge of modern management techniques and abilities in other fields also. They must be able to command a lot of economic information. In sum, entrepreneurs must be strict with themselves not only in their professional work and management, but also in their political and ideological commitment. The entrepreneurs must be able to draw lessons from other experiences, and keen to learn more knowledge in all fields, otherwise they will lag behind competitors.

At present, most enterprises are practising the contracted managerial responsibility system, and therefore there are quite a lot of problems to be studied and dealt with. The managers must explore the nature of these problems and settle them. For example, once the enterprise is contracted, it is necessary to handle sensitively relations between the state and the enterprises, and to generate enthusiasm in both managers and workers, and of how to enable smooth working relations inside and outside the enterprises.

The enterprises must pay attention to trends in international economic development. Consideration must not only be given to the problems of the managers' own enterprises, but also to the national and international economic situation. Only in this way will they become a new type of entrepreneur. All gifted entrepreneurs consider every kind of problem and like to make comparison between their own enterprises and other domestic ones within the same trade; they even like to seek out weaknesses relative to foreign enterprises. Shanghai No. 2 Textile Mill is a large factory; they have done better than others in the same trade. But the disparity in efficiency is very marked when a comparison is made with foreign mills – by a factor of five or six. Nevertheless, the gap becomes a motive force in pushing these entrepreneurs forward to carry out further reform and enhance management and competitive capability in the markets, and to pay attention to changes at home and abroad. For example, a steep drop in the American stock market may not affect us directly as we don't hold much stock or many bonds in the world markets, but it may nevertheless produce some indirect effect that we must not overlook. Another big problem in the world finance market is the devaluation of the US currency and the revaluation of Japanese Yen, which have produced anxiety throughout the world. I recently visited Japan and spoke with people in Tokyo economic circles. They held that, owing to the devaluation of the US currency, it is even less worthwhile for Japanese businessmen to invest in domestic commercial firms; instead they intended investing more heavily in the United States or in other countries and regions. Japanese businessmen have bought up a lot of American firms and will continue doing so if the US currency remains devalued.

It is conceivable that American 'sun-rise' companies might be bought by Japanese businessmen, who have said that they will greatly expand their outside investment in accordance with the international economic situation. Their aim is to gain the highest profits by any means, so as to make their capital fund constantly increase in value. The price of land in downtown Tokyo is much higher than that of New York. One square metre of the land is worth 100 million yen. It is said that the land around the palace in Tokyo is worth more than the total assets of California State. Since the revaluation of the Japanese currency, Japanese capital has flowed increasingly abroad, in the main to Thailand and other Asian countries and regions. If it is considered beneficial by businessmen, their capital will also flow to China. Recently, something happened in South Korea that it is worth paying attention to. First, the prices of the stocks of their companies that have commercial relations with ours have gone up; second, there has been a surge in the numbers learning the Chinese language. Some of their large-scale enterprises willingly provide funding to train personnel in this respect, on the grounds that it will help trade with China. This has shown that the South Korean entrepreneurs are sensitive and shrewed. We hope our entrepreneurs will follow suit. In a word, the significant changes in the world economic situation have tended to exert influence upon each country. Our entrepreneurs must pay attention to these changes in the world markets, and subject them to scientific analysis and assessment. We must find out what is to our advantage, and what is not in our interest.

With regard to the domestic situation, we are going to develop Hainan Island, which is to be granted a preferential policy by the state. This is a good opportunity for our entrepreneurs to invest in this island at the same time as foreign investment is growing. In accord with international practice, the latter may establish companies there. However, importantly, permission is not granted for the import of foreign commodities there; nor is export trade that involves evasion of tax or of foreign exchange permitted. Also we are going to develop Hainan in a planned way, rather than rush headlong into mass action.

In brief, reform has made strict demands on our entrepreneurs who have to be concerned about every aspect and every problem, to learn more things and to open up new fields of vision, and to develop their skills under conditions of market competition and risk.

6 An Approach to the Socialist Market System in China

ESTABLISHMENT OF THE SOCIALIST MARKET SYSTEM: ITS SIGNIFICANCE AND DEVELOPMENT

(1) The socialist market system is the basis for the operation of the planned commodity economy.

In October 1984, the third plenary session of the Twelfth Party Central Committee meeting adopted a 'Resolution on the Reform of the Economic System' and reiterated that the socialist economy is a planned commodity economy based on public ownership. This opened the way for the development of the theory and practice of the socialist market system. The market is an integral part of the commodity economy; a commodity economy without a market is unimaginable. As Lenin pointed out, where there is a social division of labour and commodity production, there is a market; to the extent that the social division of labour and commodity production are developed, so the market will be developed. In capitalist society, the market system, as the basis for the operation of a commodity economy, has expanded and developed to an unprecedentedly large scale, and capitalist society, relying on a continually improving market system, has pushed forward the development of the productive forces. But, it must be noted that the market system does not belong only to the capitalist economy. In a socialist society, owing to the existence of different types of ownership, the exchange of commodity ownership must be carried out by way of the market. Owing to the general existence of a specialised division of labour, each producer (including each enterprise) must realise the value of his own products and exchange them for the use value of other producers' products through the market. In the socialistic commodity economy, the market system can serve the function of coordinating and balancing the national economy through the various economic mechanisms – price, competition, supply and demand, credit, interest rate, and so on. It therefore follows that, under socialist conditions, economic operations cannot be separated from its basis in the market system, and the producers of commodities cannot be separated from the economic linkage provided by the market system. In 1985, the Party Central Committee proposed, in the seventh five-year plan, to develop a socialist commodity market and to perfect the market system. This marked another great step toward establishing a socialist economic system with Chinese characteristics.

(2) The establishment and development of the socialist market system is an important factor in constructing the new economic system.

Under the prevailing theory of the product economy, conceived within the traditional pattern of economic behaviour, the economic activity of the whole society was considered to be like that of a large factory engaged in the production of all things to meet its own direct needs, and the production and exchange of commodities was excluded as being the diametrical opposite of the planned economy. This theory has in practice led to the shrinkage of the market in means of production, the collapse of such metropolises as Shanghai, which was once the largest financial centre in the Far East, an acute shortage of consumer goods on the market owing to extensive implementation of the ration system, and the splitting up of all kinds of markets. In the meantime, a complete system of overcentralised planned administration was established. In this old model, the entire market system was replaced by an administrative system which operated a top-down system of distribution from the upper levels to the bottom in a closed system of circulation channels. It relied solely on planned, mandatory decisions and utterly ignored the regulating mechanism provided by various kinds of levers based on the law of value. The circulation, combination and disposition of productive elements were not carried out in accordance with the law of value and the law of market competition, but were made subordinate to the subjective will of men. This inevitably gave rise to serious drawbacks and abuses. The new market system we are building up through reform is unified and not segmented, open rather than closed, linked horizontally and not controlled vertically, competitive not monopolistic. The establishment of the new market system will inevitably deal a heavy blow to the old methods of planning in the circulation, financial and labour systems. With the growth of the market system, the old economic pattern will be replaced, and the framework of the new economic system will in due course be set up. We shall establish, on the one hand, a market system which is regualted by, as well as orientated and shaped by planning. On the other hand, the law of value will be the prevailing mode of operation in the market. It is only by speeding up the development and perfection of the market system, and establishing a completely new set of economic mechanisms combining plan and market, that we will make substantial progress in reform and achieve a transformation of the old into a new system.

(3) Development of the socialist market system is the way to guarantee revitalisation of the enterprises.

Revitalising the enterprises and motivating the enthusiasm and creativity of both workers and entrepreneurs are the key factors in the reform of the economic system. But without an open market, it is impossible to energise the enterprises, especially the large and medium-sized ones, and to turn them into commodity producers and managers who are self-sufficient, financially independent and equally competitive. Earlier, although we adopted a series of measures intended to maximise the benefits of extending the rights of enterprises, the efficiency and vitality of the large and medium-sized enterprises leave a lot to be desired. One of the main reasons for this is the lack of a complete market system. As the enterprises still have to rely, to a considerable extent, on administrative institutions for planned investment, distribution of materials, credit targets, and so on, it is very difficult for them to free themselves from the subordinate status this relation confers. As conditions of inequality still exist in pricing, capital investment, distribution of materials, and so forth, the legal rights of many enterprises have been infringed. Free competition and an equal exchange of value cannot be fully implemented, and the vigour and vitality of many enterprises have consequently been stifled. Owing to long-term deficits in some of the productive elements, many enterprises have been deprived of the opportunities for technical reform and investment, and thus cannot realise their objective of reforming and developing themselves. Owing to a lack of systematic and accurate market signals, it is difficult for the enterprises to make sensitive and effective responses to the regulation of macro-policy and the changes in market conditions, and they are therefore liable to make short-term decisions. After all, under the conditions of a socialist commodity economy, enterprise autonomy must find its expression only in the market. The autonomy of an enterprise is manifested not only in the fact that the enterprise is free to expand and reduce the scale of its production and to determine the direction of its development from time to time in accordance with the changing conditions of market supply and demand, but also in the fact that it can choose from the different kinds of productive elements on the market at its own discretion. Such prerogatives are fundamental to the enterprise as a commodity producer, and they are inseparable from the operation of a complete market system. If we see the enterprise as playing the leading role in the human drama of economic development and reform, then the market system is the broad and splendid stage on which it plays its part. No enterprise can possess vitality and hope, unless it has weathered the storm of free competition in the market.

(4) The development of the socialist market system is the prerequisite of, and the effective means for achieving, macro-economic control.

The socialist commodity economy established on the basis of public ownership is a unity of plan and market. All the economic activities of society should be carried out not only on the basis of the market system, but also subject to planned regulation in varying degrees. But the planned regulation of socio-economic activities should not in any way be equated with direct command by the state of enterprise production and management. The objective of our macro-administrative reforms is to bring about, step by step, a change from direct to indirect state administration of enterprises, through the effective use of the various means of economic regulation; and for that purpose a complete market system is required. First, only after the establishment of a complete market system can we take steps to establish a scientific decision-making system. The market is an important source of information for the state to conduct its analysis of the economic climate and to make decisions on regulation policy, as it can sensitively reflect the total demand and qualitative needs of society. The state, as the organiser and administrator of the economic activities of society, must take objective reality and the trend of market developments as the basis for deciding the planning policy, and reassess and modify its plans in accordance with feedback from the market. Second, it is only through the establishment of the market system that an indirect system of regulation can replace the direct system and play its role. And, with the development and perfection of the market system, economic levers such as taxation, interest rates, credit, price, and so on, can be made to play their full roles. Only then can a relationship based on the commodity economy be established between the state and the enterprises. The state must make use of the mechanism of market in order to realise its plans. In the meantime, the enterprises can no longer enjoy the privilege of 'eating from the big common pot' by relying entirely on the state, and must make sensitive responses to the signals of the market. So, it may be said that indirect control of enterprises by the state is carried out by interposing a market between the state and the enterprises. Economic and policy information from the state is transmitted to the enterprises by the market, and all manner of economic relations between the state and the enterprises are mediated by way of market mechanisms.

(5) The structure and interrelations of the socialist market system.

As the socialist market system plays a pivotal role in all the economic activities of society, it must be established in a complete and orderly form. Under the conditions of socialist public ownership, it is possible for us to structure the market system in a reasonable and planned way on the basis of our objective recognition of the inherent law of the socialist commodity economy. From a larger perspective, the aim is to establish step by step a nationwide unified, open, multi-level and network type of market system to meet the requirements of the developing commodity economy and the growing needs of the whole people in their material and cultural life.

To achieve that aim, it is necessary for the market system to have an integrated structure. In the old model, men, wealth and materials were considered to be the main factors in the planned regulation of the economy. Now we must establish the commodity market (including the market in means of production), the capital market and the service market as the mainstays of the market system, to be supplemented by the markets in technology, information and real estate, and so on. All these essential markets are interrelated, complementary and mutually promoting. They are all indispensable and should operate on a totally open basis.

Second, the market system must have unity, too. Owing to the vast expanse that comprises Chinese territory, the development and organisation of productive forces in the regions are highly asymmetrical, and the economic sectors participating in the market are ever on the increase. It is thus highly probable that the establishment of the market system in China will have to progress from regional markets to one unified market. However, care must be taken to prevent or overcome any form of regional protectionism, or monopoly and segmentation of markets on the part of certain regions or departments for their own interests. The establishment of a unified market for the whole country is a necessary condition for the development of a planned commodity economy and for the optimum utilisation of social resources.

Third, in establishing the market system, rational organisation must be considered paramount. In accordance with the different conditions of economic development in the country, markets may be formed at different levels, for example, primary markets with rural counties and towns at the core, regional markets with small cities at the core, and markets in large economic zones with big cities at the core; on this basis a nationwide unified market will be formed. The markets at different levels should be open to each other and develop lateral economic relations, so that ultimately a network will be formed. In the complete market system, the commodity market (including the market in means of production) will form the foundation, with the markets in capital technology, services and so on as its organic and component parts. With further restructuring of the economic system and the subsequent development of the socialist commodity economy, establishing and perfecting the market in means of production has become a crucial issue requiring urgent settlement. The issue of the capital market has also assumed a more prominent position. Hence, in the near future, we should concentrate on the organisation and development of the capital market and the market in means of production; in the meantime, however, we should develop the service market in an active but cautious manner.

(6) The establishment and development of the market in means of production.

The establishment of the market in means of production is an important factor in the revitalisation of enterprises and the change to indirect state control of economic operations. In contrast with the market in consumer goods, the market in means of production in China began later and developed at a lower speed; the fact that it cannot meet the growing demands of reform and construction poses an outstanding problem that calls for an urgent solution. Therefore, we must make an effort to build up in a short period of time a truly open and unified market in means of production – that is, a planned market in which the materials in circulation are not, in the main, distributed by administrative organs, and not subject to limitations of linear and regional segmentation.

The key to the development of the market in means of production is to establish a pricing structure by adopting a measure which combines regulation with relaxation, and to carry out steady reform of the pricing system and the price-regulation mechanism. In 1985, the state relaxed its control over the price of means of production operating outside the state plan, and put into effect a 'double-track price system' that allows coexistence of different prices inside and outside the state plan. This is an important experimental measure in price reform, and also an unavoidable transitional stage toward the overall reform of the price system of the means of production. The 'double-track system' serves to promote the supply, retention and replacement of the means of production, to put more capital goods into circulation on the market, and to lead the way in the rational development of the financial, industrial and production structures. What is more important is that such a measure serves to give a warning signal to the enterprises: they can no longer rely on distribution by the state at a controlled price, but should make an effort to improve their capacity to adapt and absorb change in conformity with market conditions. In that way, preparation is made for the state to regulate the price of the means of production in a planned way, thereby bringing them nearer to the equilibrium prices of the market. However, in the meantime, abuses of the 'double-track system' are becoming more and more evident. It has led to serious confusion in the market, producing a hotbed that has bred corruption and malpractice. Steps must therefore be taken to reduce the gap between the two prices and to turn the 'double track' into a 'single track'.

In connection with the development of the market in means of production, another important task at this moment is to take further steps to reform the planning system, to make appropriate reductions in the scope and scale of the mandatory plan by gradually withdrawing a large portion of the means of production from planned purchase and distribution by the state, and enlarging the scope of guiding plans and regulation through the market. In recent years, owing to the rapid reduction in the proportion of planned coal and timber distribution, these markets appear to be more stable, while the proportion of planned steel distribution remained higher, resulting in an acute supply shortage on the one hand, and large unused stocks on the other. To alleviate the situation, we must year by year reduce the amount of steel earmarked for planned distribution, and increase the supply to the markets, so as to open up new prospects for the steel industry. This is the key to the further development of the entire market in means of production. Also, in order to develop this market, it is necessary to promote actively lateral economic relations in the field of circulation and to strengthen market management, so as to produce a well-planned and properly directed operation.

(7) Establishment of a capital market and its future development.

With the change in the way our economy operates, the importance of finance for the vitalisation of the economy and implementation of macro-control becomes more and more evident. It follows that reform of the price and circulation systems and the establishment of the market in means of production must be closely coordinated with reform of the financial system. For, under the conditions of a commodity economy, the financial market, just like a heart which pumps blood into the body, directly controls the vigour and vitality of the enterprises. Thus it is necessary to establish the financial market on a sound footing and speed up reform of the financial system.

In view of the backwardness of our commodity economy and credit system, it is thought advisable to establish and develop the short-term capital market first, and then to develop, step by step, the long-term capital market – this is the natural way to create a financial market with Chinese characteristics. For the time being, we should resolve the problems involved in institutionalising a short-term loan capital market and a discounted payment market. With a view to promoting the lateral flow of capital, we should make full use of the time factor bound up with ordinary capital, as well as regional and trade differences as much as they operate distinct financial set-ups. We must establish a free-exchange loan market, and in the meantime create a discounted payment market by steadily extending to all businesses the practices of bill acceptance, discounting, loans raised against bills, and so on. The establishment of these markets is essential for the development of a capital market, and also to achieve the breakthrough point for establishing a system of credit capital.

Second, we must resolve the problems caused by the diversity that exists in the financial institutions and in their terms. On the one hand, we must break monopoly and encourage competition, allowing a network composed of different kinds of specialised banks to develop, as well as encouraging the growth of financial institutions of various kinds. On the other hand, when conditions permit, we will be able to issue securities such as stocks, bonds, cashiers' cheques, drafts, and so on, and experiment with stock exchanges.

Third, we should consider turning financial institutions into enterprises. The ordinary banks should be reformed and allowed to manage themselves in the manner of the enterprises, so as to avoid any interference by the administrative organs, to encourage free competition, and to motivate the enthusiasm and creativity of the staff and workers. Only when they achieve a higher degree of autonomy, can there be more vigour and vitality in the financial market.

THE INITIAL STAGE OF GROWTH OF THE SOCIALIST MARKET SYSTEM

Since the implementation of the reform policy, an embryonic form of the socialist market system has come into being. Some of the markets have been established in rudimentary form and have shown clear signs of their likely future achievement. They have played an active role in our economic development and have effectively pushed forward the transformation from the old to the new system and the establishment of a new mechanism of economic operation.

(1) The basic shape of the consumer goods market.

Long ago, the consumer goods market in our country was replaced by a form of planned distribution; this resulted in an acute shortage of supplies, the proliferation of receipts and documentation, and the closure and segmentation of markets. During the ten years of reform, with a rapid growth in the production of consumer goods, more and more agricultural products and industrial goods have been put into circulation, thus providing an ample supply for the market and overcoming shortages. This points to new prospects for prosperity and stability, and has laid the material basis for a thriving consumer goods market. Details of the changes are as follows:

First, the single-channel, monopolistic, closed and segmented 'market' has been replaced by markets with multiple economic sectors and multiple channels of circulation. A new commercial structure has been established, with state-run commerce as the main body, but with cooperative, collective and private commerce coexisting in partnership.

Second, new ways of purchasing and selling consumer goods have replaced the old way of monopoly purchasing and marketing, consolidated purchasing and sales, and planned distribution by the state. Now, with the exception of a handful of important consumer goods which are bought under contract or supplied on ration, the purchasing and selling of all consumer goods are carried out on the principle of free choice at negotiated prices. Industrial enterprises and the vast rural areas may dispose of and market their products independently, with the exception of a few important commodities that are sold to the state under contract. Commercial enterprises may now buy freely, thereby breaking the old rule of triple fixing (fixed object of supply, fixed district of supply, and fixed discount in pricing), and removing all restrictions on the purchase of goods by retail commercial enterprises. The number of commodities under the planned administration of the

Ministry of Commerce have been reduced from 188 in 1979 to 22, the proportion of self-marketing industrial goods has increased by about 50 per cent, and the proportion of commodities freely purchased by large retail enterprises makes up about 80 per cent of the total produced. This has greatly opened up the prospects for the development of the consumer goods market.

Third, the rapid growth in the various forms of transaction market has broken down the barriers that operate in the planned circulation of consumer goods, which functioned by way of administrative measures governed by administrative districts. In 1988, following ten years of reform and reconstruction, there were about 70 000 different sized markets in farm produce in both urban and rural areas throughout the country, which served to meet the requirements of the small commodity dealers and the broad mass of consumers in a fairly satisfactory way. In some large and medium-sized cities, the volume of vegetables passing through these markets made up some 30–50 per cent of the total volume of supply in the cities; in some cities the proportion was as high as 70–80 per cent. The total volume of these transactions amounted to more than 110 billion yuan, constituting about 18.9 per cent of the total volume of retail commodities in society. This factor has played an important role in promoting commercial prosperity, stimulating the markets, and facilitating the buying and selling of commodities. The recently established wholesale transaction markets now number some 1500 units, which provide the location for large-scale transactions of consumer goods, thereby facilitating the circulation of goods through different channels and enlarging the scale of free exchange. In the meantime, more than 2200 marketing centres for different kinds of industrial products have been set up, which have become regular market places for large quantities of commodities. This form of marketing has gradually replaced the meetings convened periodically to order the distribution and supply of goods, thus speeding up the circulation of commodities and promoting reform of the wholesale system operating in state-owned commerce.

Fourth, various methods of pricing consumer goods have replaced the single method of pricing by the state. There are now three main forms of pricing for consumer goods. (i) The prices of small industrial products, of a large portion of agricultural products, of local and special products, and of some industrial consumer goods have been relaxed, and made subject to market conditions; all sales and purchases are therefore conducted at negotiated prices. (ii) For most consumer goods, the floating price or ceiling price system has been adopted. (iii) For a small portion of important consumer goods related to the national economy and to people's well-being, prices are fixed by the state. At the present time, the proportion of floating price and market price goods is 65 per cent for agricultural products, and 55 per cent for industrial consumer commodities. That portion of consumer goods should be seen as being regulated by the market mechanism, with the law of value and the principle of equal exchange being realised in a fairly satisfactory way. Even for those goods priced by the state, much more attention is being paid to the law of value in fixing the prices.

Fifth, the consumer-goods market has become increasingly brisk and prosperous, and the scale of trade is growing continuously. The residents in urban and rural areas are guaranteed their basic food needs. The demand of the majority of consumers for a wide choice in clothing has been satisfied, and their need for functional articles of different kinds has also been met. Thus the difficulties once experienced by urban and rural residents in buying and selling goods have been alleviated, and their living conditions have steadily improved as production has developed.

(2) Markets in means of production are being gradually extended. Means of production have entered into commercial circulation.

First, the variety, quantity and scope of materials distributed under the state plan have been considerably reduced – from 689 in 1978, to 256 in 1979, to 27 in 1987. The proportion of important raw materials in the state plan has been greatly reduced: for example, steel has decreased from 73.4 per cent in 1980 to 47.1 per cent in 1987; coal, from 57.9 per cent to 47.2 per cent; timber, from 80.9 per cent to 26.2 per cent; cement, from 35 per cent to 15.6 per cent. In addition, the right of material-producing enterprises to market their own products has been granted, and users can now purchase a bigger range of materials freely.

Second, the method of pricing means of production according to the principles of combining regulation with relaxation and 'double-track price' has been adopted. Since 1979, we have, on the one hand, relaxed price controls on raw materials assigned for self-marketing enterprises in favour of the market or negotiated price, and applied a floating price to part of the means of production. The proportion of means of production affected is some 40 per cent of the total. On the other hand, we have made large-scale adjustments in the prices of means of production, especially those of raw materials. A comparison of the prices of 1986 and 1979 shows that the price of extracted industrial products has been raised by 55 per cent, that of raw-material-based industrial products by 45 per cent, and processed industrial products by 18 per cent.

Third, initial steps have been taken to develop commercial networks for materials and to increase the channels of circulation. Up to 1988, a total of 36 000 trade outlets for all kinds of materials in urban and rural areas throughout the whole country (including both the big markets in materials and small stores) had been established, – an increase of 16 000 since 1978. A number of materials producers began to be run as enterprises, and then gradually to assume the status of commodity dealers, independently managed with full responsibility for profit and loss. The circulation of materials has also been transformed from a state monopoly to a multi-channel network. The inter-regional circulation of materials and cooperation has also developed steadily, and there are already more than 8200 joint companies dealing in different kinds of materials throughout the country, of which more than 470 are of the closely linked type.

Fourth, markets for different kinds of means of production began to be set up, and now play an important role as centres for the circulation of materials. There now exist a total of 1254 trading centres and special markets throughout the country, of which 182 deal in steel, subject to examination and approval by the state institution concerned. Such markets are, in the main, run by the material departments concerned, some by the production departments, and others by large enterprises that deal mainly in ex-plan materials. In the course of the development of the market of means of production, Shi-jia-zhuang city has initiated a way of selling at a uniform price and refunding the price difference: within the confines of the city, goods are sold at market prices and a refund is given according to the quantity of planned distribution by the state. This is a form of controlled, transitional market, which has laid the foundation for the full development of the competitive market in means of production. The practice has been extended to more than ninety cities throughout the country.

(3) Initial growth of the main financial market.

The financial markets in our country have developed from short-term into long-term markets; and reform of the financial system began in the experimental cities and was gradually extended to the whole country. At present, our financial market is a short-term market that deals mainly in loans between banks, and a long-term market that deals mainly in different kinds of bonds.

The loan markets between banks have developed very rapidly and now extend almost to the whole country. In the first half of 1988, total loans in the whole country amounted to 400 billion yuan. These have played an important role in facilitating the circulation of capital through different channels, speeding up capital turnover and improving the efficacy of capital utilisation.

The institution of a bill system for commercial credits is a fundamental reform. In cities selected for experimental financial reforms, markets have been opened for the circulation of commercial bills, which serve to facilitate transfers between financial institutions and also to promote business transactions through intermediate market agencies. The development of the bill-discount market and the opening up of commercial credits for the public have played an important role in invigorating the commodity markets and promoting the trading activities of enterprises.

Primary markets in valuable securities have been set up in rudimentary form. Up to the end of 1988, the cumulative value of bonds and stocks issued in the whole country exceeded 100 billion yuan, of which bonds constituted 10.5 billion yuan, and stocks 2.5 billion yuan. In 1988, the total value of the different kinds of bonds issued amounted to 37.8 billion yuan, of which national bonds constituted 28.3 billion yuan. Since April 1988, exchange markets in treasury bonds have been set up in sixty-one cities, accounting for transactions worth some 2 billion yuan. With the steady growth in the volume of valuable securities, more and more lenders and investors have been attracted to the long-term financial markets. As a consequence, with a view to furthering the development of primary markets and improving the circulation of bonds, secondary markets in valuable securities have also been set up in the selected cities for trial financial reforms. In addition, foreign-exchange markets have gradually been established throughout the country, particularly in the cities operating separate plans and the Special Economic Zones. The control of foreign-exchange rates has been lifted, and the rates now float freely according to market conditions. In 1988, the total foreign-exchange-adjustment fund amounted to US$6.22 billion.

(4) The early development of various forms of service market.

With the reform of the service system, service markets have been developed throughout the country. Up to now, the labour departments above the level of county and city have between them established more than 3000 labour service markets, which provide the location for 'two-way selection' for both the employing units and those job-seekers, and act as the vehicle for a rational circulation of the labour force. In the last two years, the total number of people employed through the service market amounts to 1.8 million.

Another role of the labour service market is to act as a go-between to enable adjustments within the labour force – to reallocate the work and posts of those workers who are not suitably employed or who have difficulties in attending work owing to distance.

With the optimum fulfilment of labour forces in the enterprises, labour service markets have developed rapidly. Though such a form of organisation has limitations, under existing conditions it is generally welcomed by all parties concerned, as it serves to relieve the pressures in society to an extent. In some districts, the service markets of different enterprises are open to each other, and reallocation of staff between factories has been carried out with good results, which serves to promote the enterprise reform in a worthwhile way.

(5) Increasing the prosperity of technological markets.

With the development of a socialist planned commodity market, the technological advances that were formerly deployed without compensation are now penetrating, as a kind of commodity, into every sphere of society and the economy through the various forms of production transfer, consultation, service, technological investment, techno-economic contracts, and so on. Technological markets have also been developed. The main features are as follows.

First, a rapid growth in the volume of technological transactions. Since 1985, the volume has increased annually. In 1988, it amounted to 7.24 billion yuan, showing an increase of 16 per cent over that of 1981.

Second, a steady increase in technological input. According to 1987 data, the aggregate of research deployment contracts, technological transfer contracts and foreign-invested technological contracts made up 40.97 per cent of the total, showing a marked increase in technological input.

Third, the entry of large and medium-sized enterprises into the technological market. In 1988, the technological achievements that flowed into enterprises through the technological markets amounted to 179 000 hectares, which made up 68 per cent of the total volume of contracted transactions in 1988. The number, quantity and volume of transactions have increased two-fold in a year.

Fourth, a marked increase in foreign-investment contracts. The volume of technological exports in 1988 exceeded US$100 million, and in Shanghai alone was in excess of US$40 million.

The technological market serves to promote the application and popularisation of scientific and technological achievement, the adjustment of the productive structure of enterprises, and the flow of skills and intellectuals. It has also enhanced the power of self-development on the part of scientific research institutions.

(6) Initial formation of real-estate markets.

With the development of a housing market, 170 cities throughout the country have established specialised institutions for the transaction of real estate, with 330 real-estate outlets spread over more than twenty provinces, cities and autonomous regions. According to a study of these outlets, over the past three years, a total of 170 000 transactions were completed, with a total value of 1.6 billion yuan and covering an area of 10 million square metres. The service has developed from the simple buying, selling and registration of private houses to a more comprehensive service. For instance, the real-estate outlet in Chunging has provided for its customers services for the purchase, sale and renting of old houses; the sale and resale of commodity houses; the construction of houses financed by collective funds; legal consultation; house exchanges; the management of real estate, and so on. In some of the cities, housing cooperatives have also been established.

ESTABLISHING A MARKET AND REGULATING BUSINESS ACTIVITIES

(1) The necessity of establishing and regulating the market.

In the ten-year reform, we have made great achievements that have been universally acknowledged; in this time, profound changes have taken place in the social environment, the economy and the lives of the people. But, as the old system has not yet been fully replaced and the new system was still to be firmly established, the two systems coexist in a state of contradiction and friction. During the present critical moment when the systems are in transition and the future of reform is faced with many alternatives, the three problems of excessive price rise, unfair distribution of wealth, and graft and corruption have increasingly aroused the concern of the whole country. Of special concern are the few people who seek personal gains through the use of their official status. Intent on making exorbitant profits by illegally reselling goods and indulging in bribery and other malpractices, they have seriously interfered with the normal operation of the social economy, slowed down reform and infringed the interests of the entire country and its people.

At the present juncture when the establishment of a new socialist economy and the implementation of price reform are urgently required, these negative elements must be dealt with effectively. We must cleanse the soil that breeds such evils by deepening reform, in particular by firmly establishing a market order based on openness, money-based transactions and a system of billing and by regularising and legalising business activities. The establishment and perfection of the market system must be accompanied by a sound market order. This will provide an important guarantee for the new system.

(2) Problems to be solved in establishing the market order and regulating transactions.

In order to establish the new market order and to realise on open, money-based economic foundation, a billing system and standardised and legal transaction procedures, it is necessary to confront the following issues.

First, it is necessary to phase out the double-track price system, to regularise the prices of means of production, and to deregulate the price controls on consumer goods. Price is the objective standard for the exchange of commodities and the main indicator of the state of the market. At present, one of the biggest problems is the irrationality of price relations. The prices of some commodities deviate widely from their values, and do not reflect the relation between supply and demand. Such distortions lead to a vicious cycle in economic life. Another problem is that abuses of the double-track system are becoming more evident, although it did play an active role at the very beginning of the reforms. Some corporations and departments have made exorbitant profits from plan-derived materials and quotas in their hands, which is hardly compatible with the principle of equal competition. It is, therefore, necessary to carry out price reforms in an active but steady way. Price reform does not simply involve adjustments in price relations. It is intended to transform the mechanism with the ultimate aim of forming a new price system in which the prices of the great majority of commodities and services are determined by the market, and to establish a reasonable price mechanism and a standardised system of regulation.

Second, it is vital to protect and promote fair trade and equal competition. What is equal competition? It means that no economic monopoly must exist and there must be no discrimination, so that all enterprises are on the same starting line. What is fair trade? It means trade that excludes any improper measures. Some of our enterprises extend their markets not on the strength or quality of their commodities and services, but by peddling products of inferior quality at sales commissions, thus giving rise to confusion and corruption in the market. Such practices tend to have an unfavourable effect at the industrial technical level and reduce economic benefits to the country. During an investigation in Dalian, I discovered an enterprise which had instituted an award for promoting sales of overstocked and sub-standard commodities! Such a way of marketing is obviously contrary to the principle of equal exchange of value, fair trade and equal competition.

Third, we must change the method of planning. It is necessary to reduce the power of resource distribution – including materials, capital and foreign exchange – wielded by administrative departments, and implement a system of ordering goods consigned to the state by way of public tender and competitive contract, with no evidence given to any organisation. To ensure the state's supply of goods, legal protection may be taken, such as implementing the principle of preferential supply to state orders.

Fourth, we must aim to establish a unified, open market. Now, although lateral connections between regions have developed considerably, regional segmentation and protectionism are still very serious problems. In the course of carrying out the strategic policy of economic development in the coastal regions, many issues have arisen which call for serious consideration and resolution. For example, how do we resolve the contradictions between coastal and inland markets, and those between the processing-industry and raw-materials zones? Regardless of the differing regional conditions, there must be a common order to be observed by all. In carrying out the open-door policy, we must take into consideration the requirements of the international market, and act according to the customary practices of the international community.

Fifth, we must move to screen and reorganise corrupt companies and put an end to all official profiteering and speculation. The combined efforts of officials and merchant companies are able to make huge sums of excessive profits by the illicit purchase and resale of means of production and scarce consumer goods, and by pushing up prices through the different levels of circulation. This practice has seriously impaired the image of the Party and government and aroused the strong indignation of the people. Therefore strong action must be taken to screen and reorganise such corrupt companies so as to ensure the smooth progress of the reform.

Sixth, it is important to develop and perfect the organisation of trade in the market. It is necessary to establish wholesale markets and auction markets for all every kind of product and material, to formulate rules and regulations in connection with these new markets, and to give support to small wholesale merchants and material retail merchants who deal mainly with small enterprises in both town and country. We must establish a system of quoting prices openly, institute a system of anti-monopoly inside the market and prohibit wholesale trade outside the market. In addition, an asset-auditing system, and financial reports must be introduced.

Seventh, we have to speed up legislative procedures and strengthen economic supervision. It is necessary to formulate laws and regulations governing market transactions, such as a Market Transaction Law, a Wholesale Market Law, a Law of Fair Competition in the Market, a Market Supervision Law, an Anti-monopoly Law, a Private Enterprise Law, a Labour Law, and so on. In the meantime, we must strictly enforce financial and economic discipline, and perfect accounting, auditing and business accounting procedures. Further steps should be taken to strengthen financial management inside the enterprises, the management of cash and transfer payments to banks, and so on.

Eighth, government cadres, and those of the Party and army institutions must be prohibited from taking concurrent or honorary posts in enterprises and companies. Retired cadres engaged in trade activities should be deprived of all their official state retirement benefits. It is also necessary to formulate and implement the Administrative Litigation Law, and to establish an Administrative Court and mete out severe punishment to state personnel found guilty of bribery, corruption and malpractice.

7 The Restructuring of China's Macroeconomic Management System

Since the start of the reform process in China steps have been taken to reduce centralisation, over-rigid control and direct interference. A macro regulation system is steadily being formed that conforms to the principle of combining a planned economy with market forces by the integrated use of economic, administrative and legal measures.

REFORM OF THE PLANNING SYSTEM AND THE ESTABLISHMENT OF A MACRO REGULATORY SYSTEM

In 1953, when the first five-year plan had just been put into effect, in order to meet the requirements of the large-scale economic reconstruction being undertaken at that time the state oversaw the overall management of the national economy and began to establish a highly centralised and unified planning system. This system allowed the establishment of a relatively complete industrial system and improved the material and cultural life of the people. However, with economic reconstruction and the increasing complexity of economic relations, the shortcomings of the system became more and more obvious.

First, planning was overcentralised, the scope of the mandatory plan was too extensive and control over the enterprises was too rigid. The enterprises were unable to adjust production according to shifts in supply and demand, which gave rise to imbalance.

Second, the emphasis on central administration and ignorance of the law of value and market mechanisms tended to prevent direct contact between the enterprises and the market, restrict competition between enterprises and impair their performance.

Third, misdirection of investment capital, state monopoly of the purchase and sale of products, state control of revenue and expenditure, and lack of enterprise responsibility for profits and losses resulted in high production costs and low investment benefits.

116

Since 1979, and especially since 1984, in order to counteract the shortcomings of the original planning system the following reform measures have been introduced.

First, the mandatory planning of agricultural production has been abolished and farmers are now permitted to adapt their production to local conditions. Beginning in 1985 the sale and purchase of agricultural and related products such as grains, cotton, fishery products and vegetables have been deregulated and are now carried out through contracted ordering, market purchasing or free transactions on the open market.

Likewise the scope of mandatory planning of industrial products has been reduced and the decision-making power of enterprises increased. The number of industrial products managed by the State Planning Commission have been reduced from 120 to about 60, and the greater autonomy of the enterprises, especially large and medium-sized enterprises, has meant that they have begun to pay attention to the marketability of and demand for their products, thus stimulating an improvement in all-round performance.

The kinds and amount of materials under planned distribution by the state and the amount of materials managed by ministries have been reduced and organised markets for the means of production have been developed. During the period 1979–87 the number of materials under planned state distribution was reduced from 256 to 76.

Second, the power to approve investment projects has been granted to lower hierarchical levels and the procedure of examination and approval simplified. The capital limit above which items of productive construction and technical renovation become subject to examination and approval by the State Planning Commission are as follows: for decision relating to energy resources, transportation and raw materials the limit has been raised from 10 million yuan in 1984 to 50 million yuan; for other items the limit has been raised from 10 million yuan to 30 million yuan. Items of non-productive construction may be examined and approved by the ministry or officers of provinces, autonomous regions, municipalities that are under central government control or separately planned municipalities under provincial governments, provided the problems of capital, energy resources, raw materials and equipment can be solved by the units concerned.

The indiscriminate use of investment capital has been curtailed by replacing state grants to enterprises with loans from banks. Scientific research institutions, schools and administrative units, which lack the ability to repay loans, continue to receive government funding.

In the old system engineering construction work was controlled by the central administration and expenses were reimbursed to the departments and regional institutions concerned. The new system of open public bidding, without interference from departments or regions and based on the principle of equal competition and survival of the fittest, will help to promote technical improvement, speed up the construction process and ensure its quality, reduce the cost of engineering work and enhance the benefits of the investments.

The state has instituted a preconstruction planning system and formulated rules and criteria governing the proposed construction programmes. Evaluating the feasibility of large and medium-sized technical reconstruction programmes and the design of large-scale construction work has been placed in the hands of the China International Consultation Corporation. Only after feasibility is confirmed does the State Planning Commission decide whether a programme should be included in the state plan.

With a view to ensuring a stable capital source for key construction projects, thus allowing construction work to be completed in a reasonable period of time, a capital construction fund was set up in 1988. In the meantime, the state has established five investment corporations specialising in the areas of energy resources, raw materials, transportation, agriculture, and the machinery, electronic and textile industries. They are responsible for managing capital construction and technical reconstruction programmes, the periodic collection of profits and foreign exchange, the allocation of products according to the terms of contracts and helping banks to collect loan and interest payments. They keep their own business accounts, pursue management through economic measures and are working towards changing their administrative relationships with firms into relationships of economic contract.

Third, for a long time planned management centred mainly on administrative command and target allocation, utterly ignoring the law of value. Now, in accordance with the requirements of the developing socialist commodity economy, it is necessary to focus on the exchange of commodities and the law of value, and to make integrated use of economic levers such as the reform and readjustment of prices in order to promote a balance between production and demand. Construction taxes have been levied to control the scale of self-raised investment capital. Differential interest rates and interest payments in the form of deductions have been adopted to promote the development of basic industry and basic installations.

Fourth, the practice of separate planning for municipalities and large-sized enterprise groups is playing an active role in developing lateral economic relations, strengthening the centralising function of municipalities and accelerating the opening up of the country to internal and external economic forces.

In spite of the above improvements, macro management of the state is still poor and the macroeconomic regulation system has not been put on a sound basis. Although the amount of financial and material resources and foreign exchange that is handled directly by the state has been reduced and the scope of direct management diminished, a corresponding indirect system of regulation and management making use of various kinds of economic policy and regulatory measures has not been set up in its stead. Different policies and spheres of regulation are handled by different departments and their operation is not coordinated. Therefore there is no institutional and organisational guarantee that their objectives and measures are united and compatible. Economic development in different regions of China's vast territory is highly diversified and to rely solely on the central government for control and management is hardly practical. It is therefore necessary to introduce a stratified system of regulation and control and graded management. Responsibility for financial expenditure and subsidies should be divided between the central, provincial, municipal and county governments, as should taxes and other receipts.

The central government should maintain overall responsibility for macroeconomic development strategies; medium- and long-term economic development projects, the aggregate balance of the macroeconomy; important industrial, structural, financial, monetary and credit policies; and the construction of important basic installations; as well as energy supply, transportation, national laws and regulations, and so on. Provincial governments should take charge of local economic development strategies and so on. With the exception of large state-owned enterprises of national importance, which should be directly managed by the central government, the great majority of enterprises should be supervised by officers of the municipalities where they are located.

REFORM OF THE FINANCIAL AND TAXATION SYSTEMS

(1) With a view to regularising the relationship between the state and the enterprises in the distribution of profits and expanding the financial power of the enterprises, three relatively major reforms have been carried out.

First, from 1979–82 various measures concerning partial retention of profits and full responsibility for profits and losses were put into effect. Profit-making enterprises were able to retain part of their profits according to a fixed rate, the remainder being handed over to the state. Loss-making enterprises were required to compensate for their losses.

Second, since 1983 the receipts of state-owned enterprises that were originally turned over to the state in the form of profits have been treated as income and regulatory taxes. The portions retained for free disposal by the enterprises may be used for technical improvement, for the welfare of employees, for issue as bonuses and so on.

Third, since 1987, in large and medium-sized state enterprises various forms of contracted responsibility have been instituted, whereby the level of profits to be turned over to the state is contractually fixed. This system is mainly intended to promote greater effort in the enterprises and encourage them to realise their full potential, thus improving their economic benefits.

These three reforms have greatly increased the autonomous financial resources of the enterprises.

Finally, since 1983 the original method of depreciation according to overall depreciation rates has been steadily changed into depreciation according to group depreciation rates. Up to 1987 the group depreciation method was applied to all state-run industrial and communications enterprises and the depreciation rate was raised from the original 4.3 per cent to 5.3 per cent. Since 1985 the 30 per cent depreciation fund, which was originally kept by the central financial department, has been transferred to the enterprises for their own disposal. Also, any new, experimental products manufactured by enterprises have been given favourable treatment in taxation policy.

(2) The budgetary management system has been reformed so as to promote the enthusiasm of regions for financial management. Since 1980 regional financial administrations have been required to separate revenue and expenditure. Quotas have been fixed for different levels and categories of taxes, and for different levels of budgetary management. That is to say, the scope and amount of regional revenue and expenditure, and the proportion shared between the central and regional institutions, is set according to the relative status of each enterprise so as to motivate the regions to increase their production and revenue levels.

(3) Various changes have been made to the taxation system in order to develop it as an economic lever:

1. Income tax has been levied on state-owned enterprises.
2. Industrial and commercial tax has been changed to product tax, value added tax, business tax and salt tax. Tax rates have been readjusted so as to alleviate the contradictions brought about by irrational prices.
3. Resources taxes, starting with a tax on enterprises and individuals engaged in the exploitation and production of crude oil, natural gas and coal, has been introduced in order to regulate the differential receipts that result from the differences in the conditions of natural resources.
4. Some local taxes have started to be collected, such as tax on construction in cities, real estate tax, tax on the use of vehicles and boats, tax on the use of land, stamp tax and so on.
5. Certain taxes are being collected in order to regulate certain enterprises' activities, such as bonus tax, wage regulation tax, construction tax, a special tax on paraffin, tax on the occupation of arable land, and so on.

With a view to meeting the requirements of opening up to the outside world while protecting national interests and ensuring equality and mutual benefits, since 1980 various laws and regulations have been instituted concerning foreign involvement in China, such as the 'Income Tax Law Concerning Joint Ventures With Chinese and Foreign Investment', the 'Income Tax Law Concerning Foreign Firms', the 'Individual Income Tax Law' and so on. Since August 1989, income tax on the wages and salaries of foreign personnel in China have been levied at half rate.

(4) The system of financial allocation for capital construction investments within the state budget has been reformed in order to enhance economic benefits. Formerly, investment in capital construction was state funded. From 1979 experiments were conducted in certain regions and trades with an eye to changing the practice of allocating finances into a system of loans for capital construction. Since 1985 this has been extended to all construction programmes and differential interest rates have been applied to different trades. Some construction programmes are subject to an investment quota system and a bidding system has been applied to some engineering projects. These measures have served to instil a sense of responsibility and purpose on the part of construction and working units, and to a certain extent have proved instrumental in reducing total investment, lowering the cost of construction, shortening construction time and enhancing the economic benefits of the investments.

Remarkable achievements have been brought about as a result of ten years of reform in the financial and taxation systems. But as certain measures have not yet been fully implemented and regulation and control of the macroeconomy have not kept pace with the changing conditions, a number of problems still exist. For example the distribution of profits between state and enterprises has not been set in order, so a number of large and medium-sized enterprises still lack vitality. Also the proportion of state revenue in total national revenue has been much reduced and at present the revenue directly organised by the central financial department makes up less than 40 per cent of the total, which is incommensurate with central government expenditure.

Henceforth on the basis of summing up our practical experiences in the past years and in coordination with the overall reform in different respects, we shall make efforts to strengthen the role of taxation in regulating and controlling the macroeconomy so as to improve supply, suppress demand and enhance economic benefits. The main points of further reform are as follows.

First, steps must be taken to set in order the distribution relationship between the state and the enterprises, so as to cope with the development needs of enterprise groups.

Second, steps must be taken to perfect the existing taxation system. Based on the principle of fairness of taxation, promotion of competition and realisation of industrial policy, tax categories should be introduced and tax rates fixed in such a way as to give full play to the role of taxation as an economic lever. Further steps should be taken to perfect the distribution of taxes. In accordance with state economic policy and industrial policy and in tandem with price reform, product tax should be adjusted; value added tax should be increased and its scope extended. It is necessary to unify income taxes throughout the country and to study the feasibility of levying business taxes on real estate. Further steps should be taken to improve the existing system of specific-purpose taxes, such as the tax for the maintenance and construction of cities, the bonus tax, the wage-regulating tax, the construction tax and so on.

In the meantime the taxation management system should be studied and improved, taxation laws and regulations strictly enforced, and tax reductions and exemptions clearly defined so as to strengthen the function of taxation and maximise financial receipts.

STRENGTHENING THE ABILITY OF THE CENTRAL BANK TO CONDUCT MACRO REGULATION AND CONTROL

China's original financial system was modelled on the Soviet pattern and combined many kinds of financial institution into a single, unified People's Bank. Various forms of credit circulation were abolished and the People's Bank was responsible only for temporary, short-term capital loans over and above allocated quotas. This resulted in a highly centralised financial system employing administrative measures as the chief means of management. However that system did play an important role in accumulating the state's capital, centralising financial resources and providing a guarantee for key construction projects. Its main drawbacks were manifested in the fact that capital was distributed from the 'big common pot', and the bank issued money only according to the production and circulation plans formulated by planning departments. The bank was little more than an accountant or cashier and was not able to make use of its resources to bring about a flexible and effective flow of capital to promote the development of production.

Since the start of the reform process the following changes have been made.

Establishment of a financial system under the leadership of the Central Bank

The Bank of China is the central state bank. Under the leadership of the State Council, it is responsible for managing the foreign exchange fund and dealing with business concerning the international settlement of accounts, foreign trade, foreign exchange credit and business relevant to the renminbi. The Bank of China provides a doorway to the development of financial, economic and commercial relations with foreign countries and plays an important role in implementing China's policy of opening up to the outside world, especially in promoting exports and organising and utilising foreign capital.

As manager of the financial affairs of the entire nation, the bank's main duties are formulating China's guiding financial principles and policies, which are submitted to the State Council for approval and enforcement; drafting financial statutes and formulating basic financial regulations; handling the issuing of currency, regulating its circulation and maintaining its stability; setting interest rates and fixing the exchange rates between the Renminbi and foreign currencies; drawing up the state credit plan and centralising the management of credit funds;

managing nationwide insurance business; managing valuable securities, such as enterprises stock, bonds and so on; and guiding, managing, coordinating and supervising the business of the following specialised banks and financial institutions.

Specialised banks

The People's Construction Bank of China undertakes all business relating to the issuing and management of capital construction loans. The Industrial and Commercial Bank of China handles industrial and commercial credit and savings deposits, all of which were formerly the realm of the People's Bank. The Agricultural Bank is concerned with credit business in rural areas.

Other financial institutions

Rural credit cooperatives are intended to promote the development of a rural commodity economy. Similar organisations in cities are designed to make up for the shortage of banking networks; to alleviate the difficulties that industrial and commercial workers experience in opening accounts, obtaining loans and settling accounts; and to give support to the development of various economic sectors.

Investment trust institutions allow the collection of idle capital, conduct the flow of local ex-budget capital, promote the development of financial entities and help to develop fair competition among financial enterprises.

In accordance with China's policy of opening up to the outside world, permission has been given for foreign financial institutions to establish agencies and offices in China and to establish banks with foreign or joint capital in the special economic zones. This acts as a supplement to the socialist financial system.

Reform of the banking business system

Banks should be encouraged to increase their sources of capital through increasing the number of branches and services offered, providing different types of account and raising their deposit interest rates.

To extend the field and scope of credit, the right to borrow from banks has been extended to enterprises in the non-state sector and individuals. To meet the new requirements a number of new credit means have been set up; new types of deposit account have been introduced, such as housing-construction deposit accounts and trust deposit accounts; and large quantities of transferable certificates and financial bonds have been issued.

Improving and strengthening macro management by the central bank

With reform of the planning, financial, investment and other systems, the scope of the mandatory plan has become more and more reduced and macroeconomic management has been steadily replaced by indirect management. Money supply has become an important feature of the macroeconomy, and the interest and exchange rates have become a means of macro regulation. The People's Bank of China, through planning measures, determines the volume of currency issue and the size of loans to the specialised banks and others. It is able to regulate the total money supply by the use of various kinds of loan and various interest rates.

The accumulation of bank reserves has led to the establishment of a deposit reserve system, that is the specialised banks are required to deposit a certain proportion of their reserves into the People's Bank, which facilitates the balancing of state revenue and expenditure.

8 Reform of Income Distribution and the Social Insurance System

REFORM OF THE WAGE SYSTEM

In order to encourage increased production and provide workers with an incentive to step up their output, piece rates and a bonus system were introduced in 1979. Since 1983, instead of turning over all their profits to the state, state-owned enterprises have been taxed and the bonuses have been drawn from profits left over after taxation. In 1984 there was no upper limit on bonuses but enterprises whose annual bonus was equal to or below two and a half months' standard wage were exempt from bonus tax, while those whose annual bonus was above the quota were taxed gradationally. In 1985 the starting point of bonus taxation was raised from the equivalent of two and a half months' standard wage to four months, and from the end of 1986 to the beginning of 1987 the rate of the bonus tax was reduced.

As a result of these government measures the bonuses paid by enterprises reflect their economic performance and the difference between bonus levels among enterprises has grown larger and larger. Enterprises whose bonuses are linked to economic performance have the right to determine their own methods of wage distribution. Wages may be linked to output, turnover, individual work load, piece rates and so on.

A new wage system has been adopted in state organs and institutions since July 1985 following abolition of the graded work-post system. The new system is a structured one with the work-post wage (related to degree of responsibility and specialisation) as its mainstay, plus basic wage, standing wage (additional pay linked to age and length of service) and reward payments. The adoption of this system has helped to link wages to productivity and a sense of responsibility. However many of the contradictions of the old wage system have been brought into the new system and irrational wage relationships between different groups and echelons remain unresolved.

THE MAIN PROBLEMS OF INCOME DISTRIBUTION

Income distribution is not only an economic problem but also a social and political one, the successful handling of which may enable China to mobilise the forces of all social strata and bring into play their initiative and creativity, as well as maintain social stability.

During the past ten years of reform the pattern of income distribution has undergone great changes. Much helpful exploratory work has been undertaken to improve the distribution system and investigate distribution theories. There have been some positive achievements, but a series of new problems merit attention. The following sections summarise the experiences and lessons.

Policy

The prospect of being able to retain a certain proportion of profits has increased initiative among employees of local governments, departments and enterprises, promoted diversification and speeded up economic reconstruction and reform. However most government measures tend to be localised and short-term in character, or are applied in a decentralised way according to different forms of ownership, or separately for different districts and departments. Income distribution policies that are compatible with regional economic policies and industrial policies, especially those concerned with performance-related pay, have been far from adequate. As a result the demand for consumption goods is far greater than supply, and society-wide income distribution has become extremely unfair.

Distribution

Some reform of the primary distribution of urban and rural income has been undertaken. The source of income has undergone a change from work-points wages as a single form of income to multiple sources. But allowances such as staple and non-staple food, water, electricity, coal, transportation, subsidies for housing, old-age pensions and medical care have not been affected. These are supplied directly by the state and enterprises and are distributed equally per head irrespective of the productivity of individual workers, which has not only caused an immense waste of resources but also given rise to undesirable practices. 'Hidden' income has expanded rapidly and will soon become a heavy burden on the state and enterprises. Furthermore it has made the contradiction between income growth and limited consumption opportunities even more prominent.

Macroeconomic control

Though great changes have been brought about in the structure of income distribution and other economic activities as a result of ten years of reform, the growth of income has greatly exceeded the growth of national income and productivity. The macro supervisory and regulatory system has not been adapted to the changed economic pattern, nor are systems in place to balance demand with supply or supervise the multiple economic forms of society as a whole. Tax regulations and tax collection are in great need of improvement, particularly income tax. The income distribution of collective, joint-venture, village, township, private and individual enterprises is beyond control.

In short, China was ill-prepared for the difficulty and complexity of the reform process and the time it would take, and expected too much of the benefits it might bring. For a time increased consumption was advocated, which sharpened people's appetite for higher incomes and expenditure. In the absence of efficient mechanisms to ensure self-restraint among enterprises, the abnormal growth of wages bore no relation to the actual state of affairs in China and led to loss of control over income distribution.

SOLVING THE PROBLEMS OF INCOME DISTRIBUTION

The ethos of egalitarianism still exists among waged staff and workers in state organs and institutions, and in some areas and departments it has become even more intense. According to the State Statistical Bureau, in the mid to late 1980s the ratio of wages of probational research fellows to those of research fellows was reduced from 1:3 to 1:2, of doctors to chief physicians in hospitals from 1:3 to 1:2.2, of third-grade teachers to senior teachers in middle schools from 1:3 to 1:1.8, of assistant teachers to professors in colleges and universities from 1:4 to 1:2, and of office workers to bureau or department heads in state organs from 1:3 to 1:1.6.

In the current composition of wages the standard wage constitutes 56.1 per cent of total wages while bonuses and subsidies constitute 43.9 per cent, although the latter can rise as high as 60–70 per cent. Bonuses and subsidies are in the main distributed per capita and are increasing rapidly. They are also distributed in an egalitarian manner. As a result, not only have the effects of the wage reforms decreased, egalitarianism within the various strata has become even more widespread than before.

Conversely there is great disparity between the incomes of general staff and workers, cadres and intellectuals who live on wages, those who work in nonproductive areas, those who have a second occupation, private enterprise owners, and some individual labourers. The annual income of self-employed labourers is 4000 yuan on average, that of ordinary enterprise employees is 2000 yuan, while that of private enterprise owners and contractors or leaseholders is tens of thousands or hundreds of thousands of yuan. Corruption, bribery, speculation and the use of power for personal gain has not only enhanced unequal income distribution at the macro level but has also undermined social stability and unity.

The key to solving the problem of egalitarianism within workplace strata lies in adhering to performance-related and job-related pay, analysing the non-state sectors and taking appropriate measures to solve the problem step by step in a planned way. The following measures should be taken.

A mechanism should be set up whereby income is linked to performance and the kind of work being undertaken. This will help to alleviate egalitarianism and reflect the difference between intellectual and manual, skilled and unskilled work. A certain number of Chinese enterprises have already linked wages to economic performance, but many problems still exist, especially linking input to output, output to income and cost to price. This requires serious attention and bold remedial action.

There should be a review of the policies that relate to the reduction and exemption of taxes and various kinds of income. Some efforts have already been made in this respect, with an emphasis on policies that relate to tax reductions and exemptions for different kinds of company as well as collective enterprises in villages and townships. Studies must be carried out to determine which taxes should be paid to central government and which to local government.

The wage system of companies should be put under the control of a wage-administration body. The 'extra-curricula income' of all units should be investigated and rectified. The composition of the extra income of schools, hospitals and research institutes should be made clear and unjustifiable items prohibited. There must be a clear line of demarcation in applying policies and regulations concerning the various kinds of income of institutions and enterprises gained through contracts, leases and so on. Units with property rights over state-owned land or houses should not be allowed to use the income gained through leasing them for collective or individual consumption.

An incomes policy should be established for those who have a second occupation and those who are reemployed after retirement. Laws should be reinforced and administration regulations consolidated so as to eliminate income obtained through unlawful channels.

Tax collection and control should be reinforced. First of all, taxation of the income of self-employed labourers, private enterprise owners and people with high incomes should be increased. Administrative regulations should stipulate the range, locality, and activities of their businesses in order to levy differential income tax, punish unlawful activities and recover evaded tax. Some exploratory work in this field is already underway in a few cities, such as Tangshan and Chengdu. A few large and medium-sized cities should be selected to try out a new system whereby people with high incomes voluntarily declare their income for taxation, although the conditions for this to be practised in large areas are not yet ripe.

Finally efforts must be made to set a rational cost range, strengthen cost control, intensify auditing and supervision, increase the transparency of business activities and set up trial accountancy offices in areas where the conditions are in place.

THE SOCIAL INSURANCE SYSTEM

China's social insurance system, which consists chiefly of the retirement pension, healthcare, unemployment benefit and provision for the victims of workplace accidents, was set up step by step shortly after the founding of the People's Republic and has guaranteed a basic income for all. But with the development of multiple forms of ownership and the overall aging of the population the defects of the system have become clear and reform is imperative.

Social stability

Stability is a prerequisite of socialist reconstruction and its maintenance is of overriding importance. The well-coordinated and steady development of social, political, economic and cultural life requires competition and vitality on the one hand, and adequate provision and stability on the other. Reform of the social insurance system is an important component of economic reform. It can provide a minimum but secure income for those in need of financial help, such as the retired, the unemployed, the disabled and dependants of the dead. It therefore functions as a societal stabiliser. For instance, in the face of a depressed market enterprises may have to suspend or partially suspend production, so that the livelihood of employees is threatened, which can become a factor of social unrest. However a guaranteed income via social insurance means that political stability can be maintained.

The aging population

Reform of the social insurance system is also necessary to relieve the pressure brought about by the aging of the population. According to one forecast, people aged sixty and over constituted 8.2 per cent of the population in 1985 but will represent 10.7 per cent by the year 2000. In 1983 the ratio of employed people to those in retirement was about 8:1. In 1988 it fell to around 6:1 and it is forecast that by the year 2000 it will fall to just over 4:1, reaching 1.8:1 in 2030. In other words, on average 1.8 workers will have to support one retired person. The share of pension payments in total wages will increase from 10.7 per cent in 1985 to 16 per cent by 2000 and 31.6 per cent by 2030.

The main cause for concern is that the proportion of elderly is expanding much more rapidly than economic development. When China's elderly population increases out of all proportion to those in work, more than one hundred billion yuan per annum will be required to provide for them, which will be too heavy a burden on the national coffers.

At the end of 1989, the social insurance fund surplus among state-owned enterprises amounted to five billion yuan. If the system were to be expanded to include employees of village and township enterprises, privately run enterprises, self-employed labourers and the more wealthy peasants, roughly 30 billion yuan could be collected.

In general, however, current retirement funds are paid out as soon as they are collected and no reserves are being accumulated to meet future needs. Therefore it is vital that an effective insurance system be designed that will allow a reserve fund to be established and augmented to meet these needs.

Unemployment benefit

In a reforming economy it is inevitable that some enterprises will close down or go bankrupt through competition, thus making their employees redundant. Moreover, as a result of the reforms, enterprises are tending to recruit more and more contract workers, causing a labour-force flow and temporarily forcing some people out of employment. It naturally follows that an effective social insurance system should be capable of providing for the unemployed.

The present state of social insurance reform and the main problems to be resolved

Reform of the social insurance system started in 1984 with reform of the old-age pension. Older enterprises have a larger number of retired employees and thus are obliged to pay out a considerable amount in pensions. To enable old and new enterprises to compete on an equal footing in the new economic climate throughout the country, the collection and distribution of pension funds to retired employees of state-owned and large collective enterprises has become the responsibility of municipalities and counties instead of the enterprises themselves. At the end of 1989, 2200 municipal and county state-owned enterprises (93 per cent of the total) and 1400 municipal, county and township collective enterprises were included in this system, involving 40 million permanent employees, 10 million contract workers and nine million retired employees. (There is no overall scheme for new and old collective enterprises below township and country level, nor for private enterprises and individual businessmen and labourers.) The introduction of this system has allowed old and new enterprises to compete more equally whilst guaranteeing retired employees a livelihood. Trial schemes have also been introduced in some places to gain experience in unemployment and healthcare insurance.

A rural pension system has been set up in more than 8000 villages and 800 townships, with approximately 900 000 participants. More than 210 000 of the peasant population now enjoy the security of old-age pensions, but the scheme is still at the trial stage and is practised only on a very small scale. Nonetheless the convention of elderly parents being totally dependent on their male children is slowly changing.

On the whole, however, the current insurance system has diverged little from the old one and cannot meet the requirements of the reforming economy. Its main problems are as follows.

Funds are raised at various levels: provincial, district and county, the latter being the mainstay. Those in receipt of social insurance payments have usually not contributed to the system when in employment, apart from contract workers, who pay a symbolic premium. Almost all the money comes from the state and the enterprises.

Briefly, three questions can be raised with respect to the future method of collecting and distributing funds. First, should the old practice of making payments as soon as the money is raised be continued or should there be a shift towards accumulation? Second, should the emphasis be placed on private means? In other words, should personal savings and insurance provide the mainstay, with social insurance acting as a supplementary safety net? Third, should social contributions be paid to a central fund by all employed and self-employed people, or should the current practice of enterprises turning over part of their profits for the purpose be maintained?

It is generally held that insurance premiums should be paid by all members of the working population, although there are those who consider that the enterprises profit system should be improved upon and extended to all economic sectors. However there is some dispute over the solution of the first two questions and no definite decision can yet be made. Take the problem of providing for the elderly for example. On the one hand China is confronted with the pressure of a large, ever-aging population. The old-age pension is a long-term item of disbursement and suitable reserves will be required to cope with the situation. Yet the necessary prerequisites are not in place, including low inflation, favourable prices and interest rates, an investment market, appropriate investment policies, management facilities and so on. When a way of accumulating funds has been determined it will be vital that their value is not only preserved, but also increased by careful, secure investment and management.

Whilst the numbers may be greater and the social and economic conditions different, China is not alone with respect to the problems involved in future pension payments. In most of the countries of the world where old-age pensions are guaranteed by legislation, funds are still being paid out as soon as they are raised. Though some countries have planned to shift towards a system of accumulation, few have taken any practical steps. When modernising, some other countries – such as Japan – at first planned to set up an accumulation system but finally adopted a similar one to that used in other developed countries. With aging populations and decreased birth rates many governments are faced with the prospect of not being able to meet future pension payments from concurrent national insurance contributions and are thus encouraging those in employment to take out private insurance.

A particular problem in China relates to attitude. Agriculture is still the country's mainstay and 70–80 per cent of the population live in rural areas. A very large percentage of the rural population would find it difficult to accept having to pay national insurance contributions. Furthermore the large differences in income between various districts and economic sectors in China's vast territory would mean a fall in income for some if a nationwide system were to be adopted in place of benefits being paid by enterprises, which could lead to social unrest. It may be feasible to combine the two systems, for instance by encouraging employers to set up company schemes, but precisely how and to what extent are difficult questions to answer.

Problems also exist in the social insurance administrative system. First, government decrees are put into effect by various departments in the absence of coordinating and balancing mechanisms. Disputes over trifles, back and forth arguments and the shifting of responsibility onto others are common occurrences. Old-age pensions alone involve such departments as labour, personnel, civil administration, finance, industry and commerce, and planning and administrative reform, as well as banks, trade unions and the Old Age Commission. It is therefore essential that a new ministry be set up to act as coordinator.

Second, administrative and managerial duties are not kept separate. Policy making and supervision are combined with execution and management without an effective supervisory and administrative mechanism. Strengthening the administrative system is therefore most important if reform of the social insurance system is to advance.

Great care must be taken to choose the right system. Different opinions, especially opposing ones, must be considered before taking the final decision, and all possible reactions and difficulties must be taken into account. Experience to date indicates that the process is likely to be a long one and rapid results should not be expected. In addition, when individual experiments are conducted at the provincial, district or county level, attention should be paid to ensuring that these experiments dovetail with proposals for the nationwide system.

9 China's Economic Experiment: Interviews with Chinese and Foreign Journalists

A GREAT EXPERIMENT: INTERVIEW WITH THE CHIEF
EDITOR OF THE *WEEKLY NEWS*, YUGOSLAVIA

Editor: A big problem is that foreigners who come to China for the first time usually have, intentionally or otherwise, bias.

We have come to China to see its reform and modernisation, in other words we are interested in the new things in this country.

When we got here we wondered (though experienced journalists would not openly admit it) whether the things we were going to see would be typical. How could we tell whether they were or not? Lastly, would our Chinese colleagues let us see everything we'd like to see, or would they only take us to the showcases?

A few days before we set off on the journey the prestigious Hamburg weekly magazine the *Times* carried an extensive analysis of China's economic reform titled 'The Greatest Experiment in History', written by former Chancellor Helmut Schmidt, who is knowledgeable about what is going on in China. He wrote: 'Insufficient as the progress is, it is nevertheless very clear and obvious, especially in the cities. One can tell by just looking at the output growth rates from 1979 till today. To any objective economist, the progress is dramatic'.

We had the opportunity to meet well-known Chinese political leaders and economists, and with the first-hand information they gave us our concept of the Chinese economic reform and our impression of the world's greatest experiment has become more complete.

Gao Shangquan is a well-known economist and vice chairman of the State Commission for Restructuring the Economic System. Premier Zhao is the chairman. Gao and his colleagues spent a whole morning, that is, nearly five hours, patiently answering our questions. What follows is the record of our interview.

Developing a planned commodity economy

Gao: The previous economic system was established in the 1950s, and by the end of the decade we had already discovered some defects in the system. However real reform did not start until December 1978, when the Third Plenary Session of the 11th Party Congress was convened. From then on till today the reform has gone through three phases. The first phase was rural reform, which was quite successful. Now we are applying our experience to the urban area. We are still making experiments though exploring various ways. The second phase began in 1984 with the convening of the Third Plenary Session of the 12th Party Congress. Now this is a critical period, for the reform will be expanded to all areas of life.

The reform went relatively smoothly in the year following the decision on urban reform by the Party Central Committee in October 1984. Our idea was to develop a planned commodity economy. If we can make it, we think it will be a breakthrough in economic theory and practice. Our experience over the past year has told us that success is not impossible.

We are promoting horizontal integration, because without it there will be no commodity economy.

Question: What is horizontal integration?

Gao: Under the traditional system, each enterprise was tied to a particular ministry. The ministry directly guided and managed the enterprise. So two neighbouring enterprises with only a wall between them might have belonged to different ministries and therefore had no contact whatsoever. Now we are trying to promote various kinds of inter-enterprise cooperation. Horizontal economic integration is important for technical progress and the development of productive forces. The famous big enterprises should be the mainstay of this kind of integration.

There have been some good examples of horizontal integration. Take Sichuan province. The Chongqing Beverage Factory has expanded into a cross-sector, cross-region, multi-level enterprise group called the Tianfu Cola Group, with 102 member firms from 27 provinces, cities and autonomous regions. Some enterprises of different administrative ranks have also merged, because rank is no longer that important. Integration is based on mutual benefit.

In Shanghai more than 2000 cases of integration in various forms took place over six months. Shanghai is a major industrial centre but is now running short of raw materials and energy. To ensure supply it has to invest in the hinterland. So does Wuhan, another industrial centre. In Wuhan more than 400 economic units from different parts of the country developed some cooperative relations. In fact horizontal integration of independent economic entities out of their own interest is a feature of a commodity economy.

The competitiveness of Chinese enterprises is being enhanced. In the past everything was decided through planning and by administrative means, and in every detail: raw materials, equipment, cadres and so on were allocated, distributed or posted. In turn enterprises handed over their profits to the government. Since enterprise losses were subsidised by the government enterprises were not concerned about performance. Worries over losses belonged to the ministry.

The management responsibility system

Gao: We are trying to invigorate the enterprises and increase their competitiveness. It is not enough to be able to produce, enterprises must also be good at marketing and competition. Ultimately they should be responsible for management, profits and losses.

In this endeavour we are mainly aiming at large and medium-sized state-owned enterprises. At the same time we are developing collectively owned and private enterprises. Now they are advancing together, and collective private enterprises have shown particularly fast growth.

Some small state-owned enterprises are being transformed into collective ones. For instance some state-owned hotels, barber's shops and public bath houses were poorly managed. Their transformation boosted the initiative of the workers as well as the quality of services. Now the government has cut its subsidies to them.

We have carried out a number of pilot schemes, applying economic laws and the law of value.

Question: How are they going?

Gao: Now enterprises pay tax instead of profits to the government. They retain one third of the profits for their own use. The budget revenue of the government is more stable now.

The first pilot scheme for urban reform was implemented in six industrial enterprises in Sichuan. In 1980 the experiment was extended to 6500 enterprises. A comprehensive reform experiment at the city level took place later, with two cities acting as trailblazers in 1981 and 1982. Today 60 cities, including some capital cities, are carrying out comprehensive reforms.

Reform is going on in other fields too, such as education and science and technology.

But the major changes have occurred in economic management, because decentralisation calls for new management methods. In 1980 special economic zones were mapped out in Shenzhen, Zhuhai, Shantou and Xiamen.

We must reform the price system. Our price system for agri-products was irrational. For example the procurement price for pork was very low. Without reform there would not have been sufficient pork to meet the demand of city dwellers. On the other hand we still have to subsidise them. Reform will encourage the peasants to raise more pigs.

The financial and fiscal systems

Gao: One of the objectives is to strengthen the role of banks. It is a popular topic this autumn. At present the government is mostly concerned with problems resulting from the overheating of the economy. In the first half of this year industrial output went up by 23 per cent over the same period last year. Capital-consuming construction has been going on in a big way. Should this trend be allowed to continue, it will incur very high costs and present a great danger.

As a countermeasure, this summer the central bank raised interest rates by a large margin, lending rates in particular.

The emerging commodity market

Gao: We have only just taken the first few steps towards developing a commodity economy, yet the market is already growing rapidly. There are 2000 or more new trade centres. All enterprises, be they state, collective or privately owned, can sell their products there. There are markets for durable consumer goods, farming tools and the like.

The rural commodity economy is thriving too. Now some four million households are specialising in grain and food production, trade and transportation. They have promoted the development of agricultural production.

Foreign economic relations

Gao: Today we have 1600 joint ventures, 3000 organisations engaged in various forms of international economic cooperation, more than 90 foreign investment projects and more than 100 Chinese units have companies abroad.

For a long time we lived with the old, centralised economic system. Now we are all beginning to get used to a commodity economy – the masses and the cadres alike. This is no simple process. As we have achieved initial success, our people are more easily able to understand the significance of the reforms.

Question: What are your headaches now?

Gao: We are facing many problems. An over-high growth rate, overexpansion of basic construction, excessive borrowing, the shooting up of prices for certain products, and so on. We saw some destabilising elements in the fourth quarter last year. The Party and government adopted some measures and now the situation is getting better. The industrial growth rate is beginning to fall: from 14.5 per cent in October to 11.6 per cent in November.

Question: What about inflation? The statistics seem to indicate the existence of inflation and it should not be overlooked.

Gao: We have recognised the danger. Therefore we are adopting, and will continue to adopt, some measures.

Coordinated reform

Gao: A basic task is to dovetail reform and development. In the long run reform will facilitate development. But when the economy is overheating and inflation is exerting pressure, reform can hardly go on. If there is too much construction, raw materials such as steel will be in short supply, their prices will go up and the completion of projects will be prolonged. So we must control the scale of basic construction.

We used to concentrate our efforts on micro aspects, that is, on enterprise reform. From this year onwards we will pay equal attention to macroeconomic control. The economy cannot be invigorated if the micro or macro systems are in trouble. Of course intensifying macro control does not mean going back to the old ways. What we have been trying to do is to establish a new and fundamentally different economic system. And we should make the new system effective as soon as possible.

For instance, enterprises did not care whether interest rates were high or low because they were not responsible for their own performance. But with the management responsibility system in place, the attitude of enterprises towards interest rates has changed. They now have to calculate whether borrowing at a particular rate is economical or not.

We are in a period of comprehensive reform. Various measures must be taken in conjunction. This is no easy task. If reform in a specific field is to go smoothly, it must be accompanied by other necessary reform measures.

You may have heard about the farm product market that opened this summer in Beijing where peasants can sell their produce freely. When the market was first set up the department of transportation still stuck to the old rules, which forebade vegetable-loaded trucks from other regions to enter the city. Consequently truckloads of vegetables rotted at the city gate while there was a vegetable shortage in the city. Prices went up and of course people were resentful. This is a case in point showing the necessity for coordinated action in the reform process.

Question: What are the things that should be discarded, and what should be created?

Gao: The old way should be discarded, but if the new system and order are not in place, disorder will prevail.

Now the major issue is to invigorate enterprises and intensify macro management and supervision. Financial supervision should be strengthened. Our bookkeeping system leaves much to be desired, and an insufficient number of people are up to the job.

On the other hand we have a very large administrative organ. Not long ago an international symposium on the macro economy was held in Beijing. Among the attendants were renowned economists, experts and Nobel Prize winners. One speaker at the meeting said that what we are doing is like making a new car out of an old one – not impossible, but extremely difficult. But no matter what car, the driver is the major factor, because if the driver is not skilful enough, even the best car can be crashed.

We have to be aware of the complexity and the possible difficulties of the reform process. I'm afraid that we have talked too little about its difficulties, so some people think of the reform as a very simple thing. Those who get lots of bonuses decide that reform is good, whereas those who get no bonuses blame the reform.

The goal of China's economic reform

Question: What is the goal of the reform?

Gao: Put very briefly, the purpose of developing a market economy is to develop a productive force, to make our country rich and strong and to improve the life of the people. It is naturally a long process, and certain risks and costs are involved. It will take us quite some time to lay the foundation for a new economic system and we have numerous things to do in this regard.

First we must invigorate the enterprises so that they become relatively independent producers and managers. Then we must improve the market mechanism and establish a market system. Lastly the old way, that is, direct management by government, still plays the main role and macro control should be changed to mainly indirect management by government.

In order to realise our goal, we must reform the planning, price, financial, tax, employment and wage systems.

Question: Could you discuss the invigoration of enterprises in greater detail?

Gao: When we talk about invigorating the enterprises we are referring to large and medium-sized enterprises. They are very important to the national economy. They total some 5800, that is, nearly 2 per cent of the number of all enterprises, but they contribute two thirds of the state budget. However past experience shows that in our country small enterprises are much more dynamic than large ones, and are more market-flexible. This is because the large enterprises shoulder heavy burdens and do not have a flexible mechanism, so it is understandable that they are less autonomous. This situation must be changed quickly.

Giving market mechanisms a role to play

Question: How do you make use of market mechanisms?

Gao: In order to develop a planned market economy (which is our goal) we have to develop our markets. Not only markets for daily necessities, which will be the first step, but also markets for means of production, money, technology, services and real estate. We are going to set up a comprehensive market system and give market mechanisms a full role to play. Price reform is called for here.

Question: What is 'indirect management'? Does it mean that the ministries will no longer intervene in the work of economic organisations?

Gao: Under the product economy management system, production, supply and marketing, as well as all resources – human, financial and material – were controlled by various central government ministries. Since China is a vast country, and most enterprises are far away from the ministries, it is indeed difficult for the central government to manage all the enterprises. Through reform, we want to form a system with indirect management as the principal means. Of course there will be some exceptions, for instance the railway, which will continue to be centrally managed.

Economic reform necessitates institutional reform, and when ministries are no longer direct managers, they will have to get used to the new system.

Opening up to the outside world – a long-term policy

Question: It is only logical that people outside China are interested in the opening up of China. We have seen some of the distinctive measures: the emphasis is on joint investment and attracting foreign capital. But why?

Gao: We have reiterated time and again that opening up is a long-term policy that must be adhered to. We shall increase our imports, exports and foreign trade. We need foreign capital, technology and expertise. We have borrowed only very small amounts from the international capital market for commercial purposes because we do not have enough experience, and also because interest rates have been very high recently. Some loans are not at high rates, but they have various conditions attached, for instance buying things we do not need. Once we have borrowed money, we have to put it to good use. If we want to introduce foreign capital, we have to enhance our ability to make money because we must consider how to repay the debt.

Reform of the economic and political systems

Question: Without reform of the political system, will the ambitious economic reform be possible?

Gao: We realised that the two reforms must go hand in hand. Deng Xiaoping said that reform is the second revolution. Without reform of the political system, economic reform cannot go smoothly. Governmental institutions must undergo reform, their functions must change and the quality of cadres must be improved to meet the needs of the reform.

Question: Reform will take away from some people the power that was given to them by the old system. Do they realise this? Do they like the change?

Gao: The reform will enjoy the support of the people, for it will make our country and people rich and strong. Of course, for personal interest reasons some cadres are not happy about the reform and thus will have to be educated and a common understanding reached.

For example in some places we are increasing house rents to make housing a commodity. At present rents are very low, ten times lower than they should be. Those who have larger houses should pay more rent. Most people and cadres understand the importance of this reform measure, but clearly those who pay nothing for their living space will not readily welcome this reform.

In order to acquire a better understanding of what is going on in this country, we will quote some findings of a census among the Chinese youth about what they thought of the reform.

In answer to the question 'What do you think the reform will bring to you personally?' 46 per cent replied 'to lead a better life in a stronger and richer country', 27 per cent thought that reform will provide more possibilities for those who are ambitious, industrious and capable, and 2.5 per cent believed that reform will bring them economic benefits. Only 6.5 per cent had no idea what reform will bring.

Eighty-one per cent of the youths in the census indicated that they liked the idea of 'development through competition'. Only 10 per cent preferred 'stable, tranquil cooperation without competition'. In reply to the question 'What concerns you most about the reform', the majority expressed a fear that their wages might not go up as fast as inflation. But 80 per cent firmly supported the breaking up of 'the big pot' (no matter their differences in merit and contribution, all people eat from the same big pot).

Returning to the question raised at the beginning. Can the world understand what is going on in China? Will the world (as the Chinese themselves) give up their bias towards China and Chinese socialism? As Helmut Schmidt wrote in the prestigious English journal *The Economist*: 'Karl Marx did not leave any ready made models for later generations. China is carrying out the greatest experiment in the economic history of mankind.'

Interview translated from nos. 1824, 1825, 15 and 22 December 1985.

A SOCIALIST ECONOMY IS A COMMODITY ECONOMY: STATEMENTS MADE AT THE PRESS CONFERENCE OF THE THIRTEENTH NATIONAL CONGRESS OF THE COMMUNIST PARTY OF CHINA

The vice minister of the State Commission of Restructuring the Economic System responds to questions asked by Chinese and foreign correspondents at a press conference organised by the Thirteenth National Congress of the Chinese Communist Party on 26 October 1987.

Question (correspondent of the *Washington Post*): Please tell me the time arrangement of price reform. For example, when are you going to carry out the reform? When will the enterprise law and the bankruptcy law be implemented? What is your first measure in price reform?

Answer: We have paid particular attention to price reform. Many measures in this respect have been taken in the last two years. Our guiding principle now is persisting with the reform, progressing steadily and keeping prices basically stable.

Our country has attached great importance to the formulation of the enterprise law and the bankruptcy law. A state-owned enterprise law (trial implementation) was discussed and adopted by the Standing Committee of the National People's Congress. It will not be implemented until the enterprise law is carried out. Some enterprises such as the Shenyang Anti-explosive Machinery Plant have undertaken experiments with the bankruptcy law and a market in Nanchang was declared bankrupt; all achieved positive results.

We have made many revisions to the enterprise law. The process of drafting a law is one of investigation and reaching a common under-standing. After various investigations and revisions, as well as exper-imentation in selected places, it seems that the conditions are becoming more and more ripe for implementation of the enterprise law.

Question (correspondent of the *Wall Street Times*): In view of the re-cent slump in the international stock market, will Chinese economists reconsider your reform measures, such as the shareholding system, or will you reconsider the decision on opening the share market?

Answer: The slump in the international stock market, especially the New York stock market has brought about a series of reactions. But the slump has had little influence on China. That is because we have very few international stocks and bonds. The reason for this slump is what we need to study. It did not influence the reform of our financial system, nor the issuance of our shares and bonds. Shares and bonds are the products of a commodity economy, which can be used by capitalist countries and socialist countries alike. What we need to study and resolve is how to make better use of them under public ownership.

Question (correspondent of the Central People's Broadcasting Station): The hiring of labour has emerged in our country. Is this a phenom-enon of capitalism? Is it a kind of exploitation? What is the reason for its existence?

Answer: The hiring of labour and non-labour income have emerged in China, but are not the same as in capitalist countries. The difference lies in the fact that, first, the hiring of labour by China's private enter-prises is closely connected to public ownership and is under its tremen-dous influence; second, the hiring of labour by private enterprises is guided by state laws and policies; and third, the status of employees in these enterprises as masters remains unchanged. Allowing the exist-ence of private enterprises and their development to a certain extent helps to promote production and make things convenient for the people, so it is a necessary and beneficial supplement to the public economy.

Question (correspondent of the *World Economic Guide*): What kind of economic pattern are we going to set up, according to our present economic level? Since the hiring of labour is now allowed in our country, is there any change to the former provision that a private enterprise can hire a maximum of eight employees? A shareholding system is going to be introduced in various places, to what extent will it be permitted? Is this system going to be introduced in a wide range?

Answer: As to the economic pattern, 'The Decision on the Reform of Economic System by the Central Committee of Chinese Communist Party' in 1984 advanced a scientific thesis that a socialist economy is a planned commodity economy. The report of the Thirteenth Congress of the Chinese Communist Party put forward a new operational mechanism that 'the state regulates the market while the market guides the activities of enterprises', giving a further development of this thesis. Thus the original planned commodity economy has become more concrete.

With regard to the number of hired workers, someone suggested eight as the maximum. We are going to study this problem further. The concept of eight hired workers was put forward by Marx in *Das Kapital*. We could say that an enterprise that hires less than eight workers falls into the category of an individual economy while that hiring more than eight workers is a private economy. We shall wait and see what kind of limit is suitable.

As for the shareholding system, this is desirable among enterprises with horizontal ties. Various regions and sectors may buy each other's shares. We still lack experience in shareholding systems under public ownership. More experiments have to be undertaken. We consider that a shareholding system is unavoidable in a commodity economy, and we have to adopt a prudent policy of excluding it gradually after we have gained some experience to draw on.

Question (correspondent of Britain's *The Economist*): What is the reason for delaying the price reform? Is it because people have a negative reaction to price hikes? Or is it because market regulation can not be implemented; or because some people have objections? When I took a taxi in the morning the driver did not want RMB or foreign exchange certificates. What he wanted was the US dollars or Hong Kong dollars in my pocket. What measures are you going to take to normalise the monetary system. Are you going to invalidate foreign exchange certificates?

Answer: Price reform is an unavoidable problem. 'The Decision on the Reform of Economic System by the Central Committee of Chinese Communist Party' in 1984 gave a clear explanation of this problem. In our view, since the price reform involves numerous households, in practising the reform it is imperative to consider the capability of the country and the support of society and the people. So we will push forward price reform under the guiding principles of persisting in the reform, progressing steadily and keeping prices basically stable. The monetary problem you mentioned is a specific problem. It was not right for the driver to ask for US or Hong Kong dollars. You may pay with foreign exchange certificates.

Question (correspondent of the American Broadcasting Corporation): You just talked about the need to reach a common understanding. Can you tell us what is obstructing reform of the economic system? Is it from the grass-roots level, from a high level or from within the Party? The report of the Thirteenth Congress of Chinese Communist Party did not mention the enterprise law nor the bankruptcy law. Why?

Answer: Most of our comrades are in favour of the reform and support it. Is there any obstruction? I can't say no. The obstruction comes from a long-standing force of habit. Reform of the economic system is in a sense an adjustment of benefit mix. It brings benefits and advantages to the majority of people, but when it involves those who have vested interest there is some resistance. The report of the Thirteenth Congress did not mention the enterprise law or the bankruptcy law but this does not mean that the laws are not important. The report was not able to include every aspect of the reform.

Question (correspondent of the Hongkong *Wen Wei Po*): Since reform of the economic system the State Commission for Restructuring the Economic System has done a lot of work. Would you please tell us something about the internal conditions and the organisational structure of the Commission. The State Commission for Restructuring the Economic System was set up to reform the economic system. Now that reform of the political system is going to be carried out, is a similar commission going to be set up?

Answer: The State Commission for Restructuring the Economic System is a comprehensive department under the State Council to exercise leadership in the reform of the economic system. The commission has the following tasks. First, to act as staff officer and assistant to the Central Committee of the Chinese Communist Party and the State Council in formulating policies on the reform of the economic system. Second, to prepare and design the overall plan and the implementation programme for the reform of the economic system. Third, to coordinate reform activities, and fourth, to give guidance to the reform in the localities.

It is up to the Central Committee to decide whether it is necessary to set up a Commission for Restructuring the Political System. In my view the question of setting up a corresponding organisation will be considered during the reform of the structure.

Inside the State Commission for Restructuring the Economic System there are eight bureaus, one general office, the China Economic Reform Institute, a Reform of China's Economic System Magazine agency as well as a China Economic Reform Seminar.

Question (correspondent of Agence France-Presse): It has been nine years since China implemented its policy of opening up to the outside world. However egalitarianism still prevails in China. Zhao Ziyang mentioned it too in his report yesterday. He said that the Thirteenth Congress would speed up the reform. Would you please give some examples to make clear what measures are going to be taken in order to speed up the reform. Especially, what is going to be done about reform of the wage system. It will be difficult for price reform to be carried out without reform of the wage system.

Answer: One of the weak points of our original economic system was egalitarianism in distribution, that is the 'big pot' system. During the past few years we have adhered to the principle of distribution according to work. Egalitarianism has been overcome to a certain extent, though it remains the main tendency.

The main subject under discussion during the Thirteenth Congress is speeding up and deepening the reform. In reforming the enterprise operational mechanism it is necessary to implement and improve the contracted managerial responsibility system. The emphasis is on further strengthening the vitality of enterprises, especially those owned by the whole people, by separating ownership from management rights. At the same time we shall also carry out reforms in planning, investment, materials, foreign trade, banking, finance and taxation in order to combine micro-reforms with the macro one.

Reform of the wage system should be linked to reform of the enterprise operational mechanism and other reforms. Increases in wages should be matched to rises in labour productivity. At the same time the real income of office staff and workers should not be reduced as a result of price reform. It is necessary to increase gradually the real income of office staff and workers with increases in labour productivity.

Question (correspondent of Japan's *Mainchi Shimbun*): Mr Gao just said that private enterprises in China always operate within the range allowed by the law. Thus what are the laws guiding private enterprises, since there are no regulations regarding private enterprises in the current constitution. Is the constitution going to be revised? If there are laws in this regard, what is the maximum permitted number of hired workers? What is the maximum number of hired workers in private enterprises operating now?

Answer: Private enterprises are allowed to exist and develop. This is elaborated in the Thirteenth Congress report. The existence of private enterprises is helpful in expanding production. We are in the process of working out the regulations concerning private enterprises in order to ensure their legitimate rights and to lead them to develop in a correct and healthy direction.

As for the number of hired workers, it ranges from a few to about one hundred. The situation is very complex. We have to do more investigation, to promote what is beneficial and abolish what is harmful. The problem of private enterprises is a new affair in our economic development. We have to study this problem as it emerges in practice.

Question (correspondent of the Xinhua News Agency): What is the specific consideration about the enterprise contracted responsibility system?

Answer: The reasons for implementing the contracted responsibility system for enterprises are as follows. First, it is helpful in separating ownership from management rights, in making clear the relations of responsibility, rights and benefits between the country and the enterprises. Second, it is suited to the condition of our country, and to the current managerial level in our country as well. It is an effective operational pattern. That is why we make it the emphasis of invigorating enterprises, though it is not the only pattern. In order to improve and develop further the contracted responsibility system for enterprises it is imperative to solve the problem of how to prevent short-sightedness in economic activities so that (1) a self-development and self-constraint mechanism can be set up and (2) the contracted responsibility system can be combined with other reforms with a view to standardising the reform gradually.

INFLATION AND PRICE REFORM: INTERVIEW WITH A
CORRESPONDENT OF *DER SPIEGEL*

Question (correspondent of the West German *Der Spiegel*): The inflation
rate of China is now 6.5 per cent. Price subsidies account for one third of
state expenditure. Can you tell me, in the political sense, what is the limit
of inflation? Do you think the price reform will cause unrest in society?

Answer: Price reform is a complex task. Price hikes are what people
complain about most. The State Council is adopting strong measures
to stabilise prices. Prices are closely related to the issuance of paper
money. To what extent will an increase in banknotes be appropriate?
It would be advisable to make the growth of money supply a little
lower than the combined rate of economic growth and price hikes.

Question: Mr Gao, though economic reform has brought China prosperity, along with it has come inflation, a reduction in foreign exchange reserves, corruption, economic crimes and enormous financial
deficits. Is the reform pattern a failure?

Answer: We can say, the negative phenomena you have listed are not
the evidence of a failure or a crisis. In order to judge whether the
reform is a success or not, to judge whether it is good or bad, we
have to observe economic development, the strength of the country,
and see whether living standards are rising.

Question: What is your opinion on that?

Answer: Since the reform process started, gross national product and
national financial income have doubled, national power has been strengthened and living standards have risen. All of these show that our reform policy is successful.

Question: But after the trammels of production collectivisation were
removed, the peasants disregarded the production of grain.

Answer: In the past the peasants produced grain according to mandatory planning. Now the state signs contracts with the peasants. When
the contracts have been fulfilled the peasants may sell their remaining
grain directly in the marketplace. This new arrangement has created

greater enthusiasm on the part of the peasant. So on the whole, agricultural production has increased.

Question: That is true of vegetables and fruit; however the output of grain and cereals is lower than in 1984.

Answer: This problem is price-related. Since grain profits are lower than those of other agricultural products the peasants have reduced the area of grain cultivated.

Question: Don't you worry about that?

Answer: The prices of grains will have to be raised. The state will supply farming implements, chemical fertilisers and fuel for diesel machines to help grain producers.

Question: Now, 1 per cent of peasants have become households owning 10 000 yuan, but the annual income of more than 100 million peasants stands at only 200 yuan. Will China become a class society with a wide gap between rich and poor?

Answer: It is not surprising that there are differences in people's incomes. China is striving to help the poor to become rich. Backward areas will be given economic support so that they can make improvements through their own efforts. It is better to help them generate new blood cells within their own bodies than to give them blood transfusions.

Question: Can this practice eliminate wide discrepancies in income?

Answer: Our policy is to let some individuals become rich first. Eventually all the people will have a chance to prosper, but it is impossible for all to become rich at the same time. That is egalitarianism, which is no good to any of us.

Question: Is there any limit on private income?

Answer: For peasants who produce grain or vegetables there is no ceiling on income earned by hard work, but illegitimate earnings (for example from speculation) must be limited or confiscated.

Question: Currently some factories are owned by individuals, some enterprises are leased to individuals, while others issue shares. When this tendency is extended, will state-owned enterprises disappear step by step?

Answer: It is important to separate ownership from management power. There are three forms of enterprise: state-owned, collective-owned and private owned, with state-owned enterprises predominating. In 1986 the industrial output of state-owned enterprises accounted for 70 per cent of the nation's total, collective-owned 28 per cent private enterprises and other enterprises only 2 per cent.

Question: Will this proportion go into reverse?

Answer: State-owned and collective-owned enterprises will be the absolute leaders. This is unchangeable.

Question: Being the leading factor, state-owned enterprises should rank first in economic activities. But in 1986 losses were incurred by 36 000 state-owned enterprises. Why do state-owned enterprises provide such scant economic returns?

Answer: The collectively-owned enterprises are more flexible so they can develop quickly. In contrast state-owned enterprises are far from being flexible enough, though they are a little better than before. An important point in the current reform drive is to bring into full play the initiative of the enterprises and their staff and workers.

Question: How is this to be realised?

Answer: Enterprises should be given more self-management power. The responsibility system is a good way of doing this. Having attained the targets set in their contracts, the enterprises may keep and dispose of a large part of the profits. This practice has been welcomed by the enterprises and has achieved some results.

Question: This practice needs competent managers and enthusiastic workers. But so far, workers can not be fired. What do you do to workers who disobey orders?

Answer: The situation has changed somewhat. Workers who violate regulations and refuse to correct their mistakes despite repeated admonition will be fired. Lazy ones are not paid bonuses.

Question: This practice will not suffice to reduce the accumulated deficits of state-owned enterprises.

Answer: Enterprises with deficits receive subsidies from the state. If they are able to reduce their deficits they may use the remaining subsidy as a bonus. This practice should give some encouragement.

Question: But why did the number of enterprises with deficits increase by 10 per cent in 1986?

Answer: There are two reasons. First, enterprises that are managed well may also have deficits. This is because of the state fixing prices at a lower level. This is a question of policy. Second, some enterprises make little progress in management and planning.

Question: Should the enterprises of the second group be declared bankrupt?

Answer: We drew up enterprise bankruptcy regulations in December 1986. I'm in favour of it.

Question: How many enterprises have been declared bankrupt?

Answer: Less than ten. But the regulations have other active functions. For example in the past some people just idled away their time. Since the bankruptcy 'yellow plate' warning has been exerted on some enterprises they have begun to turn for the better.

Question: But foreign investors still complain about Chinese workers' low productivity, poor quality and serious bureaucratic practices.

Answer: The investment environment will continue to improve. Since China is a developing country, all these factors need time to be resolved.

Question: New investment in 1986 reduced to 3.3 billion yuan, about half the 1985 value. What you called improvement did not score any achievements.

Answer: Some investors do not understand our policy. They are afraid that the anti-bourgeois liberalisation drive will infringe upon their interests. That is a misunderstanding. The policy of reform and opening to the outside world will never change.

Question: Is there any antithesis between fundamental interests? Foreign investors (for example the Shanghai Motor Plant) want to open up the large Chinese market, while China wants enterprises with strong production forces that produce sophisticated goods in order to give priority to exports.

Answer: This contradiction can be resolved. But we can not only import goods, we must also increase exports.

Question: Eleven years ago China published a book titled *Why there is no inflation in China*. This has gone with the wind. Reform has brought this capitalist disease to China.

Answer: Inflation is a problem that prevails throughout the world. In the past there was no inflation in China. China had neither foreign debts nor internal debts. People were used to that situation. Now, price reform is a must in the process of modernisation. In such conditions prices have to increase or decrease. Recently the prices of wrist watches has begun to drop, though the price level as a whole is rising. Due to government subsidies the prices of some products are on the low side. As far as housing is concerned, the rent for one square meter is less than 20 fen and is not sufficient to cover the maintenance fee.

Question: The state-fixed prices for grains are too low.

Answer: Yes. When the peasants can not get reasonable prices for their grain they will produce other agricultural products instead. Thus there are only two possibilities: raising the prices of grains or subsidising the producers. Price hikes will give rise to grievances among the people, while government subsidies will add to the burden of the state.

Question: Then how do you solve this problem?

Answer: Prices will have to fluctuate according to the law of value and to conditions of supply and demand. But the fluctuation should not be too often or too rapid. People have to be able to adapt themselves to it gradually.

Question: Unrest broke out in Poland because of price hikes. Are you afraid of a similar situation taking place in China?

Answer: The situation in China is stable. Of course people have been dissatisfied with price hikes. However the state has given subsidies to urban consumers.

Question: But this practice can not balance the price hikes in general.

Answer: Of course not, but please think of this: in the past, tomatoes were rather cheap but they were barely available; now you may buy tomatoes even in winter. But since they are grown in hothouses they cost more.

Question: But this can not overcome people's dissatisfaction with price hikes. It is difficult, too, for the country to support more subsidies. Now subsidies account for about one third of the expenditure of your country.

Answer: One of the purposes of our reform is gradually to cut down state subsidies.

Question: This is of great urgency, because there is already a big hole in your finances.

Answer: We had no deficit in the past. Having a financial deficit is a big change. But the most important question is how to use the funds we have borrowed. If we use the funds to develop economy, having a little debt will be no bad thing.

Question: Which influence is the most dangerous at present, right-wing bourgeois-liberalisation thinking or the left-wing, rigid way of thinking.

Answer: Right and left are mere definitions. But we can say that our opposition to bourgeois liberalisation is because we aim to implement our reform policies and open up to the outside world while adhering to a socialist orientation.

Question: Which school will persist, reformist or conservative?

Answer: We have neither reformists nor conservatives. We are all in favour of reform. Reform is the only road we can follow.

Question: Gorbachev understands that there can be no economic reform without political reform. Does China need greater democracy?

Answer: Deng Xiaoping said that when economic reform develops to a certain point, it can not achieve further success without political reform. Our opposition to bourgeois liberalisation does not mean opposition to democracy and freedom. Our aim is to uphold the leadership of the Communist Party and to keep to the socialist road.

PRICE REFORM IS THE KEY TO THE SUCCESS OF ECONOMIC REFORM: INTERVIEW WITH BBC TELEVISION

Vice Minister Gao Shangquan met a six-member BBC TV team led by correspondent Gavin Esler and producer Barbara Vant on the afternoon of 12 April 1989. Gao briefly introduced the ten-year economic reform in China, the main aspects of reform deepening and the problems with the current reform. He then answered questions put to him by the correspondents.

Question: What is the extent of the inflation in China? It is reported that the inflation rate reached 18–30 per cent. What measures are you going to take to solve this problem?

Answer: Inflation has appeared in China. The main measures to curb inflation are as follows:

1. To control the scale of investment, especially investment in capital construction projects.
2. To curb the increase in consumption, especially the growth of extravagant consumption by government departments, institutions and enterprises.
3. To tighten the money market and control the volume of loans and currency issue.
4. To reduce financial expenditure, especially administrative expenditure, and to encourage hard work and thrift.

In addition we are deepening the enterprise reform in order to improve economic performance and readjust the economic structure, including the structure of the system and the enterprise structure, the investment mix and the export and import mix. China's reform is an overall reform. We are in the course of comprehensive economic improvement and rectification. The current target is to keep this year's inflation rate significantly lower than that of last year. At present inflation is being curbed, investment in capital construction has been reduced, savings have increased, consumption by government departments and enterprises has been reduced, the hike has been checked and we intend further to increase the supply of essential products.

Though we have achieved some results in curbing inflation we must not be overoptimistic. The task is arduous but we have confidence.

Question: Price reform is inevitable in the course of China's economic reform. Chairman Deng said that in carrying out the price reform, some difficulties have to be overcome. What do you think of that?

Answer: The Central Committee of the Chinese Communist Party has pointed out the importance of price reform. 'The decision on the Reform of the Economic System by the Central Committee of the Chinese Communist Party' in October 1984 stated that price reform is the key to the success or failure of the overall reform of the economic structure. Without price reform, economic relations can not be normalised and market mechanisms can not function. That is why Chairman Deng said that the difficulties of price reform have to be overcome. The orientation of price reform is clear. Market and enterprises should play a regulatory role in promoting economic growth.

Question: Why did the pace of price reform slow down?

Answer: Because we have to consider the following factors. First, price reform is not a short-term task, it is a long-term process. Second, price reform is not a solitary task. It has to be combined with enterprise reform, macroeconomic regulation and control as well as reforms in finance, banking and taxation. Third, due consideration must be given to the ability of society and the enterprises to accept price reform. The panic purchasing last year is an example. People did not understand. So we must pay attention to people's thinking and their ability to accept the reform.

I have to make clear two other points. First, slowing down doesn't mean that we have stopped the reform of prices. We adjusted the prices of more than 20 kinds of commodity last year. We have just slowed down the pace of the reform. Second, it is necessary to curb inflation. But in order to do that we have to carry out a series of price management practices in order to lay down the foundation for further price reforms and the deepening of economic reform.

Question: In the West it is natural to have different opinions over a certain problem. Now, different views do exist in terms of economic reform. What is the opinion of Chinese leaders?

Answer: The curbing of inflation and the deepening of economic reform are not contradictory. At present inflation is an outstanding problem. We have to solve it first. It is imperative to undertake comprehensive rectification. Necessary administrative, economic and legal means must be taken and great attention has to be paid to political and ideological work. The old practice of using administrative management alone does not work any more. It is necessary to use economic means and macroeconomic regulation and control. It is also necessary to change the mechanisms and to deepen the reform through increasing the supply of essential products and optimising economic structures to improve economic performance.

Generally speaking, the curbing of inflation and the deepening of structural reform are consistent. They do not contradict each other.

Question: Is there any contradiction between a market economy and a planned economy? What is Chinese leaders' opinion?

Answer: Our recognition of the importance of market regulation has been through several stages. In the old economic system, attention was only paid to planning. The function of the market was denied. In 1984 the idea of a planned commodity economy was advanced. We knew that a planned economy and a commodity economy were not contradictory. In order to practise a planned economy it is necessary conscientiously to observe the law of value. At that time we had a tentative understanding of the need to bring into play the function of the market.

It is necessary to combine plan with market with a view to forming a socialist market system. Both planned regulation and market regulation are needed. This bears no essential relation to social systems. A socialist system may use both means in order to regulate. The essential distinction between a socialist system and a capitalist system lies in the difference of ownership.

In order to combine a planned economy with market regulation it is imperative to set up and develop a socialist market with a view to bringing into play the function of market mechanisms on the one hand, and gradually narrowing the scope of mandatory planning while expanding that of guidance planning on the other hand. Since the reform the mandatory planning of industrial products has reduced from 120 items to 60, and market regulation has played its role.

Question: In the long run, the target of reform is to combine the advantages of the socialist system and those of capitalism. But what do you think of the phenomenon of corruption?

Answer: Corruption takes place all over the world, though specific situations are different. There is no inevitable relationship between corruption and reform. The double-track system of prices in the reform offers opportunities to some speculators to use the price differences to obtain illegal profits, thus creating a hotbed of corruption. Of course, without reform corruption would still exist. We have decided to sweep away corruption by means of reform, education and supervision.

Question: Please explain the essence of the socialist commodity economy.

Answer: The socialist commodity economy is a planned commodity economy based on public ownership. We are maintaining public ownership as the dominant factor. That means we will never undertake privatisation. Of course we do not exclude a private economy. Our constitution provides for the development of a private economy. The individual economy is encouraged too.

To run a socialist commodity economy is to adhere to the principle of distribution according to work while at the same time developing other forms of distribution and allowing the existence of other, non-labour income.

In my view, when studying China's socialist commodity economy it is also necessary to pay attention to uniquely Chinese features. First, China's population has reached 1.1 billion and is increasing at the rate of 15 million per year. Second, although China is a big country abounding in natural resources, resources per capita are rather poor. The area under cultivation is reducing at the rate of five million mu annually. Due consideration must be paid to these two characteristics.

Question: What is the relationship between economic reform and political reform? Are they promoting each other?

Answer: When economic reform has developed to a certain point, political reform must be carried out in order to ensure the achievement of economic reform and facilitate its development.

These two kinds of reform combine and overlap in some areas. For example, in structural reform it is necessary to reform the administrative system in order to separate enterprises from politics, while in enterprise reform the responsibility system is in force. These two practices are included in both reform of the economic system and that of the political system.

TEN YEARS OF REFORM HAS CAUSED HISTORIC CHANGES IN CHINA: INTERVIEW WITH MORTIMER B. ZUKERMAN, CHIEF EDITOR OF US NEWS & WORLD REPORT (22/2/90)

Question: What is the motive force of China's economic restructuring? What are the merits and defects of the economic reform over the last ten years? To what extent should you return to the centrally controlled economy? How could you manage to return to the centrally controlled economy without putting an end to the devolution of power to a lower level and the promotion of the private sector?

Answer: In our economic restructuring drive, we depend mainly on the leadership of the Chinese Communist Party and bring into full play the initiative and creativity of all workers, peasants, intellectuals and cadres. At the same time we have to bring into play the initiative of the central and local governments and the enterprises. These are the fundamental reasons behind the great success of China's economic reform over the last ten years.

Our reform was initiated in the economic sphere and gained initial success in rural areas. We have combined urban reform with rural reform and made the two reforms promote each other while carrying out political restructuring step by step and under proper leadership. Since the 10-year reform great changes have taken place in our country. Gross national product, national income, national financial income and fixed assets formed by new investment as well as the per capita income of the urban and rural population have more than doubled compared with the values before reform. National capabilities have been significantly strengthened and people's well-being has improved.

However some problems have cropped up: relatively acute inflation, alternately overheated or overcooled economic development, unfair distribution of income, and corruption. But these phenomena will be completely overcome in the course of improving the economic environment, rectifying the economic order and deepening the reform.

In the current drive of improvement and rectification, since in the past undue attention was given to decentralisation, we have to put more stress on concentration, expanding gradually the proportion of national financial income in total national income and increasing the share of central government income in total national financial income. But it does not mean that we intend to return to the old economic system in which the central government exercised too much power. We shall flexibly adjust the relationship between centralisation and decentralisation in accordance with the principle of combining the planned economy with market regulation and in light of the actual situation of the development of the national economy. For example, in trades and industries that are essential to the national economy and people's well-being, emphasis will be put on planning and centralisation, while in the common trades and industries more stress will be put on market regulation and the devolution of power to a lower level. All these practices will depend on the actual situation in different periods and in different trades.

The individual sector and the private sector are necessary and useful supplements to our socialist economy. There is no change in the policies worked out by the Party and the government towards them. We shall continue to permit their existence and development while at the same time intensifying the management and guidance over them, mobilising any positive factors that serve the national economy and people's well-being and restricting negative roles that are harmful to the national economy and people's well-being.

Question: What is the main problem in agriculture at the present? Have you achieved any progress? Do you have to change the contracted responsibility system in the rural areas?

Answer: The main problem in agriculture at the present is stagnation in the production of grain and cotton for four consecutive years (1985–8). This stagnation can be attributed to the fact that our misjudgement of the agricultural situation resulted in some errors in guidance and macro policy making. The input into agriculture was reduced and basic agricultural construction neglected, so that agricultural productivity was not raised much. In concrete terms, after the bumper harvest in 1984 we were too optimistic in our assessment of agricultural production, especially grain production, and overestimated the prosperity of the peasants, with the result that agricultural production was neglected or slackened. In price policies, some measures led to a curbing of grain and cotton production. The main measure was the change in the purchasing price policy. The policy of purchasing at higher prices the grain output in excess of the purchase quota was changed to one of mixed prices. This practice reduced the income of the peasants in the new grain areas. In addition the prices of essential means of production were raised and the restriction on the prices of many cash crops, livestock products and aquatic products was lifted, thus reducing the relative income of grain and cotton production. The enthusiasm of peasants for growing grain was dampened.

In 1989 we defined anew the concept that agriculture is the foundation of the national economy, adjusted some policies, increased the input into agriculture, launched an upsurge in irrigation and water-conservation projects and strengthened the capability of agriculture to withstand natural calamities. Besides these measures, the sale of chemical fertilisers, plastic sheeting and pesticides were monopolised, the price hike of essential means of agricultural production was curbed, the purchase prices of grain and cotton were raised and policies were worked out for grain- and cotton-producing regions to sell to other areas, thus arousing the enthusiasm of peasants to grow grain and cotton. In 1989 the total grain output was 407.45 million tons, an increase of 3.4 per cent over 1988, 140 000 tons more than the bumper harvest of 1984, and all-time high. The output of such cash crops as cotton reduced due to the natural calamity.

Investment in agricultural projects (farming, forestry, water conservancy, meteorology) has continued to decrease since 1978. In 1978 capital construction investment in agriculture amounted to 5.334 billion yuan, reducing to 3.666 billion yuan in 1986. Although investment increased to 4.498 billion yuan in 1988 the share of agricultural investment in total capital construction investment is on the decline, falling from 10.6 per cent in 1978 to 3.1 per cent in 1986 and 2.9 per cent in 1988.

As for the proportion of the fulfilment volume of national capital construction investment, the proportion of the fulfilment volume of agricultural investment increased from 4.3 per cent to 4.4 per cent in 1988. We are making an effort to solve this problem. The central authorities are considering increasing the proportion of agricultural investment in total capital construction investment.

The contracted responsibility system in rural areas will be extended and improved, mainly through extending the land contract period. In the developed coastal areas and the countryside around large and medium-sized cities the development of village and township enterprises has made it easy for surplus labourers to change their trade. We are encouraging the concentration of land in good farming hands. When conditions allow, efforts will be made to expand farming on a proper scale, or a collective economy in rural areas will be developed on a voluntary basis. We shall establish a service system for the entire process of agricultural production, that is, before, during and after the farming season, in order to raise agricultural labour productivity.

Question: What kind of role do foreign investment and foreign technology play in China's economic growth? To what extent are you in urgent need of them? In the face of the reaction of foreign countries to the incident that occurred in the late spring and early summer of 1989 in China, how can you attract foreign investment? Deng Xiaoping said that, to open to the West in order to import technology and develop the economy it is inevitable that some 'flies' will come in through the window. These 'flies' came in from abroad, bringing with them the freedom of speech and the idea of restricting the power of the Communist Party. Did they have some influence on the demonstrations in late spring and early summer 1989? If you continue to open the window to the West, how can you prevent 'flies' from coming in again? What is the impact of the economic sanctions that foreign countries exerted on China? How can you make foreign investors feel assured that China has returned to normal?

Answer: Foreign investment and foreign advanced technology have played a positive role in China's economic growth. The share of foreign funds in China's total fixed assets investment was 5.6 per cent and 6.1 per cent in 1988 and 1989 respectively. The proportion of the industrial output value of Sino–foreign joint ventures, cooperative enterprises and wholly foreign-funded enterprises accounts for less than 3 per cent. According to the statistics of the relevant departments, China spent US$ 27 billion in the 1980s to import foreign advanced technology. Sixty per cent of the increased annual output value came from increased earnings through importing new technology. Investment in such basic industrial sectors as energy, transport, communications and raw materials stands at 43.2 per cent of imported technology.

We hope that foreign funds will go to the following areas: advanced technical products, especially those that fill the gaps in technology in our country; production of import substitutes; export products to earn foreign exchange; and basic industrial facilities projects such as energy, transport, communications and raw materials.

To a certain extent the economic sanctions that Western countries exerted on us affected China's policy of opening up to the outside world but had little influence on China's economic development. This is because our economy is still import-oriented and is not dependent on the world market. In 1988 the total volume of our export products accounted for only 7.5 per cent of total national industrial and agricultural output, and the total volume of export and import trade was 16 per cent of total industrial and agricultural output.

In order to reassure foreign investors the central government, local governments at all levels and the departments concerned have restated again and again that there has been no change in China's policy of opening up to the outside world, in its policy on special economic zones and opening experimental regions in the provinces of Guangdong, Fujian and Hainan, and in its policy of developing an export-oriented economy in coastal areas. The investment environment for foreign businessmen has been improved and legislation to protect the legal rights and benefits of foreign businessmen has been formulated and perfected.

The martial law imposed on parts of the capital was lifted on 11 January in order to prove that public order has returned to normal.

China imports foreign funds and advanced technology with a view of speeding up its modernisation. We warmly welcome all foreign businessmen and friends who come to China to invest in our economic reconstruction. In the course of reform and opening up to the outside world it is inevitable that some Western capitalist ideas and values will have some influence on us. But we are overcoming and eliminating these negative influences by strengthening the socialist legal system and political ideological education. Just as when we open a window to breathe fresh air, we fix window screening on it to prevent flies from coming into the room.

Question: Due to the reaction of international business circles and financial circles towards China after the June incident, did China change the pace of its economic growth, the process of its economy and technology and the policy of joint venture?

Answer: Our policy of improving the economic environment, rectifying the economic order and deepening the reform is not a measure that was adopted after the turmoil and counterrevolutionary rebellion in late spring and early summer last year; nor a countermeasure of the economic sanctions Western countries exerted on China. The Third Plenary Session of Thirteenth CPC Central Committee decided in September 1988 to carry out economic improvement and rectification measures so as to slow down the pace of economic growth, control the volume of credit and currency issue, control total investment in fixed assets, and curb the growth of consumer demand. This is because, since 1984, some problems have cropped up, such as overheated economic growth, huge investment, uncontrolled credit and currency issue, excessive growth of consumer demand and continuing price hikes. In view of this situation we have taken some measures to stabilise the economy and the markets and to set people's mind at ease. By improving the economic environment, rectifying the economic order and deepening the reform we shall see to it that our inflation rate is controlled at less than 10 per cent, and our economy is to witness a sustained, stable and coordinated development.

There is no change in our policy of opening up to the outside world and engaging in Sino-foreign joint ventures. We think there is no need for such a change. If there is any change, we hope that the direction of foreign investment will correspond to China's industrial policy. We shall import foreign funds and start Sino-foreign joint ventures, cooperative enterprises and wholly foreign-funded enterprises in compliance with international practices, and redouble our efforts to improve our investment environment and make things more convenient for foreign businessmen.

Question: What is your inflation rate? And what are the inflation rates of the prices of food, consumer products and essential materials?

Answer: So far we have not formally calculated the inflation rate. What the statistics department uses is a general index of national retail prices, which hit 18.6 per cent in 1988 and 17.8 per cent in 1989. We had planned in the fourth quarter of 1988 to make the inflation rate in 1989 significantly lower than that of 1988. In the light of the actual situation this target was not fulfilled satisfactorily. The inflation rate decreased by only 0.7 per cent. But the momentum of the rising price index was checked and is now on the decline, from 27 per cent in January last year to 6.4 per cent in December. In 1989 the index of consumer product prices rose 17.5 per cent, of which food was 16.2 per cent and essential materials 21.2 per cent.

Question: The price reform is to be carried out to what extent and in which respects? Are you going to abolish the dual price practice which led to corruption? To what extent? What policy is to be its substitute?

Answer: Price is a comprehensive reflection of the national economy. Price reform is the most sensitive problem in our economic activities. Our Party and government have always been very prudent and reliable in making policies on price reform. Over the last ten years we have systematically adjusted the prices of farm products, industrial raw materials, energy and transport. We have lifted the price restrictions on certain small articles and have allowed some general industrial processed products to have various price patterns, such as state-fixed prices, state-guided prices and prices regulated by the market. These price reform measures have played an important role in promoting industrial and agricultural production, enlivening both urban and rural markets and making things convenient for the people, but along with these measures have come such problems as price hikes.

In order to avoid possible defects brought about by the 'double track' price system we have adopted a series of new economic management measures. First, we have monopolised the management and sale of some essential commodities and materials that are in short supply, such as steel, non-ferrous metal, agricultural means of production, colour TV sets and brand-named quality cigarettes and spirits, and have strictly forbidden the resale of these goods and the reaping of huge profits. Second, with regard to products from which price restrictions have been lifted, price rises must be approved by the relevant authorities. Third, without the authorisation of the State Council, no department concerned may adopt any new or major measures regarding price change. Finally, market order has been rectified and control and supervision of market prices tightened. These practices have begun to produce significant effects. The price increase rate in 1989 was lower than in the previous year. Nationwide market prices are in the main being kept stable, while the price of some articles has decreased.

In the course of improving the economic environment, rectifying the economic order and deepening the reform we shall steadily and gradually push forward price reform on the basis of strengthening macro-regulation and control. As for the products from which price restrictions have been lifted, there will be no change. When necessary we shall fix a price ceiling for certain articles or enforce the system of having to report raised prices to a higher body. We are exerting ourselves to the utmost to keep stable the price of daily necessities.

We have come to the realisation that the 'double-track' price system is responsible for the chaos in the economic order and for corruption, and its defects are becoming more and more evident. For this reason we are going to adjust the price system during this year and next. First the price of coal, which is subject to centralised distribution, will be changed from the double-track system to a single-track one. Then the double-track system that is applied to some commodities will be abolished. However it will be difficult to abolish the double-track system of certain goods in a short time. We shall make an appropriate adjustment to their centrally planned prices and strictly control the demand for these goods, while tightening the management of the prices of those articles whose sales are through individual channels in order to narrow the gap between the two prices.

Question: The Chinese government has made efforts to curb the inflation rate and slow down the growth rate of the overheated economic development. Is there any progress in these regards? Did the growth rate slow down too much? How do you plan to reactivate the economy? How does the Chinese government plan to deal with the problem of urban and rural unemployment?

Answer: As I have mentioned before, according to the statistics the general index of national retail prices in 1989 was up 17.8 per cent over the previous year, a decline of 0.7 per cent compared with 1988. The general index of national retail prices in January 1989 stood at 27 per cent, decreasing to 6.4 per cent in December and continuing to reduce to 5 per cent in January this year. We plan to reduce the price index to less than 10 per cent through a three-year economic improvement and rectification programme. The annual growth rate of gross national product is on average 5–6 per cent. The growth rate of industrial output value last year was 6.8 per cent (or 8 per cent if village enterprises and enterprises below the village level are included), while the gross national product increased 4 per cent and the agricultural output value 3.3 per cent, basically fulfilling the expected target. However, since last September the growth rate of industrial output value has slowed down (the growth rate was 0.9 per cent in September 1989, 2.1 per cent in October, 0.9 per cent in November and 3.4 per cent in December. The growth rate in January 1990 decreased 6.1 per cent compared with the same period the previous year, but calculated by comparable factors it rose 4.3 per cent). The fact that the growth rate of industrial production has dropped has aroused the concern of governments at all levels. In the light of the actual situation we have to give priority to improving our economic performance.

The percentage of people waiting for employment in cities and towns was 5.7 per cent in 1979, decreasing to 2 per cent in 1988. According to primary estimates the percentage of people waiting for employment was about 3 per cent in 1989. We shall open up new avenues to create more employment opportunities. In the past, employment opportunities in cities and towns were basically offered by the state. Since the reform this policy has been changed. People are being encouraged to find jobs by themselves. Efforts to set up collective economic undertakings, individual industrial and commercial business and private enterprises are being supported. There is no change in our policy towards the development of individual and private economic undertakings, however these should be under proper management, guidance and supervision. Currently 14 million individuals are engaging in industrial and commercial business (including more than 220 000 private enterprises), with more than 23 million employees. In rural areas, surplus personnel should be shifted out according to plan. Our policy is to absorb surplus agricultural labour on the spot, mainly through promoting village and township enterprises, and individual and private economic undertakings. In addition, where conditions permit, efforts should be made to set up an agricultural service system of production, supply and marketing with a view to offering jobs to some surplus labour in the rural areas. By the end of 1989 more than 10 million peasants had returned to rural areas throughout the country to obtain employment.

PUTTING HOUSING REFORM AT THE TOP OF THE AGENDA: INTERVIEW IN THE NEWSPAPER *CONSTRUCTION DAILY*, 28 AUGUST 1987

Recently a senior leader of the State Council pointed out that urban housing reform must be put at the top of the agenda. So far the housing reform proposal for the city of Yantai has been approved by the State Council, and was implemented on 1 August 1987. Housing reform proposals for other cities are also being worked out. Since there is considerable interest in this issue among the general public, correspondents from this newspaper interviewed Mr Gao Shangquan, vice chairman of the State Economic Reform Commission and deputy chairman of the Housing Reform Committee of the State Council.

Question: Many people do not understand why the present housing system must be changed. Could you please talk briefly on this issue?

Answer: Since 1949 urban housing in this country has largely been the responsibility of the state. Investment in housing is by the state, and rents are substantially subsidised. More than thirty years of experience has shown that the housing problems in our cities will not be solved if this system is to continue.

At the moment the average rent per square metre is only 0.13 yuan, which is not enough to meet the cost of running the elevator in some high-rise blocks. Funds allocated by the state for housing have no return whatsoever, making further commitments by the state to finance housing construction an increasingly heavy burden. At the same time, the state has to pay huge subsidies for maintenance and renovation. The result is that the more houses that are built, the heavier the state's burden will be, leading to a vicious circle and a host of problems in distribution.

Housing is a factor of living, but it should also be commercial property. At the present, however, housing is not being treated as commercial property and rents paid for housing are nothing more than symbolic, representing just over 1 per cent of urban family expenditure. Because the state monopolises housing and individuals can only expect to receive it from the state, there is nothing individuals can do to improve their housing conditions. The average consumer has to concentrate his consumer spending on refrigerators, colour television sets, washing machines and the like instead of housing. This has done nothing to help tackle the housing problem. Indeed the country's industrial structure and economic development in general have been adversely affected.

The low rent has exerted tremendous pressure on the demand for housing, and has led to malpractices in the housing distribution process. The more housing is built, the greater the housing problem seems to be. According to statistics, during the sixth five year plan period alone, state expenditure on public housing amounted to more than 100 billion yuan, which is 21.8 per cent of the country's total expenditure on fixed asset investment. Six hundred and forty eight million square metres of housing were constructed, almost equal to the total constructed during the past 30 years. The speed of construction has exceeded that of advanced countries, and per capita housing has increased from 4.2 square metres in the early 1950s to 6.36 square metres today. Nevertheless more than ten million families, or one quarter of the whole population, still do not have adequate housing. A solution to this urban housing problem must be found during the reform process.

But it should be noted that housing reform is faced with difficulties. This is not only an adjustment in economic interest, but also a revolution in traditional mentality. It has long been taken for granted among cadres and the rank and file that low rent is a manifestation of the superiority of socialism, that housing is a sort of perk associated with status, and that housing should be provided and not paid for. This sort of mentality has hindered housing reform. Housing reform affects the state, enterprises and the individual. It is also related to the reform of central planning, fiscal policy, finance, taxation and the price system. This reflects the complexities and difficulties of housing reform. However difficult reform may be, it must be implemented. Solutions to problems will have to be found along the way. Otherwise burdens will become heavier by the day.

Question: Many people are convinced that the old housing system has reached a dead end, and that there will be no solution without reform. Now, what kinds of measure should the housing reform include?

Answer: As early as April 1980 Deng Xiaoping made the following comments on housing reform: 'A series of policies should be formulated to tackle the urban housing problem. Urban residents should be able to purchase houses or build their own houses. New houses may be sold; so may the older ones. . . . Once rents are higher, low-income people should be subsidised. These policies should be formulated as an integral package'. This pointed to a new direction in housing reform.

The objective of urban housing reform is to commercialise the housing sector. That is, physical distribution will be replaced with monetary distribution. Consumers buy or rent houses, turning housing into a consumer market. This will give investment in housing a real return, thus increasing housing construction and providing a new solution to the country's housing problem.

So far, according to the experiences of various regions, housing reform is mainly centred on the following issues. First, rents should be raised to a rational level while occupants of public housing receive a subsidy. Second, the public should be encouraged to buy or build their housing and channel their savings into improving their housing conditions. Third, a rational source of finance for housing constructions should be found. At the same time central planning, fiscal policy, the price system and housing management should be reformed. A framework should be established for the healthy flow of housing finance, which will promote the development of the real estate industry, the construction industry and related financial services. Housing reform also requires complementary measures on other reform fronts.

Question: Housing reform will inevitably have a ripple effect on other reform measures. Which aspects of reform will be affected?

Answer: Housing reform is a major decision by the government to solve the housing problem once and for all. The successful implementation of housing reform will boost reforms in a number of other areas.

When the housing reform scheme is up and going, housing finance will be able to flow in a healthy manner, reducing the burden on government expenditure, enabling the more rapid development of housing construction, and rationalising consumption and the industrial structure of the economy.

The successful implementation of housing reform will almost certainly be the engine of development of the construction industry and the real estate industry, turning the construction industry into one of the economy's pillar industries. The commercialisation of housing will give incentives to private purchasers of houses, channelling public savings into the real estate market.

Politically, the commercialisation of the housing market will remove malpractices in the distribution of public housing. This will contribute towards social stability.

Question: A lot of people now worry about the effect of higher rents on their living standards. Could you please tell us something about your view on this?

Answer: It is the general public who will benefit most from the housing reform. The healthier flow of housing finance and the development of housing construction will help to solve the housing problem and create favourable conditions to meet the public housing demand.

As average income in the country is still relatively low, once rents are raised, subsidies will be provided by the government. On the whole, therefore, an increase in rents will not necessarily imply a reduction in living standards. It must be pointed out that those who occupy more or better housing than the average public will have to increase their housing expenditure while those who lack housing will see their income rise as a result of housing subsidies, which could be used as savings for the purchase of housing in the future. Personally, I think this is reasonable and acceptable to the public. Once on the market, just like other goods such as food, clothing and domestic appliances, housing could be traded freely. The public could make their own choices according to their requirements and financial means.

Special rent deduction policies will be implemented where and when appropriate on a case-by-case basis.

Question: It has been reported that housing construction costs have been rising steadily, particularly in the big cities where construction costs are now more than 1000 yuan per square metre. At such a cost very few people will be able to afford to buy houses or flats of their own.

Answer: One of the major objectives of housing reform is to sell houses to the general public. Whether houses can be sold or not will depend on how rents and prices are set. Once housing is commercialised and rents are increased substantially, there will be more incentive for the public to buy rather than rent houses. At the same time, pricing is just as important to successful sales. Excessive increases in property prices should be stopped. We believe that a solution will be found as proposals for housing reforms are prepared in different regions according to their own conditions.

It is reasonable to assume that a substantial number of people can afford to buy houses. As of the end of July this year, urban bank savings amounted to 183.3 billion yuan, which is an indication that the disposable income of the pubic is higher. At the beginning of this year a survey of newlyweds conducted in Beijing found that, on average, each pair had spent 5945 yuan on their wedding. More than one third of them had spent over 7000 yuan, while a few had spent well over 10 000 yuan. The spending was mainly on quality furniture, domestic appliances, jewellery, fur and other quality consumer products. If only a proportion of that money could be spent on housing the effect on the housing problem and stability of the market would be substantial. In recent years apartment blocks for newlyweds have been built in many cities and have proved extremely popular among buyers. This is yet another indication of public interest in commercially sold houses.

As far as those who lack cash are concerned, a special programme will be introduced in the form of mortgages, long-term low-interest housing loans, price reductions and tax deductions.

Question: Could you please talk briefly about the cities where housing pilot schemes are being implemented?

Answer: The cities of Bengbu, Tangshan, Changzhou and Shengyang have all worked out proposals, which are being scrutinised. These are expected to be implemented as soon as possible. Another twelve cities, including Xingtai, Zhenjian, Jinzhou, Shijiazhuang, Lanzhou, Chongking and Wuhan, are currently working on their proposals, which they expect to implement next year.

The proposals can be categorised into the following groups. 'Raise rents and issue subsidies' is the approach adopted by the city of Yantai and a number of other cities. Your newspaper has made a detailed report on this. I will therefore not elaborate on it.

'Raise funds and rents' is another approach that attempts to pool available funds. Housing subsidies are paid out of these funds. Property owners settle with the issuer to exchange subsidy certificates for cash. Yet another approach is to start with profitable and cash-rich enterprises and then go on to other enterprises and work units to complete the housing reform.

Because the housing reform schemes have been formulated individually by the localities under the guidance of the government, they are all different and there may be even better ones.

Question: Housing reform has been proposed for many years. A lot of people believe that the earlier it is implemented, the more benefits it will produce. Now, how can this scheme be better implemented?

Answer: Up to now, Yantai is the only city where housing reform has started. The other cities will soon follow suit.

Efforts will have to be made to help the public recognise the relationship between housing reform and their own interests. The policies and proposals of housing reform should be presented to the public to allow public participation in the project.

The different cities' housing reform schemes must be carefully examined and placed at the top of their agenda.

Housing reform affects central planning, fiscal policies, finance, income policy, taxation, the price system and city planning. There must be coordination among the departments involved.

Housing reform has difficulties. But if carried out properly, recognised by the government and accepted by the general public, housing reform will make rapid progress and contribute to the success of the overall economic reform programme.

A NEW ORDER IN BUSINESS ACTIVITIES: INTERVIEW IN THE *PEOPLE'S DAILY*, 10 SEPTEMBER 1988

Recently Mr Gao Shang-quan, vice chairman of the State Economic Reform Commission, expressed his views on the problems of the business sector and gave suggestions on the establishment of a new order of business activities. This correspondent had an interview with him recently.

Question: It appears extremely appropriate that you are emphasising the importance of establishing a new order in business activities as the economic reform programme reaches a vitally important crossroad. I sometimes wonder what really caused the price hikes, the illegal profiteering and corruption. Some people maintain that this is the result of the development of the commodity economy. I can not agree with them. But I can not find convincing arguments against them.

Answer: It should be made clear that these negative phenomena are not the inevitable consequences of a commodity economy, but the result of the coexistence of two inherently different economic systems.

The essence of a commodity economy is that all economic relationships are embodied in monetary relationships. And demand and supply are regulated through open market competition, forcing enterprises to cut down costs and enhance product quality and economic efficiency by ensuring a rational allocation of resources. Speculative trade in factors of production or consumer goods that are in short supply stems mainly from the exchange of power for money. Because the traditional system has not been fully replaced by the new one, government agencies still enjoy a substantial amount of power over the allocation of resources, and certain departments still have an industry monopoly. The power-related business activities belong neither to market transactions in the real sense, nor to planned allocation under the tradition system. Besides, the so-called 'double-track' price system has been employed during economic reform, which has led to huge discrepancies between the regulated price and the market price. The problem has been further worsened by less than perfect market organisation, backward trading methods and an incomplete legal framework. All these have created opportunities for the abuse of power for personal benefit. This is a manifestation of the imperfection of the market system. In order fundamentally to solve these problems, further reform measures must be implemented to create a new market system.

Question: Could you elaborate on that?

Answer: A market system requires open, monetary transactions within a legal framework.

Open business transactions are essential for the establishment of a transparent market system. Transactions must be conducted in the market as opposed to privately concluded deals. Wholesale transactions must be based on legal agreements and contracts. Important production materials and consumer goods must not be traded privately. Companies or individuals entering the market have to meet certain qualification requirements. Prices and commissions involved in a transaction must be clearly stated in the contract or other relevant papers. Open market information is conducive to the establishment of direct contract between buyers and sellers, cutting out unnecessary middleman and curbing unnatural price rises.

The current reform is also a monetarisation process for the economy. Administrative allocation of resources should gradually be replaced by monetary transactions. Each year the Commerce Department buys food from provinces that have surpluses and sells it to those with shortages. It would be more appropriate if these provinces could deal directly between themselves. Barter trade is used by some steel companies to sell their over-quota products. Scarce material thus becomes a sort of hard currency, enabling tax evasion.

A legal framework is indispensible for the creation of a new market system. Legislation should be speeded up to provide a fair and open environment for competition. At the same time, measures should be taken to develop adequate accounting and auditing systems and standards to foster effective financial discipline for enterprises. Corruption must be dealt with according to law. The government should gradually pull away from the market and assume the role of a referee.

Question: Given the present status of our economy, it seems that we still have a long road ahead of us.

Answer: That is true. There are a number of issues we should try to address now. First, the so-called double-track price system must be removed to allow a truly meaningful market price. Prices are severely distorted at the moment, and do not reflect demand or supply. Another problem is that the defects of the double-track price system are becoming increasing obvious. Some government departments and 'companies' that are nothing more than disguised government agencies are abusing their power by profiteering. Therefore price reform must be implemented to enable the formation of market prices for most goods and services, which will be a time-consuming process.

Second, fair and open competition should be promoted and protected.

Question: This issue has been raised by the press many times during the past few years, but so far no attempts have been made to address the issue. A large number of township enterprises are paying fat commissions in order to fill the market with inferior goods. Good quality products from state-owned enterprises, on the other hand, are placed at a disadvantage because of the lack of similar sales techniques. Besides, state-owned, collectively owned and privately owned companies pay different rates of tax, which has caused the producers of better quality products to shoulder a heavier burden. According to some reports, some local governments are using administrative measures to protect backward industries that might otherwise be threatened with the loss of investments, bank loans and allocated raw materials.

Answer: These problems do exist. State-owned enterprises enjoy a stable supply of raw materials, but they are also subject to stringent controls. Township enterprises have much more flexible management methods, but suffer from a shortage of raw materials. Of course they enjoy certain tax advantages. In order to tackle these problems, further reform measures must be implemented to change the tax system, the accounting system and the material allocation system. Appropriate legislation should be introduced, for instance an anti monopoly law. Government control of resources (including raw materials, finance, foreign exchange) should gradually be replaced by market mechanisms.

Question: If open and fair competition can be assured, a healthy and stable market order will emerge.

Answer: The level of organisation of the market should be enhanced. A well-organised market is an indication of the development of a market system. For this purpose, commercial organisations incorporating a group of companies or integrating manufacturing and marketing should be developed. These should be engaged mainly in wholesale businesses and become elements of stability in the market. The government should not be involved in commercial activities. Wholesale companies affiliated with commerce or material-allocation authorities must cut their ties with the government and become independent business entities dealing with retail concerns and private businesses. Finally, markets for different goods and services should be developed. There should be plans to develop markets for factors of production, agricultural products and raw materials. Experiments with a futures market should be conducted as part of the plan to provide a mechanism for open transactions. All the markets should be open and provide services, but should not engage in transactions themselves.

Appendix

THE MAJOR EVENTS OF THE TEN-YEAR ECONOMIC
REFORM: DECEMBER 1978 TO DECEMBER 1988

1978

18 December   The third plenary session of the Eleventh Central Committee of the Chinese Communist Party is held in Beijing. The Party's
line on Marxist thought, and its political and organisational programmes
are reaffirmed, and the policy of concentrating on socialist modernisation is launched. The plenary meeting makes a commitment to reform
in a thorough going way those production relations and aspects of the
superstructure that are not adapted to the development of the productive forces, and to reform all backward methods of management,
activities and thinking. The reform, therefore, is to be an extensive
and deepening process. China's economic restructuring began at this
moment.

1979

11 January   The Party's Central Committee distributes the document
'The Resolution (Draft) on several Issues Regarding the Rapid Development of Agriculture' to all rural areas for consultation. The draft
stipulated that the proprietary rights and decision-making power of the
production brigades and production teams are to be protected; and that
property cannot be transferred and occupied without remuneration. The
draft also pointed out that commune members' family plots, family
side-lines and country market places are indispensable supplements to
the socialist economy, and are not to be banned as 'capitalist tails'.

31 January   The Party's Central Committee and the State Council
decide that an industrial district is to be established in Shekou, Guangdong
Province; it is to be organised and run by China Merchants of Hong
Kong, who are to raise funds for it.

23 February   The State Council decides to restore the Agricultural
Bank of China in order to better manage the funds that have been
raised to support agriculture.

1 March   The State Council decides that, starting from March, the purchase price of eighteen agricultural products, including grain, cotton, edible oils and live pigs, will be raised – an average increase of 24.8 per cent. It is estimated that the peasants will benefit by increasing their income by a total of some 7 billion yuan.

3 March   The China Enterprise Management Association is founded.

10 March   The State Council approves the report made by the People's Bank of China on regulating the interest paid on bank deposits. From April, the rate applying to all urban and rural residents' savings deposit accounts will revert to the level of the pre-cultural-revolution period.

13 March   The State Council approves the report made by the People's Bank of China on restructuring the Bank of China. The two are to be separated, and the latter will be directly controlled under the leadership of the State Council.

14 March   In the cause of providing a unified leadership on financial and economic matters, the Party's Central Committee decides to establish a Financial and Economic Commission of the State Council to act as a policy-making organisation.

30 March   Deng Xiaoping gives a speech on Adherence to the Four Cardinal Principles at the Party's meeting to discuss ideological guidelines.

5–28 April   The Party's Central Committee working party proposes a policy of restructuring, reform, rectification and improvement to improve China's national economy. Li Xiannian makes an important speech at the meeting.

13 April   The Party's Central Committee and the State Council approve the report 'Several Suggestions on Improving Current Capital Construction' submitted by the leading party group of the State Construction Commission, and order its conscientious implementation.

25 May   Six departments, including the State Economic Commission and Ministry of Finance, give notice to begin experiments in reform of enterprise management at eight enterprises, including Capital Iron and Steel Plant, and Shanghai Motors in Beijing, Tianjin and Shanghai.

June   The Financial and Economic Commission of the State Council decides to found a Research Group for the study of Restructuring the Economic System, headed by Zhang Jingfu.

18 June–1 July   The second plenary session of the Seventh National People's Congress is held in Beijing. It sets a time scale of three years for improvement of the national economy under the policy of restructuring, reform, rectification and improvement. It adopts the 'Law of the People's Republic of China on Joint Ventures with Chinese and Foreign Investment', which is to come into force upon promulgation on 8 July.

28 June   The State Council approves the report made by the Ministry of Posts and Telecommunications and resolves to restructure the postal and telecommunications systems.

3 July   The State Council transmits the draft of Several Regulations related to the Development of the Commune-or-Team-managed Enterprises to the lower levels and requests that a trial be commenced. The Regulations stipulate that the newly established commune-or-team-managed enterprises should enjoy the exemption from taxation for two or three years.

8 July   Xinhua Agency reports that the State Council has approved the establishment of China International Trust and Investment Corporation (CITIC).

13 July   Five documents are issued by the State Council to all regions and departments requesting that experiments begin in a few selected enterprises. The documents include 'The Provision for Expansion of Decision-making power in State-operated Industrial Enterprises', 'The Provision for Practising the Retention of a Share of the Profits Earned by the State-run Enterprises', 'The Temporary Provisions for the Taxation of Fixed Assets of the State-operated Enterprises', 'The Temporary Provisions for Raising State-operated Enterprises' Fixed Assets Depreciation Rate and Improving the Means of Using the Depreciation Charge', and the 'Temporary Provisions for Utilizing the Credits of Circulating Funds in the State-operated Enterprises'.

Xinhua Agency reports that, from the beginning of the year, Sichuan Province has been operating, on an experimental basis, the devolution of decision-making power to one-hundred industrial enterprises throughout the province, and has met with good results.

15 July   The Central Committee approves the reports of Guangdong and Fujian Provinces; it is decided that 'a special policy and flexible measures' will be adopted in these two provinces to deal with overseas economic relations.

23 July   The State Council transmits a document, 'The Summary of a Forum on the Transformation of State Farms into an Agricultural, Industrial and Commercial Complex', and asks for trials on selected state farms.

26 July–9 August   The State Council calls a national meeting on prices and wages. The meeting decides to raise the selling prices of eight non-staple foods including pork, as well as those consumer goods that use these non-staple foods as their main raw materials. At the same time, price subsidies are extended to all staff and workers, and 40 per cent of the workforce are promoted to a higher grade.

13 August   The State Council promulgates The Provisions on Developing Foreign Trade and Increasing Foreign Exchange, stipulating that the competence of the regions and the enterprises to handle foreign trade will be strengthened; that enterprises will be permitted to retain a share of the foreign currency earned; and that preferential rates of taxation will apply to those commodities that are imported for use in export manufacture.

28 August   The State Council transmits 'The Report on the Trial Measure of Loans for Capital Construction Investments' put forward by the State Planning Commission, State Construction Commission and the Ministry of Finance. The State Council announces a trial in converting capital construction appropriation into bank loans.

28 September   The Party's fourth plenary session of the Eleventh Central Committee passed the 'Resolution on Accelerating the Development of Agriculture'.

20 November–21 December   The State Council called a national planning conference to discuss and draw up the national economic plan for 1980. The meeting also resolved to restructure the financial system. Comrade Li Xian-nian gave a talk at the meeting.

3 December   The Group Responsible for Restructuring the Economic System, under the State Council Financial Commission, suggests 'An Overall Restructuring of the System of Economic Management'. This is the first programme of its kind.

1980

16 January   Deng Xiaoping makes a speech entitled 'The Current Situation and Tasks' at a cadres' meeting called by the Party's Central

Committee. He raised the prospect of our achieving the four modernisations with Chinese characteristics within twenty years.

22 January   The State Council distributes the document 'The Trial Measures for the Retention of A Share of the Profits Earned by the State-run Industrial Enterprises, and requests trials in selected enterprises. This is a revised version of 'The Provisions of Practising the Retention of a Share of the Profits Earned by the State-run Enterprises', promulgated by the State Council in July 1979. The main revision was to specify that, rather than retaining a share of the total profits, enterprises would retain a share of basic profits plus a share of increased profits.

1 February   The State Council transmits to the lower levels 'The Temporary Provision on the System of Financial Management' stipulating the basis upon which income and expenditure between central and local authorities was to be apportioned and responsibility delegated to the different levels for their own profits and losses. The new regulations are to apply to all provinces and cities, with the exception of a small number that would adopt different measures.

9 February   The State Council issues a resolution on the restructuring of the customs management system. The old system based on local regions is to be taken under centralised management by the government in the form of a General Administration of Customs.

12 February   The 13th Meeting of the Standing Committee of the Fifth National People's Congress resolve to establish a State Council Machine-building Industrial Commission, which will assume centralised control of the machine-building industry.

24 February   The Party's Central Committee and the State Council give notice of a drive to reduced non-production expenditure and combat waste.

29 February   The State Council gives notice of a restructuring of the system of export and import commodity inspections. The Commodity Inspection Bureau under the auspices of the Ministry of Foreign Economic Relations and Trade is to be redesignated the State General Bureau of Commodity Inspection.

17 March   The Standing Committee of the Political Bureau of the Party's Central Committee resolves to establish a Central Finance and Economic Leading Group headed by Zhao Ziyang. The former Finance and Economic Commission under the State Council is to be dissolved.

1 April The State Council issues a resolution on the raising of the interest rate on urban and rural residents' fixed deposit accounts and on the Ren Min Bi deposit accounts of Chinese investors living abroad.

The State Planning Commission, The State Economic Commission and the Labour Bureau distribute the document 'Temporary Measures (Draft) Governing the Payment of Piece Work Wages in the State-run Enterprises' to the regions and departments at all levels to undergo trials where conditions permit.

25 April The Ministry of Finance resolves to reduce or waive taxation on those collective enterprises that place young people awaiting employment.

4 May Five departments, including the State Construction Commission and State Planning Commission, issue a resolution on 'Interim Provisions on Expanding the Decision-making Power of Management for the State-run Construction Enterprises'.

8 May The State Council decides to establish an Office of Structural Reforms under the State Council to take charge of drawing up the overall reform programme and coordinating all aspects of reform. Du Xingyuan is appointed director.

17 May The State Council and the Military Commission of the Central Committee of the CPC issue a resolution on the future organizational structure of the Civil Aviation Administration of China.

21 June The State Council approves and transmits the document drawn up by several departments, including the State Economic Commission, 'Interim Provisions on Tapping the Latent Power of the Industrial and Communication Enterprises' in the Cause of Renovation and Reform, and requests studies and trials.

1 July The State Council draws up interim provisions on advancing the scope of economic association.

12 July Nanjing Radio Corporation of China is established. It is the first corporation in the field of electronics to be formed jointly by the ministry-owned enterprises and regional enterprises.

21 July Xinghua News Agency reports that at present 6600 selected industrial enterprises are experimenting with the expansion of decision-making power. These enterprises account for about 16 per cent of the country's total. Their output value and profits account for 60 per cent and 70 per cent of the total respectively.

26 July The State Council promulgates two regulations: 'Rules on Registration of Joint Ventures with Chinese and Foreign Investment' and 'Regulations on Labour Management of Joint Ventures with Chinese and Foreign Investment'.

18 August Deng Xiaoping makes an important programmatic speech, 'Reform of the System of Party and the State Leadership', at an expanded meeting of the Political Bureau of the Central Committee. (The substance of the speech was agreed by the Political Bureau on 31 August.)

26 August The 15th Meeting of the Standing Committee of the 5th National People's Congress resolved to establish Special Economic Zones in Shenzhen, Zhuhai and Shantou in Guangdong Province, and in Xiamen in Fujian Province. At the same time, the meeting approved the 'Regulations on Guangdong Special Economic Zones of the People's Republic of China'. The meeting also decided to set up State Energy Resources Commission, and passed the 'Interim Regulations of Lawyers of the People's Republic of China'.

30 August–11 September The Third Meeting of the 5th National People's Congress was held in Beijing. The meeting passed the 'Income Tax Law of the People's Republic of China Concerning Joint Ventures with Chinese and Foreign Investment' and the 'Individual Income Tax Law of the People's Republic of China'; these are due to come into force following promulgation on 10 September.

2 September The State Council approves and transmits the report on experimental expansion of the decision-making power of enterprises and on future work practices. It is proposed that the enterprises whose decision-making power has been expanded may practise various kinds of retention of a share of the profits. The expansion of decision-making power will be introduced throughout the state-run enterprise sector.

8 September The Office of Structural Reforms under the State Council issued a report, 'Preliminary Suggestions Regarding Economic Restructuring', indicating possibilities for the orientation of economic restructuring and the work to be done in the near future.

27 September The Party Central Committee distributed the document 'The Matter of Further Strengthening and Perfecting the Systems of Agricultural Responsibility'. The Central Committee requested its immediate transmission so as to achieve a clear understanding of the policy in people's minds.

17 October The State Council introduce interim regulations on developing and safeguarding socialist competition. The regulations will be promulgated on 29 October.

30 October The State Council issues interim regulations on the management of foreign enterprises resident in China.

12 November The State Economic Commission, the Ministry of Finance and the People's Construction Bank of China issue a joint notice decreeing that, starting in 1981, funds arranged by the State Economic Commission and the Ministry of Finance for the Tapping of Latent Power, Renovation and Reform will switch from state allocation to bank loan.

18 November The State Council approves and transmits the report on the issuing of loans rather than allocations for capital construction projects put forward by several departments including the State Planning Commission. It is decided that, from 1981, all enterprises responsible for their own accounting and with the capacity for reimbursement will operate on the basis of capital construction loans rather than allocation.

7 December The State Council issues the 'Notice Concerning Severe Control of Prices and Rectification of Negotiated Prices'. The State General Bureau of Commodity Prices, the Ministry of Commerce, the Ministry of Grain, All-China Federation of Supply and Marketing Cooperatives and the State Administration Bureau for Industry and Commerce request the practical implementation of the Notice.

10 December The State Council approves the 'Rules for the Implementation of the Income Tax Law of the People's Republic of China Concerning Chinese–Foreign Joint Ventures' and 'Rules for the Implementation of Individual Income Tax of the People's Republic of China'. These two Documents are to be promulgated by the Ministry of Finance and to come into force on 14 December.

16–25 December The Party's Central Committee calls a working conference in Beijing. The meeting decides on further economic regulation. Deng Xiaoping gives a speech on 25 December entitled 'To Carry Out the Regulation Policy and to Pledge Stability and Unity'.

18 December The State Council promulgates the 'Interim Regulations on Foreign Exchange Control in the People's Republic of China'; this was passed on 5 December, to become effective on 1 March 1981.

1981

16 January   The State Council draws up regulations on the proper implementation of the encouragement and reward system, and declares that the indiscriminate granting of bonuses must be stopped.

21 January   The State Council promulgates 'Interim Regulations on the Imports of Technology and Equipment'.

26 January   The State Council resolves to balance revenue and expenditure, and rigorously to enforce financial management.

29 January   The State Council issues resolutions on the strengthening of credit management and on the strict control of money supply.

20 February   The Party's Central Committee and the State Council resolve to expand educational opportunities for staff and workers.

3 March   The State Council draws up regulations to strengthen the planning and management of capital construction projects and to limit their scale. Henceforth every stage of capital construction must be vetted by the Planning Commission.

6 March   The Party's Central Committee and the State Council transmit the State Agricultural Commission's 'Report on the Active Development of Diversified Undertakings', and stress that these undertakings are the key to developing a commodity economy.

1 April   The State Council approve and transmit the report 'Outlines of the Forum on Restructuring the Industrial Management System' prepared by the State Economic Commission and the Office of Structural Reforms under the State Council. The 'Outlines' suggest that the trial expansion of decision-making power should be consolidated, but that the range of selected enterprises not be enlarged. It is also recommended that the reorganisation of industrial and communications enterprises be energetically carried forward and, in the cities, the heat-treatment, electroplating, casting and forging industries be rationalised.

4 May   The State Council issues new regulations governing the commune-operated enterprises responsible for carrying out national economic policy.

20 May   Ten departments, including the State Economic Commission and the Office of Structural Reforms under the State Council, jointly issue 'Interim Provisions concerning the Expansion of Decision-making

Power in accordance with the Related Documents issued by the State Council, and Specific Enforcement Regulations on the Consolidation and Improvement of the Expansion of Decision-making Power'.

31 May The State Council issues supplementary provisions on the issue of bonuses. It is proposed that these be paid out by the responsible production unit, and that the bonus level should preferably be between one and two months' wages, and must not exceed three months.

12 June The Office of Structural Reforms under the State Council issue a 'Proposal on Economic Restructuring in the Regulating Period'.

27 June The sixth plenary session of the Eleventh Central Committee of the CPC passes the 'Resolution on Certain Historical Issues since the Founding of the Republic adopted by the Central Committee of the Communist Party of China', which points out that 'Our socialist system is still in the primary stage'.

7 July The State Council issues policy provisions on non-agricultural self-employment in cities and towns. These encourage and offer support to young people awaiting for employment to engage in self-employed enterprise by leasing or sub-contracting work to them on a small scale in the handicraft industry, repairing trade, service trade and commerce.

13 July The Party Central Committee and the State Council transmit 'Interim Provisions on The Workers Congress of the State-run Industrial Enterprises', which defines the rights of the Workers Congress.

31 July The State Council agrees to the comprehensive reform of the economic system in Changsha, Hubei Province.

8 August The State Council transmits 'Interim Provisions on the Management of the Market in Industrial Means of Production', which proposes that the surplus part of production may enter into the market to be sold and purchased freely.

17 October The Party's Central Committee and the State Council propose provisions on the free movement of people in order to re-energise the economy and solve the problem of unemployment in the cities and towns. They also propose that collective enterprises practise a variety of labour employment systems, including contract labour, temporary labour, and regular labour.

29 October The State Council issues 'Some Proposals on the Practice of the System of Economic Responsibility in Industrial Production' made by the State Economic Commission, Office of the Structural Reform under the State Council.

6 November The State Council approves the establishment of Shanghai Gaoqiao Petrochemical Corporation, which is the first large-scale cross-trade integrated complex in our country. The corporation is composed of seven factories and one research institute, and represents a significant break-through in the reform of our industrial management system.

11 November The State Council approves and transmits 'Interim Provisions on the Practice of the System of Economic Responsibility in Industrial Production', which were suggested by a forum discussing the new system. The forum was organised by seven departments, including the State Economic Commission, the Office of Structural Reform under the State Council, and the All China Federation of Trade Unions, with personnel invited from five provinces and cities including Beijing, Tianjin, Shanghai, Liaoning and Shandong.

30 November–13 December The Fourth Meeting of the Fifth National People's Congress is held in Beijing. Premier Zhao Ziyang gives a 'Report on the Work of the Government', which outlines ten new policies for economic construction. The meeting agree the 'Economic Contract Law of the People's Republic of China' and the 'Income Tax Law of the People's Republic of China Concerning Foreign Enterprises', which will come into force on 1 July 1982 and 1 January 1982 respectively.

15 December The State Construction Commission, the Ministry of Finance, the General Bureau of Labour and the People's Construction Bank of China issue 'Provisions for the Pursuit of the System of Economic Responsibility in Enterprises in the Building Trade'.

28 December The State Council approves the operation of a licensing system on the extra-plan export of eleven varieties of materials, including petroleum, coal, steel products, pig iron, non-ferrous metals, timber and grain.

31 December The State Council approves the establishment of the China Motor Industry Corporation.

1982

1 January The Party's Central Committee approves and issues 'The Summary of Minutes of the Meeting on All-China Rural Work', which proposes that rural areas adopt a variety of systems, including contracts that calculate remuneration according to quotas; specialised contracts that calculate remuneration according to output; production-related labourer contracts; production contracted to the household and to the team; all of which are socialist, collective systems of economic responsibility in production.

2 January The Party's Central Committee and the State Council issue 'Interim Provisions on the work of Factory Directors in State-run Factories, which put forward the basic principles of enterprises management – collective leadership by the Party Committee, democratic management and by staff and workers, administrative command by the factory director.

The Party Central Committee and the State Council issue a resolution on the need for overall improvement in state-run industrial enterprises.

13 January The State Council draw up management measures, for a three-year period, on the system of responsibility for the purchase, marketing and allocation of grain that is to be practised in the provinces, cities and autonomous districts.

18 January The State Council resolves that existing enterprises will pursue a drive for technological reform.

6 February The State Council issues 'Provisions on Advertisement Management', which will come into force on 1 May.

17 February The State Council approves 'Rules for the Implementation of the Income Tax Law of the People's Republic of China Concerning Foreign Enterprises', which come into effect on 12 February, the date set by the Ministry of Finance.

25 February The Office of Structural Reforms under the State Council puts forward 'The Overall Plan for Restructuring the Economic System', indicating the targets of reform and steps to be implemented.

1 March The Party's Central Committee approves and issues 'The Summary of Minutes of the Forum held by the Provinces of Guangdong and Fujian', and proposes continuation of the experimental Special Economic Zones.

2 March A report on the structural reform of the State Council, is given by Premier Zhao Ziyang to the Standing Committee of the National People's Congress, proposing the establishment of the State Commission for Restructuring the Economic System. This body will take charge of the overall plan for structural reform, while the State Economic Commission will take responsibility for implementing the restructuring of the economic system for the current year.

4 March   The speech made by Premier Zhao Ziyang in the Industrial and Communications Working Conference stresses that it is necessary for the process of restructuring the economic system to adhere to the principles of 'big plan, little liberty, great concentration and little dispersion' in order to coordinate national activities and arouse the enthusiasm of localities.

8 March   A resolution is passed by the 22nd Meeting of the Standing Committee of the National People's Congress stating that they approve in principle the State Council's structural reform plan, and give assent to the establishment of the State Commission for Restructuring the Economic System, confirming that the premier of the State Council would concurrently hold the post of director of the Commission. The Meeting also decided to dissolve the State Agricultural Commission, the Machine-building Industrial Commission, the Natural Resources Commission and the Financial and Trade Group under the State Council, and to re-establish the State Economic Commission, with expanded powers and operational scope.

16 March   The State Council issues 'Interim Provisions on the Management System of Nation-wide Specialised Corporations', and proposed that all specialised corporations should not be listed among the administrative organisations of the State Council but, rather, operate under the leadership of the departments concerned. The corporations are to have decision-making power and act as economic entities.

10 April   The State Council issues a notice regarding protectionism in the purchasing and marketing of industrial products. 'Regulations Concerning Rewards and Disciplinary Sanctions for the Staff and Workers' was issued on the same day.

17 April   The State Council approves and transmits a forum report written by the State Construction Commission and National Bureau of Urban Construction regarding the trial marketing of houses in urban areas, and requests the authority to begin selling urban houses to the staff and workers on an experimental basis.

30 April   The State Council approves the comprehensive restructuring of the economic system in Changzhou City of Jiangsu Province.

4 May   The State Council appoints Comrades Bo Yibo, Du Xingyuan, An Zhiwen and Tong Da-ling as vice-directors of the State Commission for Restructuring the Economic System, which was formally established today. The Commission has responsibility for drawing up the overall plan of reform, and for helping to coordinate the nationwide restructuring of the economic system.

The 23rd Meeting of the Standing Committee of 5th National People's Congress approves implementation of the plan to restructure the departments and commissions under the State Council. The Meeting also approves the establishment of a Ministry of Labour and Personnel.

12 May   The State Council approves the establishment of the China Shipbuilding Industry Corporation.

17 June   The State Council resolves to open up the channels of urban and rural commodity circulation, and to enable an increase in the flow of industrial products to the rural areas.

6 August   The State Council issues 'Interim Provisions on the Management of Prices' and makes it known that these provisions represent important laws and regulations in the field of prices.

9 August   The State Council issues 'Rules on the Registration of Industrial and Commercial Enterprises'.

23 August   The 24th Meeting of the Standing Committee of the 5th National People's Congress passes 'The Trademark Law of the People's Republic of China', which will come into force on 1 March 1983.

1 September   The 12th National Congress of the Communist Party of China opens today. Deng Xiaoping emphasises in his opening speech that the restructuring of the economic system is one of the important guarantees in the construction of the four modernisations. Hu Yaobang reaffirms in his political report that 'Our socialist society is still in the preliminary stage of development', and suggests a number of basic principles for the restructuring the economic system.

16 September   The State Council decides to relax the prices of 160 small commodities in order that they be regulated by the market.

Over the last ten days of the month, the State Commission for Restructuring the Economic System, the State Construction Commission, and the Ministry of Finance jointly convened a forum to discuss the system of industrial economic responsibility. Personnel from eleven provinces, cities and autonomous districts were invited to the forum.

Following discussion, the forum put forward several proposals to improve the system of industrial economic responsibility. These proposals were subsequently approved by the State Council and made known to the lower levels on 8th November.

17 October   The Party's Central Committee and the State Council give notice of a 'Report on the Rapid Development of Fresh Water Fisheries prepared by the Ministry of Agriculture, Animal Husbandry and Fisheries.

27 October   The State Council issues provisions on solving the problem of enterprises that represent a social burden.

29 October   The State Commission for Restructuring the Economic System draws up 'An Outline Report regarding the Restructuring of the Economic System in the Period of the Sixth Five-Year Plan and in 1983'.

30 November   Premier Zhao Ziyang gives a speech, 'Report on the Sixth Five-Year Plan', at the Fifth Meeting of the 5th National People's Congress.

4 December   The Fifth Meeting of the 5th National People's Congress agrees 'The Constitution of the People's Republic of China', which stipulates that the systems of economic and enterprise management should be perfected, and that various forms of socialist responsibility were to be practised.

7 December   The Party's Central Committee issues a notice regarding the restructuring of local Party and political organs. In the economically developed regions, the regional organs will be merged with those of the cities; the cities will administer the counties and their enterprises.

24 December   The State Council issues a supplementary provision on the strict control of the scale of fixed-asset investments. All self-raised funds that break through the quotas of the state's plan would have to pay 30 per cent more for natural resources and towards the funds for major communications construction.

1983

2 January   The Party's Central Committee issues a notice regarding 'Certain Problems with the Current Rural Policy', which stresses that reform of the rural economy should progress step by step in accordance with national conditions, and that the road of socialist development must have Chinese characteristics.

3 January By the end of 1982, 120 000 contract workers had been recruited from among the unemployed in the cities and towns. This was the first encouraging sign to emerge from the reform of our labour system.

20 January The State Council decides to lower the prices of chemical fibre fabrics, and at the same time to raise the prices of cotton textiles.

5 February The State Council issues 'Management Regulations applying to the Urban and Rural Fair Trades'.

8 February The Party's Central Committee and the State Council approve 'The Report of Proposals Regarding the Experiment in Comprehensive Reform to Restructure the Economic System in Chongqing City' submitted by the Sichuan Provincial Party Committee and Provincial Government. Chongqing was given separate status in the state's plan, and thus exercised its own economic management at the provincial level.

11 February The State Council approves and transmits the report submitted by the State Commission for Restructuring the Economic System and the Ministry of Commerce regarding the proposed regulations on the reform of the system of rural commodity circulation.

17 February The State Council issues a notice approving the report by the Ministry of Agriculture, Animal Husbandry and Fisheries regarding 'Regulations on the Development of the Integrated Complex of Agricultural Reclamation, Agriculture, Industry and Commerce'. The State Council asks for active support to be given to the reform of the agricultural reclamation system.

19 February The Party's Central Committee and the State Council approve the establishment of the China General Petroleum and Chemical Industry Corporation.

3 March The State Planning Commission, the State Economic Commission, the Ministry of Labour and Personnel, and the People's Construction Bank of China issue 'Proposed Measures on the Practice of the Contracted Responsibility System for Capital Construction Programmes'.

5 March   The Party's Central Committee and the State Council issue instructions regarding the development of urban and rural retail and service trades.

7 March   *The Economic Daily* reports that, according to statistics of the supply and marketing cooperatives, 613 counties (31 per cent of the total) have undertaken to carry out trials with restructured systems, and among them, 237 counties have established county-associated cooperatives.

21 March   The 10th Meeting of the Standing Committee of the Sixth National People's Congress passes 'The Economic Contract Law of the People's Republic of China concerning Foreign Nationals', which will come into force on 1 July.

25 March   The State Council assents in principle to the reform plan of the Changjiang shipping system submitted by the Ministry of Communications, and requests that it be put into practice, and then extended to other areas, before the end of 1984.

28 March   According to statistics, by the end of 1982, 2636 million industrial and commercial enterprises held business licenses, employing a total of 3198 million employees.

1 April   The State Council promulgates 'Interim Provisions on State-run Industrial Enterprises'.

The State Council approves the establishment of the China General Corporation of Non-ferrous Metals Industry.

13 April   The State Council promulgates provisions on cooperative undertakings by city and town labourers, and supplementary provisions to 'Policy Provisions concerning City and Town Non-agricultural Individual Undertakings' (promulgated in June 1981).

14 April   The State Council promulgates interim provisions on the policy towards the collective-ownership economy in cities and towns.

15 April   The State Council approves and transmits the 'Report on Wage and Bonus Problems in the Current Practice of the System of Economic Responsibility' submitted by the State Economic Commission, the Ministry of Labour and Personnel and the Ministry of Finance, and requests implementation in accordance with the report.

24 April   The State Council approves and transmits the working conference report submitted by the Ministry of Finance on the nationwide practice of replacing profits on turnover with taxation. It also approves

'Proposed Measures to Replace Profits on Turnover with Taxation in the State-run Enterprises', which has been in force since 1 January 1983.

29 April The Ministry of Finance issues 'Interim Provisions on the Levy of Income Tax on the State-run Enterprises', which stipulates that, starting from this year, income tax would be based on 55 per cent of the profits achieved by the state-run enterprises. The Ministry of Finance also draws up provisions for handling the financial affairs of the state-run industrial, communications and commercial enterprises where the changeover to taxation was in practice.

20 May The State Council issues a notice on strengthening the control of markets and prices, and requests thoroughgoing implementation in order to stabilise prices.

6 June Premier Zhao Ziyang gives a 'Report on the Work of the Government' at the First Meeting of the 5th National People's Congress. He expounds on the task of restructuring the economic system.

25 June The State Council approves and transmits a report submitted by the People's Bank of China regarding the circulating fund of the state-run enterprises, which is to be put under the bank's control. From July, the circulating fund, controlled by the state, would be replaced by a loan from the bank.

19 July The General Office of the Central Committee and General Office of the State Council transmit the report 'Some Proposals on Current Rural Scientific and Technological Work and Restructuring of the System' submitted by the Party group in the State Science and Technology Commission.

21 July The Organisation Department of the Central Committee of the CPC convenes a nationwide work forum. It is proposed that, from now on, the major tasks of organisation are to speed up the 'four modernisations', to inculcate the leading groups with the spirit of reform, to pay attention to the make-up of the 'third echelon', and to make efforts to improve the quality of the cadre ranks.

26 July The State Council promulgates provisions to check disorderly rises in the cost of the means of production, and clarifies the lines of policy demarcation.

28 July *The People's Daily* publishes 'The (Proposed) Outline of the Ideological Work for Staff and Workers in State-run Enterprises', which has been approved and transmitted by the Party's Central Committee.

8 August   The State Council promulgates 'Provisions on the Construction Engineering Reconnaisance Designing Contract' and 'Provisions on Building Instalment Contracting'.

10 August   The State Council issues a notice on rectification and strengthening of the management of allocated goods and materials.

22 August   The State Council promulgates 'Provisions on Arbitration of Economic Contract of the People's Republic of China'.

1 September   The State Council agrees to relax further the prices of 350 petty commodities.

2 September   The Second Meeting of the Standing Committee of the Fifth National People's Congress passes the revision of Articles 5, 8 and 9 'Income Tax Law of the People's Republic of China Concerning Joint Ventures with Chinese and Foreign Investment'.

5 September   The State Council resolves to introduce a national system of examination to select the leading cadres of nationwide enterprises.

17 September   The State Council resolves that the People's Bank of China should exercise the functions of a Central Bank. The new Industrial and Commercial Bank of China willl take charge of industrial and commercial credits and business deposits, which were originally managed by the People's Bank of China.

20 September   The State Council calls a meeting to discuss the improvement of enterprises under the departments concerned. The leading group suggests that the regulation work should be completed before the end of December. A checking process would follow and, if work was not up to standard, remedial action would have to be taken.

20 September   The State Council promulgates 'Rules on the Implementation of the Law of the People's Republic of China on Joint Ventures with Chinese and Foreign Investment' and 'Interim Measures on the Levy of Building Tax'.

23 September   The State Council promulgates 'Regulations on the Tobacco Monopoly'.

4 October   The State Council approves and transmits the 'Report on the Further Implementation of the Policy of "Price According to Quality" in the Manufacture of Industrial Products', which was issued by the State Price Administration and the State Economic Commission.

6 October   The Ministry of Commerce draws up 'Interim Stipulations Regarding the Practice of Overall Payment of Pensions for those Retiring from the Ministry of Commerce and Its Affiliated Organisations'.

22 November   According to a report in Xinhua News Agency, the Party's Central Committee and the State Council have issued a notice requesting the separation of government administration from commune management, and the establishment of Village Governments. It is proposed that this reform should be accomplished by the end of 1984.

8 December   The Third Meeting of the Standing Committee of 5th National People's Congress passed 'The Statistics Law of the People's Republic of China', which will come into force on 1 January 1984.

28 December   According to the resolution made by the State Council, the Industrial and Commercial Bank of China would be established on 1 January 1984.

December   According to statistics issued by the State Statistics Bureau, by the end of 1983 there were 5863 million production teams practising the system of contracted responsibility with remuneration linked to output – for 99.5 per cent of the total. Of these, 98.3 per cent (5764 million production teams) were practising the system of all-round contracts.

1984

1 January   The Party's Central Committee issues a notice on rural work for the year 1984, proposing that a continuous effort be made to stabilise and perfect the system of production responsibility. This will necessitate extending the period over which land is leased – in general in excess of fifteen years.

6 January   The State Council resolves to strengthen statistical work.

10 January   The State Council promulgates 'Interim Provisions on the Licensing of Imported Commodities'.

23 January   The State Council promulgates 'Purchasing and Marketing Regulations Applying to Industrial and Mining Products' and 'Purchasing and Marketing Regulations Applying to Agricultural Products'.

10–23 February   The State Council calls a nationwide economic working conference. The conference urges maximum effort to enhance economic performance.

1 March   The Party's Central Committee and the State Council transmit a report issued by the Ministry of Agriculture, Animal Husbandry and Fisheries and its leading Party, group 'Report on Opening up New Prospects for the Communal and Team Enterprises', and approve the redesignation of the latter as town and township enterprises. These will become the main component of the new, diversified economy, and the mainstay of agricultural production.

The Party School of the Central Committee and the State Commission for Restructuring the Economic System conduct a research class on restructuring. The forty trainees signed up for the first half-year term are mainly deputy mayors of those selected cities engaging in trials involving comprehensive reform, or those in charge of restructuring organisations in the provinces, cities and autonomous regions.

5 March   The State Council promulgates 'Cost Management Regulations for State-run Enterprises'.

12 March   The Fourth Meeting of the 6th National People's Congress passes the 'Patent Law of the People's Republic of China', which will come into force on 1 April 1985.

10 April   The State Science and Technology Commission and the State Commission for Restructuring the Economic System issue a notice on implementation of the proposed trial reform whereby the operational expenses of research-institute development are covered by the compensatory contract system, and request thoroughgoing experimentation in this area.

16 April   The State Council issues a notice on the problems of state-run enterprises granting bonuses. It stipulates that bonuses not exceeding two and half months average wages will be exempted from the bonus tax, but that the tax will be levied for the amount exceeding the limit.

4 May   The Party's Central Committee and the State Council issue a notice on 'The Summary of a Forum Held by a Number of Coastal Cities', and agree to the proposal made by the forum to open a further fourteen coastal cities, namely Dalian, Qinhuangdao, Tianjin, Yantai, Qingdao, Lianyungang, Nantong, Shanghai, Ningbo, Wenzhou, Fuzhou, Guangzhou, Zhanjiang and Beihai. These coastal cities and the four Special Economic Zones of Shenzhen, Zhujiang, Xiamen and Shantou will become the advance regions of our open-door policy.

10 May   With the approval of leading cadres of the State Council, the State Commission for Restructuring the Economic System issues

'The Summary of a Forum Discussing the Experimental work of Re-structuring the Urban Economic System'. The forum suggests that, in addition to the selected cities approved by the State Council for trying out comprehensive reform, where conditions permit, the provinces and autonomous regions may select one or two cities to add to the trial. (The forum was organised by the State Commission for Restructuring the Economic System at Changzhou, 16–25 April.)

The State Council draws up interim regulations on further expanding the decision-making power of state-run enterprises.

15 May Premier Zhao Ziyang gives a 'Report on the Work of the Government' at the Second Meeting of the 7th National People's Congress, and stresses emphatically that restructuring and opening up to the outside world would be two key factors in future economic work.

21 May The General Office of the Party's Central Committee and the General Office of the State Council issue a document approving the inclusion of Wuhan among the areas participating in the economic restructuring trials permitting the city to operate according to a separate plan.

28 June The State Council promulgates 'Interim Regulations on the Bonus Tax Levied on State-run Enterprises'. The tax will be levied on enterprises whose annual bonuses exceed two and half months at the average wage.

30 June Deng Xiaoping talks with Japanese friends on the subject of 'Constructing Socialism with Chinese Characteristics'.

11–13 July The General Office of the State Council issues successive documents giving the approval of the State Council to further trials involving economic reforms in Shenyang, Nanjing and Dalian, and the granting them the power of economic management at the provincial level, and permitting them to operate a separate plan.

14 July The State Council issues approval of the report made by the Ministry of Commerce, 'Several Problems Arising from the Current Reform of the Urban Commercial System'.

19 July The State Council approves and issues the 'Report on Improving the Circulation of Rural Commodities' prepared by the State Commission for Restructuring the Economic System, the Ministry of Commerce, and the Ministry of Agriculture, Animal Husbandry and Fisheries.

20 July The secretariat of the Central Committee of the CPC resolves to reform the system of cadre administration: to transfer administrative power over cadres to the lower levels, and thereby to restrict the scope of Central Government power over cadres.

3 August The State Council approves and issues a 'Report on the Major Effort Devoted to the Development of Industry by the Commercial Departments' put forward by the State Economic Commission, the Ministry of Commerce and the Ministry of Finance.

6 August The State Council issues a notice approving the report prepared by the Agricultural Bank of China, 'Report on the Reform of the Credit Cooperative Management System', and proposes running the credit cooperative as a genuine mass cooperative financial organisation.

31 August The State Council approves and issues a 'Report on Proposals to Restructure the Management System of the Machine-building Industry' put forward by the Ministry of Machine-building Industry, and requests its implementation.

August A book entitled *The Current Restructuring of China's Economic System*, edited by Zhou Taihe, is published this month.

7 September The State Economic Commission and the Guiding Commission for the National Examination of Cadres in Economic Management issues a report on the first batch of enterprise managers and factory directors to sit the new examination. A total of 9019 managers and directors entered the examination; the pass rate was 94.47 per cent. The two commissions also outlined certain problems that remained to be solved. The report was to be issued by the general office of the State Council on 27 September.

9 September Zhao Ziyang writes to the Standing Committee of the Political Bureau of the CPC Central Committee, putting forward 'Proposals regarding three Problems in the Restructuring of the Economic System'.

15 September The State Council approves and issues a 'Report on the Reform of the Foreign Trade System' prepared by the Ministry of Foreign Economic Relations and Trade, and insists on the necessity of separating government administration from enterprise management, and on the need to simplify the administrative organisations and transfer management power to the lower level in the course of restructuring the foreign-trade system.

18 September   The State Council draws up interim regulations on the restructuring of the management system of the house-building trade and capital construction, and requests that the investment contract responsibility system applies to all construction programmes.

The State Council approves and issues reports prepared by the Ministry of Finance: 'Report on the Second Step of the Reform Regarding the Change from Profits on Turnover to Taxation in the State-run Enterprises' and 'Trial Measures' outlined for this policy.

29 September   The Party's Central Committee and the State Council make a commitment to reassess the situation in the poor regions as soon as possible.

4 October   The State Council approves and issues a notice on the report put forward by the State Planning Commission, 'Some Temporary Regulations on the Improvement of the Planning System'.

5 October   The State Council approves and issues a report prepared by the State Planning Commission and the State Commission for Restructuring the Economic System, and grants approval to Harbin, Guangzhou and Xi'an to continue to work for their own plans, with the power of economic management at the provincial level.

11 October   The State Council approves and issues a report prepared by the Ministry of Urban and Rural Construction and Environmental Protection: 'Report on the Extension the Trial Sale of Urban Public Housing with the Aid of Subsidy'.

20 October   The Third Plenary Session of the 12th Central Committee of the CPC is convened in Beijing. The plenum unanimously passes 'The Resolution put forward by the Central Committee on the Restructuring of the Economic System'. This resolution advances the scientific thesis of the planned commodity economy, and expounds the necessity of speeding up the overall reform of the economic system. The plenum also assesses the orientation, characteristics and policies of reform. The report is a programmatic document intended to guide the restructuring process.

10 November   The State Council approves and issues a report prepared by the State Planning Commission: 'Several Proposals Regarding the Reform of Engineering Design'.

15 November   The State Council promulgates 'Interim Regulations on Tax Reductions or Exemption from Enterprise Income Tax and Industrial and Commercial Tax for the Special Economic Zones and Fourteen Coastal Cities'.

17 November The Party's Central Committee and the State Council issue a notice regarding the strict control that exists over the establishment of nationwide organisations.

3 December The Party's Central Committee and the State Council issue a resolution strictly forbidding Party and governmental institutions and Party and government cadres to engage in trade or to run enterprises.

8 December The State Council issues a notice regarding the term of office for factory directors (managers) in the state-run enterprises. This will come into effect from 1 January 1985.

15 December The State Council issues a notice allowing thirteen cities to be designated 'large cities' and to draw up their own laws and regulations when necessary in accordance with national legislation.

These thirteen cities are: Tangshan, Datong, Baotou, Dalian, Anshan, Fushun, Jilin, Qiqihar, Qingdao, Wuxi, Huainan, Luoyang and Chongqing.

December According to statistics, in 1984 every production team was practising the system of contracted responsibility with remuneration linked to output. By the end of 1984, some 58 000 small-scale publicly owned commercial firms had been granted commercial freedom in the country, and 2248 urban trade centres had been established.

1985

1 January 'Ten Policies Drawn up by the Central Committee of the CPC and the State Council Regarding Further Enlivening of the Rural Economy' are issued for enforcement. The document suggests reform of the system of unified purchase and the sale of agricultural products.

10 January The State Council draws up interim regulations on the transfer of technology and on the operation of a market in technology.

20 January The State Commission for Restructuring the Economic System organises a forum to discuss the restructuring of urban economic systems of Shandong, Shanxi, Henan, Hebei, the Interior of Mongolia, Beijing and Tianjin. The forum is held at Shijiazhuang, with the main intention of discussing Shijiazhuang's experience of comprehensive reform.

21 January The Ninth Standing Committee Meeting of the Sixth National People's Congress passes 'The Accounting Law of the People's Republic of China', which will come into force on 1 May.

31 January The State Council approves and issues a report prepared by the National Tourism Administration: 'Report on Problems Arising from the Current Reform of the Tourist Trade'.

8 February The State Council approves and issues a report prepared by the State Economic Commission, the Ministry of Finance and the People's Bank of Cina: 'Interim Regulations on the Policy of Advancing Technological Progress in the State-run Enterprises'.

The State Council promulgates the 'Interim Regulations on Retaining the Construction Tax'.

18 February The Party's Central Committee and the State Council approve and issue a report on 'The Summary of a Forum Held by the Regions of Changjiang, Zhujiang Delta, Xiamen, Zhangzhou and Quanzhou'.

26 February The State Council promulgates 'Regulations on Export and Import Duties' and 'Customs Export and Import Tax Regulations'. These will come into effect on 7 March.

6–13 March A forum to discuss nationwide trials in restructuring the urban economic system is held in Wuhan. The participants include the leading cadres of fifty-eight experimental cities that have been conducting trials involving comprehensive reform of the economic system. (The General Office of the State Council are to issue a summary of the forum of 27 March.)

7 March Deng Xiaoping gives a talk at the All-China Scientific and Technological Working Conference. He discusses two subjects: 'To Restructure the Scientific and Technological System is to Liberate Productive Forces' and 'Unity relies on Ideals and Discipline'.

13 March The Party's Central Committee's resolution on the restructuring of science and technology is issued.

14 March The State Council approves and issues a report put forward by the People's Bank of China. From 1 April, the interest rates applying to deposits and loans will be further adjusted in certain regions.

21 March The State Council promulgates regulations on the system of financial management. This involves the differentiation of taxation categories, appraisal and decision-making on income and expenditure budgets, and the assignment of responsibility to each level.

21 March   The tenth meeting of the Standing Committee of the Sixth National People's Congress passes and promulgates the 'Law of the People's Republic of China Concerning Foreign Economic Contracts', which will come into force on 1 July.

27 March   Premier Zhao Ziyang reports on the work of the government at the Third Plenary Meeting of the 6th National People's Congress. In the second part of the report, he emphatically expounds on the policy of restructuring.

2 April   The State Council promulgates 'Management Regulations of the People's Republic of China with regard to Foreign Funded Banks and Joint Venture Banks involving Chinese and Foreign Investment in the Special Economic Zones'.

10 April   The Third Plenary Meeting of the 6th National People's Congress resolves to authorise the State Council to draw up rules and regulations when necessary on reforms and on the open-door policy.

11 April   The State Council promulgates 'Interim Regulations of the People's Republic of China on Collective Enterprises' Income Tax'.

22 April   Premier Zhao Ziyang gives a talk in Wuhan on the subject of 'Making a Good Job of Urban Reform and Giving Full Play to the City's functions'.

26 April   The State Council promulgates 'Proposed Regulations on Fixed Asset Depreciation in the State-run Enterprises'.

30 April   The State Council approves and issues a report put forward by the Ministry of Railways and the State Bureau of Commodity Prices on the programme to adjust short-distance passenger rail fares and freight charges. The programme will be put into practice on 15 May.

24 May   The State Council promulgates 'Management Rules of the People's Republic of China concerning contracts for Imported Technology.

27 May   'The Resolution of the Central Committee of the CPC on the Restructuring of the Education System' is issued.

4 June   The Central Committee of the Party and the State Council issue the 'Notice on the Reform of the Wages Scales Applying to Personnel Employed by Government Organisations and Institutions'.

3 July   The State Council promulgates the revised 'Interim Regulations on the Bonus Tax Levied on State-run Enterprises'. The starting point of the levy changes from two and half months at the average wage to four months. The State Council also promulgates the 'Interim Regulations on the Tax to Regulate wages in the State-run Enterprises'.

22 July   The State Council approves and issues a report submitted by the People's Bank of China on the adjustment in deposit and fixed-asset loan interest rates.

27 July   The State Council promulgates 'Regulations on the National Treasury of the People's Republic of China'.

14 August   The State Council approves 'Interim Regulations on the Registration of Corporations'. (The document will be promulgated by the State Administration Bureau for Industry and Commerce on 25 August and come into force on the same date.)

16 August   The State Council approves and issues a 'Report on the Success of Buying and Selling Vegetables in the Cities' prepared by the Ministry of Commerce, the Ministry of Agriculture, Animal Husbandry and Fisheries. The State Council requests that great care be taken in the introduction of this reform.

24 August   The State Council promulgates 'Interim Regulations on the Bonus Tax levied on Collective Enterprises'. The bonus tax will be levied from 1985.

28 August   Deng Xiaoping gives a talk entitled 'Reform is the only way to develop China's productive forces' at a meeting with some African guests.

29 August   The State Council promulgates interim regulations on the work of auditing.

2–7 September   The China Research Institute for the Restructuring of the Economic System, the Chinese Academy of Social Sciences, and the World Bank jointly hold an International Symposium of Macroeconomic Management – called in short the 'Bashan Steamer Conference' because it is held on the Bashan Steamer sailing from Chongqing to Wuhan. The meeting discusses the theory of macroeconomic management in its application throughout the world. Relations between planning and the market are also discussed.

11 September   The State Council approves and issues 'Interim Rules on Instilling Vitality into Large- and Medium-scale State-run Enterprises', which were submitted by the State Economic Commission and the State Commission for Restructuring the Economic System.

18 September Zhao Ziyang gives a talk at the National Congress of the CPC on proposals to draw up the seventh five-year plan. It is proposed that the foundations of the new economic system should be laid in the period of the seventh five-year plan.

20 September The State Council promulgates the 'Interim Rules on the Bonus Tax Levied on Institutions', which lay down the principles of the tax levy: three months basic wages for enterprise management units, and between one and half and two months for others.

23 September The National Congress of the CPC agrees 'Suggestions on the Drawing up of the Seventh Five-year Plan for the Development of our National Economy and Development', which stipulates the fundamental principles behind the restructuring of the economic system.

24 September The State Council promulgates 'Temporary Management Measures Applying to the Wage Fund'.

30 September The State Council promulgates 'Proposed Regulations of the State Council of the People's Republic of China on Preferential Treatment for the Construction of Ports and Wharves, Involving Chinese and Foreign Investment'.

31 October The Party's Central Committee and the State Council issue a notice curbing the imposition of cash levies upon peasants.

2 November The State Council approves and issues a report submitted by the State Economic Commission: 'Report on the Problem of Organising the Production and Management of Petty Commodities'.

17 December The General Office of the State Council approve and issue a report put forward by the State Commission for Restructuring the Economic System and the State Planning Commission regarding the work of ascertaining and improving the plans of the seven cities.

1986

1 January The Party's Central Committee and the State Council issue a document on the mapping out of rural work. The document stresses the necessity of implementing policy and deepening rural economic reform. (The document is to be published in full on 22 February.)

6 January   The Secretariat of the Central Committee of the CPC call a meeting of cadres of the central organs in Beijing. Tian Jiyun gives a talk at the meeting on the current economic situation and the problems of restructuring the economic system.

7 January   The State Council promulgates 'Proposed Rules of the People's Republic of China on the Management of Banks' and 'Proposed Rules of the People's Republic of China on the Income Tax Levied on Individual Urban and Rural Industrialists and Businessmen'.

13 January   Premier Zhao Ziyang talks about the tasks of restructuring the economic system at the All-China Planning Meeting and at the All-China Economic Working Conference.

24 January   The Party's Central Committee and the State Council issue a notice on the 'Report on the Reform of Professional Status and on the Employment of Specialists'.

30 January   By the end of 1986, China had approved the establishment of 2300 joint ventures based on Chinese and Foreign investment; more than 3700 cooperative enterprises; and 120 ventures exclusively based on foreign business investment.

4 February   The Party's Central Committee and the State Council issue a notice on regulations to curb further the power of Party and government organisations, and to prevent Party and government cadres engaging in business or running certain enterprises.

7 February   The State Council approves and issues 'The Summary Minute of the Working Conference on the Special Economic Zones', and requests maximum effort to ensure their success.

3 March   Our first joint venture bank based on Chinese and foreign investment, the Xiamen International Bank, is formally founded.

8 March   The State Council approves and issues the 'Report on Advancing the Restructuring of the Industrial Management System' submitted by the Ministry of the Electronics Industry.

10–16 March   The State Council calls an all-China conference on restructuring the urban economy in Beijing. Vice-premier Wan Li presides over the opening ceremony, and Vice-premier Tian Jiyun presents an imporatnt report in the light of the current situation and the task of restructuring the economic system. On 15 March, after hearing reports from the conference, Premier Zhao Ziyang stressed that the development of lateral economic associations might achieve benefits and accelerate reform.

23 March The State Council promulgates 'Regulations on Some Problems of Further Accelerating Lateral Economic Associations'. The State Statistical Bureau, the Ministry of Finance, the People's Bank of China, the State Bureau of Supplies, the State Administrations of Industry and Commerce each draw up concrete provisional measures to deal with the problems.

25 March Premier Zhao Ziyang gives a 'Report on the Seventh Five-year Plan' at the fourth meeting of the sixth National People's Congress. In the third part of the Report, he expounds on the restructuring of the economic system that will take place during the period of the seventh Five-year plan.

The State Council issues a notice on the establishment of the Leading Group under the State Council for Studying the Plan for Restructuring the Economic System. The task of the Leading Group is to study and draw up the reform programmes and the major measures for the next two years. The Leading Group is headed by Tian Jiyun.

31 March The State Council approves and issues a notice on the practice of the contracted responsibility system in the Ministry of Railways. The programme was proposed by five departments including the State Planning Commission. The State Council requests that every department works hard to implement it.

7 April The General Office of the State Council transmits the 'Report on Doing a Good Job in the Buying and Selling of Vegetables in Cities' put forward by four departments including the Ministry of Commerce.

12 April The Fourth Meeting of the Sixth National People's Congress passes and promulgates the 'Law on Foreign Funded Enterprises' which is to come into force immediately. The meeting also approves in principle the seventh Five-year Plan (1986–1990) for Developing the National Economy and Society of the People's Republic of China'.

13 April The State Council issues a notice on exerting more control over extra-budgetary funds.

19 April The State Council promulgates temporary provisions on extending the decision-making power of the scientific and technological research institutes.

21 April   The State Council promulgates 'The Provisional Regulations on the Management of Taxation', which will come into effect on 1 July.

23 April   The State Council issues a notice on strictly limiting levies of money upon enterprises.

28 April   The State Council promulgates 'Provisional Regulations for a Levy to Provide Additional Educational Funds'.

7 May   The conference of directors of labour departments (bureaus) of all the country's provinces ends today. The conference proposes that the focal points in the restructuring of labour, wages and personnel during the period of the seventh Five-year Plan should be reform of the recruitment system and the related work of restructuring governmental organisations.

30 May   The state approves and issues a report submitted by the State Commission for Restructuring the Economic System and the Ministry of Commerce: 'Report on the Problems of Restructuring the Commercial System in 1986'.

4 June   The State Council revises and promulgates 'Regulations on Rewards for Rationalisation Proposals and Technological Innovation'.

25 June   The sixteenth meeting of the Standing Committee of the 6th National People's Congress passes 'The Regulative Law on Land'.

26 June   China gives statistical data on its urban population for the first time: the country has 324 cities with a total population of 212 million.

3 July   The State Council promulgates 'Regulations on Registered Accountants', which will come into effect on 1 October.

4 July   The State Council issues resolutions on the strengthening of administration of industrial enterprises.

5 July   Chen Muhua announces that, from 5 July, the exchange rate between Ren Min Bi and foreign currencies will be reduced by 15.8 per cent.

9 July   The State Council issues 'Regulations on Controlling the Scale of Fixed Asset Investments'.

With the agreement of the leading cadres of the State Council, the State Commission for Restructuring the Economic System and the Ministry of Labour and Personnel issue a 'Summary of a Forum to Discuss the Experimental Work of Structural Reform in some medium-sized cities'. Sixteen medium-sized cities were selected as the first batch to try out structural reform. They are: Jiangmen, Dandong, Weifang, Suzhou, Wuxi, Changzhou, Ma-an-shan, Xiamen, Shaoxing, Anyang, Luoyang, Huangshi, Hengyang, Zigong, Baoji and Tianshui. The forum was held between 15 and 20 of May in Jiangmen City.

12 July   The State Council promulgates four documents regarding regulations on reform of the labour system: 'Interim Regulations on the Practice of the Labour Contract System in State-run Enterprises', 'Interim Regulations on Recruiting workers for State-run Enterprises', Interim Regulations on Dismissing Employees Who Violate Disciplinary Codes in State-run Enterprises', and 'Interim Regulations on Insurance for Those Awaiting Jobs in State-run Enterprises'. These Regulations will be promulgated on 9 September, and will come into force on 1 October.

17 August   Xinhua News Agency reports that the People's Bank of China has announced that, from 1 August, the interest rate on deposit accounts held at special banks was adjusted.

18 August   The total number of self-employed industrialists and businessmen in both urban and rural sectors is now 17 million – one hundred times the total of ten years ago.

15 September   The State Council promulgates 'Interim Regulations on House Property Tax' and 'Interim Regulations on Vehicle and Vessel Duties'. They will come into effect on 1 October.

The Party's Central Committee and the State Council promulgate 'Working Regulations Governing Factory Directors in Publicly Owned Industrial Enterprises', 'Working Regulations Governing the Primary Organisations of the Chinese Communist Party in Publicly Owned Industrial Enterprises', and 'Regulations Governing the Workers Congress in Publicly Owned Industrial Enterprises'. The Committee also issues a notice requesting further trials of the system whereby overall responsibility is exercised by factory managers in publicly owned enterprises.

16 September   The State Commission for Restructuring the Economic System and the People's Bank of China issue a notice transmitting instructions given by leading cadres of the State Council on the trial restructuring of the financial system. In January, it was determined that five cities, Guangzhou, Chongqing, Wuhan, Shenyang and

Changzhou, would experiment with reform of the financial system. Now, seven more cities, Dalian, Dandong, Nanjing, Suzhou, Wuxi, Ningbo and Wenzhou, will join them.

20 September   The trials of the system whereby overall responsibility is exercised by the factory manager in publicly owned enterprises has made significant headway; the number of enterprises taking part is now in excess of 27 000.

25 September   The State Council promulgates 'Interim Regulations on Individual Income Tax', which will come into effect on 1 January 1987.

28 September   The sixth plenary session of the 12th Central Committee of the CPC is held in Beijing, and passes 'The Resolution of the Central Committee on the Guiding Principle of Cultural and Ideological Progress'. The resolution stresses the necessity of remaining resolute in the task of restructuring the economic system, and reiterates the theory that China's socialism is still in the primary stage.

7 October   The State Council issues a notice on the restructuring of the road and traffic-management system.

11 October   The State Council resolves to encourage investment from foreign businessmen.

15 October   The State Council resolves that Qingdao City will work to its own plan, and be granted the power of economic management at provincial level.

30 October   Xinhua News Agency reports that, according to resolutions made by the Party's Central Committee and the State Council, from next year auditing departments would practise to a greater extent an auditing system whereby factory managers were held responsible for costs.

11 November   The Party's Central Committee and the State Council issue a supplementary notice requesting implementation of the three regulations on publicly owned industrial enterprises, stressing that the factory manager, who is the head of the factory and has central authority, will play the vital role.

24 November   The General Office of the State Council issues a notice transmitting the summary of a conference that discussed the trial reform of the housing systems in five cities, Yantai, Tangshan, Bengbu,

Changzhou and Jiangmen. The conference was held on 21 October in Yantai City.

2 December The eighteenth meeting of the Standing Committee of the 6th National People's Congress passes 'The Insolvent Enterprises Law (Trial)'. The meeting also resolved to establish a State Commission on the Machine Building Industry and dissolve the Ministry of Machine Building Industry and the Ministry of the Ordnance Industry.

5 December The State Council promulgates regulations on deepening the reform of enterprises and improving their vitality, as well as regulations relating to the reform of enterprises in 1987: the further expansion of decision-making power and reduction of the tax rate applying to bonuses.

6 December The State Council calls a meeting at Qingdao to discuss reform of the management system of the five ports: Qingdao, Huangpu, Lianyungang, Yantai and Nantong.

19 December The first commodity housing foundation in the country – Shanghai Commodity Housing Foundation – is established.

1987

1 January *The People's Daily* issues a New Year message stating that restructuring of the economic system would continue in 1987.

3 January Deng Xiaoping is host to some Japanese guests, and gives a talk on 'Overcoming all Obstacles in the Way of Implementing the Reform and Open-Door Policies'.

14 January The State Council issues a notice on the further control of prices, and the need for fundamental market-price stability.

15 January The State Council approves and transmits a report made by the State Economic Commission, the Auditing Administration and the Ministry of Finance, 'Recommendations on Curbing the Imposition of Apportioned Charges on Enterprises', and requests its implementation.

16 January The Enlarged Meeting of the Political Bureau of the Central Committee of the CPC gives notice that the meeting unanimously accepted Comrade Hu Yaobang's resignation from the post of General Secretary of the Central Committee, and unanimously elected Zhao Ziyang as acting General Secretary of the Central Committee. The meeting also stressed the need to continue the drive for overall reform, and to implement policies to invigorate the domestic economy and open up to the outside world.

20 January The State Council issues regulations on further advancing reform in the scientific and technological fields, and in the scientific research and design units of large and medium-sized industrial enterprises.

22 January The nineteenth Meeting of the Standing Committee of the 6th National People's Congress passes and promulgates 'The Customs Law of the People's Republic of China', which will come into effect on 1 July.

22–25 January The All-China Working Conference on the Economy was held in Beijing. The meeting set the central task for the year: deepening reform of the enterprises, striving to increase production and make economies, and enhancing all-round economic performance.

24 January By approval of the State Council, the State Economic Information Centre was established in Beijing.

26 January With the approval of leading comrades of the State Council, the People's Bank of China and the State Commission for Restructuring the Economic System issued 'The Summary of Third Forum on the Urban Experiment in Restructuring the Finance System', and laid down the guidelines for. It decides that Guangdong will be the trial province, in addition to which the following cities would participate: Shanghai, Beijing, Tianjin, Harbin, Xi'an, Qingdao, Shijiazhuang, Lanzhou, Chengdu, Hangzhou, Changchun, Fuzhou, Weifang, and Shashi. In due course, a total of twenty-seven cities and thirteen towns formerly assigned cities (including Baoji) become participants in the experimental restructuring of the finance system.

29 January Zhao Ziyang gives an important talk at the Spring Festival mass meeting, and confirms that the overall reform policy will remain unchanged. He stresses that, since the third plenary session of the Central Committee of the CPC, there have been two fundamental stands to the line: one, adherence to the Four Cardinal Principles; two, adherence to the reform and open-door policies.

4 February With the approval of leading cadres of the State Council, the Research Group on Restructuring the Economic System under the State Council is established, headed by Comrade Tian Jiyun. The

Group will take charge of preparing and implementing the plan of next year's programme of economic restructuring. The existing body responsible for this work is automatically dissolved.

5 February Xinhua News Agency reports that The State Science and Technology Commission, the State Commission for Restructuring the Economic System, and the Office of the Leading Group in Science and Technology under the State Council has designated Shenyang as the city that will conduct trials into the restructuring of science and technology.

14 February *The People's Daily* reports that, with the approval of the State Council, the programme of restructuring the management system of China's civil aviation has already begun. The Civil Aviation Administration of China (CAAC) was no longer running the aviation enterprises directly. Six main aviation corporations were established throughout the country; they practised independent accounting and were solely responsible for their profits and losses.

26 February According to the State Statistical Bureau, Xinhua News Agency has made public the following figures. There are 74 experimental cities, including 67 engaged in comprehensive reform and 16 undergoing structural reform. Nine cities are experimenting with both: they have active economies, with a total industrial output value last year of 453.9 billion yuan, accounting for 43.4 per cent of the country's total. This represents an increase of 11.5 per cent on previous year, a little higher than the average increase across the country.

27 February Xinhua News Agency reports that, with the approval of the State Council, Ningbo City will operate its own plan, and that it will exercise the power of economic management at provincial level.

2 March The Ministry of Finance and the State Science and Technology Commission issue a notice regarding the tax on bonuses paid by scientific research institutes which came into effect on 1 January.

23 March The third issue of the periodical *China's Restructuring of the Economic System* publish statistics relating to those cities experimentally restructuring their economic systems. By the end of February, the total engaged in comprehensive reforms was 72; those trying out a single element of restructuring numbered 86.

25 March Zhao Ziyang delivers a report on the work of the government at the fifth session of the sixth National People's Congress.

27 March   The State Council promulgates 'Interim Provisions on the Management of Enterprise Bonds'.

The restructuring of the system of transportation management within the Ministry of Communications came under review. Those parts directly subordinate to the Ministry and to industrial enterprises will be transferred to the localities, and the Ministry of Communications will exercise the government functions of trade management and macro-control.

28 March   The State Council issues a notice on tightening up the management of stocks and bonds.

1 April   The State Council promulgates 'The Interim Provisions of the People's Republic of China on Land Royalties'.

2 April   The State Council issues a notice on transmitting the 'Interim Provisions Regarding the Operation of Separate Plans in Large-scale Industrial Complexes' made by the State Planning Commission.

7 April   The State Council approves 'The Measures Adopted by the Bank of China Regarding Loans to Foreign-funded Enterprises', which will be promulgated and come into force on 24 April.

8 April   The State Council resolves to give serious attention to the tax laws and to tighten up taxation procedures.

11 April   Chairman Li Xiannian appoints Li Tieying as director of the State Commission for Restructuring the Economic System, and removes Zhao Ziyang from the post.

17 April   The State Council decides to improve the system of raising funds for key construction projects in the realms of energy resources and communications. All collective enterprises and self-employed labourers who have not been levied must pay in accordance with this regulation.

22–25 April   The State Commission for Restructuring the Economic System and the Ministry of Labour and Personnel jointly convene a second forum to discuss experimental structural reform in medium-sized cities. The forum is held at Weifang in Shandong Province. The participants share experiences of reform, and put forward proposals on furthering its progress. Among the sixteen experimental cities, eight have already entered the enforcement stage; these are Dandong, Weifang, Baoji, Tianshui, Ma'anshan, Anyang, Zigong and Jiangmen.

23 April   The Office of the Research Group on Restructuring the Economic System under the State Council put forward 'Review of the Process of Restructuring the Economic System and Directions for Future Reform', which will be sent to every department for their views.

23–27 April   The State Economic Commission calls a forum in Beijing to discuss the contracted managerial responsibility system, and to study and map out the programme for introducing this system in all large and medium-scale enterprises.

3–7 May   The China Research Society for Restructuring the Economic System calls a meeting in Beijing to discuss the transformation of the macro-economic managerial system. A Japanese economist gave an introduction at the meeting, Japan's experience and the measures the country adopted in its postwar economic transformation. Both Chinese and Japanese economists discussed the ways that China might control the transformation of its economic system.

5 May   Xinhua News Agency reports that the State Commission for Reconstructuring the Economic System and the Ministry of Labour and Personnel called a forum at Qingdao to discuss the overall plan for introducing a contributory pension scheme. The participants came from the provinces, cities and autonomous regions. The meeting resolved that such a pensions scheme would be introduced throughout the country.

8 May   The State Council promulgates 'Some Regulations on Strengthening Control of the Cost of the Means of Production', and on checking unnecessary price raises, as well as curbing the high cost of collection.

10 May   The Students of Beijing University and the People's University of China come onto the streets to discuss the subject of reform; the audience amounted to some twenty thousand.

13 May   Zhao Ziyang gives an important talk at a cadres meeting. Participants include cadres in the fields of theory, propaganda, the press and the Party school. He stresses the need to concentrate on the work of forming public opinion.

21–22 May   The Propaganda Department of the Central Committee invite a number of theorists and journalists to an informal discussion on improving pro-reform propaganda and research facilities for this work.

22 May Five Departments including the State Science and Technology Commission and the State Commission for Restructuring Economic System jointly issue a document approving the selection of Nanjing, Harbin, Guangzhou and Huangshi as cities that will conduct trials into the restructuring of the Scientific and Technological Systems.

23 May The Secretariat of the Central Committee and the State Council decide to regulate the distribution of cadres in order to strengthen political–legal departments and the units responsible for economic supervision and regulation. The Organisation Department of the Central Committee and the Ministry of Labour and Personnel call a working conference on 16–20 May in Beijing to discuss the control and regulation of the cadres system.

29 May The State Council issues a notice dissolving the Chinese Corporation for the Motor Vehicle Industry, and establishing the Chinese Federation of Motor Vehicle Industries, granting it the necessary trade and administrative functions.

1 June The Propaganda Department of the Central Committee invites Comrade Gao Shangquan, the deputy director of the State Commission for Restructuring the Economic System to give a talk to the press circle of Beijing on the current situation in the restructuring process. Gao Shang-quan gave a twelve-point summary of the significant results that have been achieved during eight years of reform.

10 June The State Council approves and issues reports submitted by the State Commission for Restructuring the Economic System, the Ministry of Commerce, and the Ministry of Finance: 'Suggestions Concerning Further Restructuring of the Commercial System', and 'Suggestions Concerning Further Restructuring of the System of Supply and Marketing Cooperatives', and requests implementation in accordance with local conditions.

12 June Deng Xiaoping meets Koloshez, the member of the Presidium of the Yugoslavian Communist Alliance. He stresses that there is no alternative but to speed up the pace of reform.

23 June The twenty-first meeting of the Standing Committee of the 6th National People's Congress passes and promulgates 'The Law Applying to Technological Contracts', which will come into force on 1 November.

25 June The State Council promulgates 'Interim Provisions on the Building Construction Tax', which will come into effect on July. At the same time, 'Interim Measures for the Levy of Building Construction Tax', promulgated by the State Council in September 1983, will be repealed.

29 June Deng Xiaoping meets the former president of the United States of America, Jimmy Carter. He stresses that China's Reform and open-door policies must be accelerated.

29 June–3 July The China Association for the Restructuring of the Economic System holds its 1987 annual meeting at Changsha. The meeting agrees regulations for the Association and elects its president, vice presidents, secretaries, and other officials. An Zhiwen is elected president. Li Tieying attends the meeting and gives a talk.

1 July *The People's Daily* publishes in full an important essay, 'Reform of the Party and Government Leadership System' written by Deng Xiaoping, and carries an editorial entitled 'Schedule for Restructuring the Political System'.

4 July Deng Xiaoping, at a meeting with the president of Bangladesh, states that a faster pace of reform and opening up to the world will bring about faster development.

Deputy Premier Tian Jiyun interviews trainees of the Seventh Research Class in Restructuring the Economic System, which has jointly conducted by the Central Party School and the State Commission for Restructuring the Economic System. He stresses the need to speed reform.

6 July Xinhua News Agency reports that at the end of 1986 China's 353 cities accounted for 22.3 per cent of the country's total population.

8–12 July The State Commission for Restructuring the Economic System convenes a forum at Shenyang to discuss the restructuring of the urban economy, and in particular the document 'Review of the Restructuring of the Economic System and Directions for Future'. The meeting also discusses the problems involved in improving the contracted managerial responsibility system. Director Li Tieying presents a progress report.

16 July Deputy Premier Yao Yilin reaffirms the policy of strictly controlling self-financed capital construction investment.

28 July The State Council promulgates 'Management Regulations Governing Equipments of Publicly Owned Industrial and Communication Enterprises'.

31 July   The State Council promulgates 'Interim Regulations on Handling Labour Disputes in the State-run Enterprises', which will come into force on 15 August.

1 August   Yantai City undertakes a trial reform of its housing system by adopting measures to raise rents and issue subsidiary tickets.

5 August   Xinhua News Agency reports on the working conference held in Changchun to discuss market management throughout the country, and stresses the need for a tightening of supervision and control, and strict prohibition on the fraudulent selling of scarce commodities and major means of production.

5 August   The State Council promulgates 'Provisional Regulations on the Management of Urban and Rural-employed Industrialists and Businessmen', which will come into effect on 1 September.

7 August   The General Office of the State Council issues 'Summary of the Forum to Discuss the Reform of the Town and Township Housing Systems'. The forum was called by the Leading Group of Housing System Reform under the State Council and held in Beijing on 7–9 July. The Summary indicates that the main strands in the reform of town and township housing are: raising rents, increasing wages, and encouraging staff and workers to buy houses. In the initial stage of reform, the housing certificates issued to staff and workers were only used for paying rent.

8 August   The State Council promulgates provisional regulations on the income tax rules applying on to the salaries of foreign personnel in China. Some will pay at half the normal rate; others will be exempt. The regulations came into force on 1 August.

19 August   The State Council issues a notice modifying market regulations and strengthening price control.

20 August   The General Office of the Central Committee of the CPC and the General Office of the State Council issue a 'Report into Structural Reform in Medium-sized cities' drawn up by the Ministry of Labour and Personnel and the State Commission for Restructuring Economic System, and request its implementation.

24 August   The General Office of the State Council approve and issue a 'Report on the Continued Success of Producing Vegetables in the Cities' recommended by the Ministry of Commerce.

25–29 August The State Economic Commission, the Organisation Department, and the All-China Federation of Trade Unions jointly call a meeting to organise the factory managers' responsibility system. The meeting, held in Beijing, decides that all large and medium-scale enterprises must introduce the system this year, and that publicly owned industrial enterprises must all be operating this way by the end of 1988.

31 August The General Office of the State Council issues 'Suggestions on furthering the Reform of the Enterprises and Improving the Contracted Managerial Responsibility System'.

1 September The General Office of the State Council issues a notice on personnel in the Leading Group for Restructuring the Material System under the State Council. Zhang Jingfu is the leader.

3 September The Deputy Manager of the World Bank praises China's economic reforms as 'The most significant economic experiment in the twentieth century'.

8–12 September The State Commission for Restructuring the Economic System and the People's Bank of China jointly call a fourth forum to discuss the restructuring of the financial system. The forum, held in Dalian, studies the outline plan to extend the process of restructuring the finance system. Chen Muhua and Li Tieying address the forum.

10 September The largest Sino-foreign cooperative project to date – the Ping-su-an-tai-bao coal mine goes into production. Deputy Premier Li Peng attends the inauguration.

11 September The State Council promulgates 'Price Control Regulations', which shows that our price-control policy and supervision is on the right course. The 'Interim Regulations on Price Control', which was promulgated in 1982, is superseded.

12 September *The People's Daily* reports that the ten provinces and autonomous regions have established fourteen districts that will conduct trials in rural reform.

The State Council revises and promulgates 'Export and Import Duties Regulations'.

17 September The State Council promulgates 'Provincial Regulations on Penalization for Profiteering and Speculating'.

26 September The State Council approves the 1988 plan for restructuring the foreign trade system drawn up by the Ministry of Foreign Economic Relations and Trade. Light industry, crafts and clothing will be the first trades to be reformed.

22–29 September The All-China Planning Meeting and the All-China Working Meeting to Restructure the Economic System are held in Beijing. Deputy Premier Li Peng gives a talk at the opening ceremony. He points out that the holding of the two meetings reflects the close relation between economic development and economic restructuring. Zhao Ziyang gives a talk on 29 September, stressing the success that has been achieved in the contracted management of enterprises, in stabilising the economy, and in the control of the extra-budgetary investment programme – major tasks in the planning and restructuring of our economy. Comrades Yao Yilin and Li Tieying also address the subjects of planning and reform. The meetings contribute to the discussion on national economic planning for 1988 and the vital task of furthering the process of economic restructuring.

10 October The State Planning Commission, the Ministry of Finance, and the People's Construction Bank of China jointly issue regulations on the restructuring of the management mechanism of the state-run construction enterprises so as to promote a combination of responsibility, authority and benefits.

14 October With the approvals of the State Council and Anhui People's Government, the trial reform plan for town and township housing in Bengbu City are formally promulgated and put into practice. The major components of the trial were the raising of rents and the issuing of subsidiary tickets.

15 October Premier Zhao Ziyang meets with specialists from six countries as well as Chinese representatives to participate in the 'International Seminar on the Reform of Enterprise Mechanisms'. The Seminar was jointly held by the State Commission for Restructuring Economic System and the World Bank in Beijing from on 12–16 October. Zhao Ziyang welcomed the suggestions put forward by the foreign specialists on the subject of enterprise reform, and thought that these would be put into effect.

19 October *The People's Daily* reports that the system of economic law was gradually taking shape. In the past eight years, some five hundred laws and decrees were enacted; of these, economic legislation accounted for some 70 per cent.

20 October   The Seventh Plenary Session of the Twelfth Central Committee of the CPC was held in Beijing and issued a bulletin. The meeting approved in principle 'The Overall Plan for Restructuring the Political System', and recommended that the great proportion of the plan be included in the Report to the Thirteenth National Congress of CPC.

22 October   The State Council issues a notice on the strict curbing of price rises of agricultural products and hoarding.

25 October–1 November   The Thirteenth National Congress of the CPC is held in Beijing. Zhao Ziyang gives a report on 'The Advance along the Socialist Path with Chinese Characteristics', and outlines the fundamental policies for future economic and political restructuring. The meeting revises a number of articles in the Party constitution, and confirms that the party's enterprise committee would play a supervisory role. The meeting gives a press conference for both foreign and domestic correspondents, with Du Runsheng and Gao Shangquan answering questions on our programme of economic restructuring.

26 October   The State Council promulgates 'Regulations on the Management of Advertisements', which will come into force on December. This annuls 'Interim Regulations on the Management of Advertisements', promulgated by the State Council in February 1982.

30 October   The State Council issues a notice on the need to strengthen the work of developing the economy of the poor districts.

8 November   Xinhua News Agency reports that the pattern of our planned economy has undergone a profound change during the nine years of reform. The part of the economy that is subject to a high degree of planning has dropped to 50 per cent from the original 100 per cent. The various markets in technology, finance and labour have sprung up energetically throughout the country.

24 November   The Twenty-third meeting of the Standing Committee of the Sixth National People's Congress accepts the resignation of Comrade Zhao Ziyang from the post of premier; this will be submitted to the Seventh National People's Congress for confirmation. Comrade Li Peng will assume the role acting premier.

12 December   Acting premier Li Peng gives a talk at the All China Finance Working Conference, indicating that the key task of financial work next year will be to stabilise the economy and deepen the reform process.

16 December   The Second Meeting of the Political Bureau discusses and approves in principle the structural reform plan of the Central Committee and the State Council.

18 December   Some leading cadres of the Central Committee including Zhao Ziyang and Li Peng interview the trainees of the Eighth Research Class in Restructuring the Economic System, which was jointly conducted by the Central Party's School and the State Commission for Restructuring the Economic System. Zhao Ziyang told them that economic restructuring next year would take many forms; the focal points would be the further improvement and development of the enterprise mechanism as well as establishing the contract system in foreign trade.

30 December   The State Council holds a plenary meeting. Li Peng stresses emphatically that all departments under the State Council must perform preparatory work for structural reform, and that the key task of 1988 would be to extend reform and stabilise the economy.

December   According to data provided by the State Statistical Bureau, the state-run industrial enterprises in the 28 provinces, autonomous regions and municipalities which have practised the factory manager responsibility system account for 68 per cent of the total. Among the large and medium-scale 82 per cent have introduced the new system; of those small-scale state-run industrial enterprises that have become collectively run or that operate as leased and individually contracted enterprises, the figure is 46 per cent. More than 60 per cent of the large and medium-scale state-run commercial enterprises practise the system.

By the end of 1987, there were 6780 lateral associations above county level that had industrial enterprises as their main component; the investment funds for these enterprises reached 12.57 billion yuan. A total of 6792 commercial economic associations had an annual turnover of at least 15.5 billion yuan. In all, there are eleven enterprise groups with separate plans.

1988

1 January   *The People's Daily* carries a New Year Message 'Greet the Tenth Year Reform', stating that it is necessary to tackle the central issues in order to spur on other work.

3 January   The State Council issues a notice regarding improvement of the tripartite policy – the linking of grain, contracts and purchasing by order.

9 January   The third plenary session of the Central Political Bureau approves in principle the revision of the 'Law (Draft) of the People's Republic of China on Publicly Owned Industrial Enterprises' and recommends that it be submitted by the State Council to the Standing Committee of National People's Congress for their consideration.

11 January   The State Council promulgates 'Provisional Regulations Regarding Price Control over the Major Means of Production and Communication and Transportation Charges' and 'Provisional Measures for Unifying Limited Price Controls over Extra-Budgetary Means of Production throughout the Country'.

The State Council approves and responds to Tangshan City on the planned trial restructuring of their housing system.

11 January   The Twenty-fourth meeting of the Standing Committee of the Sixth National People's Congress made a resolution to promulgate 'The Draft Law of Enterprises', and asked for submissions.

12–17 January   The State Commission for Restructuring the Economic System calls a forum at Harbin to discuss urban trials and maps out plans for further deepening the process of urban reform.

13 January   With the approval of the State Council, the State Administration Bureau for Industry and Commerce promulgates the revision of 'The Enforcement Rules and Regulations of the Law of Trade Marks'.

14 January   The Propaganda Department of the Central Committee of the CPC and the State Commission for Restructuring the Economic System issue a notice requesting all departments to issue propaganda supporting the restructuring of the economic system by representing the practice of reform in ways that can be understood by the masses.

18 January   The General Office of the State Council transmits a notice drawn up by the State Science and Technology Commission regarding scientific and technological personnel who hold another post in their spare time.

8 February   The Political Bureau of the Central Committee of the CPC hold their fourth plenary meeting to discuss the economic situation and current work on the economy.

9–12 February An all-China forum on the enterprise contracted managerial responsibility system is held in Beijing. Acting Premier Li Peng addresses the meeting on the views of the State Council on this reform. The Council considers it to be one of the four major issues to be tackled.

12 February The results of an appraisal of China's most able economic reformers are announced. Fifteen factory managers win prizes of golden cups, while eighty-four factory managers win prizes of silver cups.

25 February The State Council issues a report drawn up by the Leading Group for Restructuring the Housing System, regarding its view of an enforcement plan to restructure the housing system in stages and in separate batches in towns and townships throughout the country, and requests that all localities push ahead with this reform.

The General Office of the State Council issues a notice based on a recommendation by the Leading Group for Restructuring the Housing System to encourage staff and workers to buy old houses.

27 February The State Council promulgates 'Interim Provisions Concerning the Contracted Managerial Responsibility System in Publicly Owned Industrial Enterprises'.

27 February The State Council approves the recommendations made by the State Commission for Restructuring the Economic System in 'The Overall Plan of Deepening Economic Restructural Reform in 1988', which will be promulgated on 19 April.

28 February The Central Committee of the Communist Party of China proposes to the Standing Committee of the National People's Congress a revision of certain articles of the Constitution: to permit the existence and development of the private economy within the scope of legal provisions; to transfer income from the land within the scope of legal provisions.

February A Collection of Plans for China's Economic Restructural Reform (1979–1987), edited by the State Commission for Restructuring the Economic System, is published by the Central Party's School Publishing House. The fourteen plans included in the book are being made known to the public for the first time.

4 March The People's Daily reports that the State Council has recently approved the report submitted by Shanghai's local government regarding the deepening of reform, speeding up the process of opening up to the outside world, and accelerating Shanghai's transformation to an export-oriented economy. The State Council gives approval to Shanghai practising the basic quota contract system, which will operate for at least five years.

4–8 March The State Council calls a meeting of the coastal areas opening up to the outside world to discuss the plans to develop their economies. The deputy premier Tian Jiyun stresses at the meeting that the key is to increase exports and earn foreign exchange. The Central Committee invites the participants of the meeting to Zhong Nan Hai to attend a forum on 7 March. The meeting stresses the urgency of the reforms, and the need to improve efficiency, and to strengthen scientific and technological services.

8 March Shanghai House Auction Shop established. This is the first house auction shop to open in China.

12 March Xinhua News Agency report, that the State Council recently mapped out a new plan for accelerating the reform of the foreign-trade system. The major measures to be carried out are the introduction of the contracted managerial responsibility system in foreign trade, the contracting of localities to turn over their foreign exchange, and introduction of economic benefits quotas.

15 March Guangdong Provincial Government announces that the State Council recently approved Guangdong Province as an experimental region to try out comprehensive reforms – to begin reform and open up to the outside world in advance of other areas.

17–19 March The State Commission for Restructuring the Economic System calls a forum in Beijing. The participants are the directors of the Commission for Restructuring the Economic System of Coastal Provinces and Cities. The meeting discusses how to promote the strategy of developing the coastal economies. Comrade Li Tieying stresses that the key is to pursue economic reform boldly.

25 March The first plenary session of the Seventh National People's Congress is held in Beijing. The acting premier Li Peng delivers a 'Report on the Work of the Government'.

2 April The results of appraisal of outstanding entrepreneurs were announced today. Twenty factory managers were honoured by the State Economic Commission.

8 April Xinhua News Agency reports that The State Council has issued a resolution on enlarging the scope of the coastal development areas to 140 cities and counties. The forward open zones will now number 288 cities and counties with an increased area of some 320 000 square kilometres, pushing the population up to 160 million. The new areas include Shenyang, Nanjing, Hangzhou, Tangshan, Dandong, Weihai and Wuzhou.

9 April The first plenary session of the National People's Congress resolves to appoint Li Peng as the premier of the State Council, and approved in principle the structural reform plan mapped out by the State Council including the dissolution of the State Economic Commission, the Ministry of Labour and Personnel, the Ministry of Coal Industry, the Ministry of Petroleum Industry, the State Commission for Machine Building Industry and others. In total, twelve ministries and commissions will be scrapped, and of nine new ones, including the Ministry of Labour, the Ministry of Personnel, the Ministry of Supplies, the Ministry of Energy Resources and the Ministry of Mechanical Electronics, established.

12 April The first plenary session of the Seventh National People's Congress agrees 'Amendments to Articles 1 and 2 of the Constitution of the People's Republic of China'. The plenary session also votes on members to the State Council. Chairman Yang Shangkun issues Order No. 2 appointing Li Peng as Director of the State Commission for Restructuring the Economic System.

13 April The first plenary session of the Seventh People's Congress is held. The session agrees the 'Law on Publicly Owned Industrial Enterprises', which will come into effect on 1 August, and the 'Law on Joint Ventures involving Chinese and Foreign Investment'. It is resolved that Hainan Province will be a Special Zone.

14 April The State Council approves and issues the summary of a forum called to discuss the further opening up of Hainan Island and the speeding up of its economic reconstruction.

17 April *The People's Daily* reports that the State Council has recently approved in principle the report submitted by Fujian Province regarding its development of an export-oriented economy. The province will undertake a number of comprehensive reforms, which will put it ahead of the field.

18 April The State Council agrees that Xiamen City will pursue its own plan, and grants it the power of economic management at the provincial level.

20 April The ninth annual meeting of the China Society of Enterprise Management is held in Beijing. The leading comrades of the Central Committee and the Central Government award prizes for excellent management to twenty outstanding entrepreneurs and ten enterprise representatives.

28 April The Central Committee of the CPC issue a notice regarding implementation of the 'Law on Publicly Owned Industrial Enterprises' and request that all levels of Party organisation and all Party members take the lead in implementing the law.

The State Council promulgates the 'Interim Regulations on the Overfunding of Enterprises'.

30 April Yao Yilin represents the Central Committee of the CPC and the State Council at the awarding of May Day prizes organised by the All-China Federation of Trades Unions. He urges the working class to live up to its traditions by actively participating in and supporting reform.

3 May The State Council issues regulations supporting investment on Hainan Island, and on the operation of a more flexible economic policy in Hainan Special Zone.

4 May The State Council issues 'Extending the Plan to Restructure the Provision of Materials' to all the lower levels.

8–12 May A meeting to discuss the restructuring of the vegetables sector in ten cities is held in Xi'an. Li Peng gives a speech on 11 May, stressing the necessity of adhering to reform, increasing production and ensuring stability in price of vegetables.

13 May *The People's Daily* reports that, from 15 May, the retail prices of pork, (beef and mutton), eggs, popular vegetables and sugar would rise, and that staff and workers would be granted a 10-yuan subsidy. It is also reported that most cities throughout the country will adopt the same measures starting in May.

12–18 May The State Commission for Restructuring the Economic System calls a forum in Luoyang to enable all enterprises groups to discuss the problems of developing and improving themselves. In all, sixty-four representatives attended.

17 May The first annual meeting of the Chinese Society for the Industrial Economy is held in Beijing. This society is a group that provides service to the industry and encourages greater macro-control.

18 May   The State Council approves the recommendations of the Ministry of Labour and the Ministry of Personnel regarding ascertainment of the employment power of foreign-funded enterprises.

19 May   Xinhua News Agency reports that the State Council has recently resolved to deal with the problems of pushing ahead with further restructuring of the scientific and technological systems, and indicates that the contracted managerial responsibility system should be a key feature.

21 May   With the approval of leading cadres of the Central Committee the Organisation Department of the Central Committee and the Ministry of Personnel jointly issue 'Recommendations on the Introduction of a Competition Mechanism and the Restructuring of the Personnel System in the Publicly Owned Industrial Enterprises', and confirm that the process of inviting applications for enterprise managers will continue.

The General Office of the State Council issue a notice regarding the resolution made by the office of premier that since the dissolution of the State Economic Commission, the guiding work of enterprise reform and management would be undertaken by the State Commission for Restructuring the Economic System.

24–27 May   The International Seminar on Macro-economic Management, jointly conducted by the Chinese Society for Study in the Restructuring of the Economic System and the Albert Foundation of Federal Germany is held in Beijing. It has met to discuss price reform. Premier Li Peng meets the German specialists on 28 May.

1 June   The Political Bureau of the Central Committee calls the ninth plenary meeting to discuss the necessity of proper resolution of problems raised during the course of reform. It is necessary to control prices, to solve the wages problem, and to establish a new economic order adapted to the socialist commodity economy. All these might be done by deeper restructuring of both the economic and political systems.

While listening to the report concerning the branch directors meeting of the People's Bank of China, Premier Li Peng states that the banks should speed up their reforms and change their ways of working as soon as possible.

3 June   Premier Li Peng issues State Council Order No. 1 on the promulgation of 'Rules of the People's Republic of China on Registration of Persons Legally Responsible for Enterprises', which will come into effect on 1 July.

5 June   Premier Li Peng issues State Council Order No. 2 on the promulgation of 'Interim Regulations on the Lease Management of Small-scale Publicly Owned Industrial Enterprises', which will come into force on 1 July.

8 June   Deputy Premier Yao Yilin gives a talk at the closing meeting called to discuss the restructuring of the Materials system, calling for the pace of reform to be accelerated. He stresses that the market in means of production must be well run, and that loopholes in the system of materials circulation must be closed so as to prevent illegal profiteering.

19 June   There has been significant reform in the investment management system. Six investment corporations are now established to take charge of operational investment in the following fields: energy resources; raw materials; communications; machinery, electricity, light industry and textiles; agriculture; and forestry.

23 June   Xinhua News Agency reports that China now has 225 000 private enterprises with 3.6 million employees and an output value accounting for 1 per cent of total national industrial output value.

24 June   The results of an appraisal of outstanding youth entrepreneurs are announced. The appraisal activities were jointly organised by the Central Committee of Communist Youth League of China and the State Commission for Restructuring the Economic System. Ten youth factory managers won the title of Outstanding Youth Entrepreneur of China, and ninety youths won the title of Outstanding Youth Factory Manager of China.

25 June   Premier Li Peng signs and issues the State Council Order No. 4 promulgating 'Interim Regulations Covering Private Enterprises', which will come into effect on 1 July.

Premier Li Peng signs and issues State Council Orders No. 5 and No. 6 promulgating 'Interim Regulations of the People's Republic of China on the Levying of Income Tax upon Private Enterprises', 'Regulations of the State Council on the Levying of Personal Income Tax on Private Enterprise Investors' respectively. These two regulations will have effect from 1988.

29 June   The functioning department of the State Council – to take charge of overall planning and control of the circulation of the means of production in the whole country.

1 July The second meeting of the Standing Committee of the Seventh National People's Congress concludes its business. Chairman Wan Li gives a talk entitled 'Advancing Reform with One Heart and One Mind, and Working Towards a New Order Based on the Socialist Commodity Economy'. He stresses the necessity of pushing through legislative work in the next five years and uniting the whole people in support of reform.

2 July Premier Li Peng talks to visitors from six Japanese press organisations about our combined wages and price reform. The State Council has set up a Commission on Prices which is drafting a medium- and long-term reform plan.

2–12 July A Working Conference on Taxation is held in Beijing. After listening to the report of the meeting, Li Peng insists that a new system of laws must be introduced to cover taxation. The meeting proposes unifying taxation on domestic income and abolishing the regulating tax levied on publicly owned enterprises.

3 July Premier Li Peng issues State Council Order No. 7 promulgating 'Regulations of the State Council on Encouraging Taiwan Compatriots' Investment'.

The State Council resolves to expand the powers of examination and approval exercised by the inland provinces, autonomous regions and cities to dealing with the inflow of foreign investment. This measure will increase the total invested to 10 million yuan from the current 5 million yuan.

7 July The China Industrial and Commercial Trust and Investment Corporation is established today. This national financial enterprise will operate a share system and conduct trials into restructuring of the financial system.

8 July China's first tendering for land use is announced in Shanghai. The Japanese Sun Corporation will take up tenure for fifty years.

12 July The regular meeting of the State Council decides that thirteen provinces and cities including Jiangsu, Liaoning, Beijing and Chongqing will begin to operate a financial contract system this year; the trial will run for three years.

12–16 July The State Commission for Restructuring the Economic System calls a forum in Beijing to discuss the contracted managerial responsibility system in enterprises. The meeting stresses that economic benefits must be enhanced so as to create conditions for price and wage reform. Li Peng and other leading comrades of the State Council interview the participants on 13 July.

15–24 July An All-China Finance Meeting was held in Beijing. On 23 July, the leading cadres of the State Council, on hearing the report, decide that we must increase receipts and retrench expenditure by every possible means so as to reduce the financial deficit. The meeting also proposes that our financial budgetary system must be thoroughly reformed, for example, by changing from the single-entry budget to the double-entry budget system, and making a clear distinction between 'meal money' and 'construction money'.

16 July The State Council holds its second plenary meeting. Premier Li Peng gives a talk on the next half-year's work, stressing the need to ensure that reform assumes the dominant role, and to work continuously to implement the policies of deepening reform and stabilising the economy.

17 July Shanghai has established twenty-seven industrial trade societies, with a further twenty in the pipeline. These societies act as bridging and information services.

21 July The General Office of the Central Committee and the General Office of the State Council issue a notice regarding the settlement of the issue involving separation of the government administration from enterprise management.

23 July *The People's Daily* reports that Beijing City is practising the optimum organisation of labour in some 160 industrial enterprises. The same system has been introduced in commercial service enterprises, sixty-seven of which have completed the experiment.

24 July *The People's Daily* reports that Hubei province has advertised for enterprise managers. Half of the total number of factory directors, managers and new employees will be engaged in this way.

25 July *The People's Daily* reports that Liaoning Province has been conducting a trial in the operation of 147 'special factories' in Shenyang, Anshan and Dandong. These factories have had success in implementing special policies and are considering wholesale reform.

With the approval of the State Council, from 28 July the price of cigarettes and quality wines will be deregulated, and thereafter be subject to the market. At the same time, the prices of some top-grade and or medium-grade cigarettes and spirits will be raised.

The Economic Daily reports that The Anshan Iron and Steel Complex is advising staff and workers to transform their consumption fund into a production fund. They have issued 980 000 share certificates worth 49 million yuan. They have also issued financial bonds worth 30 million yuan through the Anshan Jingang Trust Investment Corporation.

27 July   With the approval of leading comrades of the State Council, the State Commission for Organisational Establishment issues the 'Triple-fixed' Plan of the State Commission for Restructuring the Economic System'. The major tasks of the State Commission for Restructuring the Economic System are to draw up an overall design for restructuring the economic system of the whole country; to study and coordinate the operation of enterprise reform; and to guide the enterprises to improve their economic management. The Commission will have a general office and eleven business bureaus with three hundred cadres.

1 August   With the formal implementation of the 'Law of Enterprises', the Commission of Legislative Affairs of the National People's Congress calls a forum to promote and carry through the Enterprises Law and Bankruptcy Law.

5 August   *The People's Daily* reports that Shenyang Golden Cup Motor Vehicle Limited Company is our first large-scale industrial enterprise to issue shares. Subscriptions have amounted to 50 million yuan in less than two weeks. The company was established on the basis of sharing out the assets of the Shenyang Motor Vehicle Industrial Company.

8 August   Premier Li Peng signs and issues State Council Order No. 11 promulgating 'Interim Provisions of the People's Republic of China on Stamp Tax', which will come into force on 1 October.

The Press and Publications Administration of China notifies the State Commission for Restructuring the Economic System that they have agreed to set up a Reform Publishing House in order to serve the needs of reform and the open-door policy. It will publish mainly works and data relating to economic and political restructuring.

Xinhua News Agency reports that China has established overseas a total of 458 joint ventures, cooperatives and sole-investor enterprises. Total investment amounts to US$1.838 billion. These enterprises supply materials that are in short supply domestically, and aid the export of technological equipment and commodities.

10 August   According to the report furnished by the Ministry of Construction, at least two hundred cities in the past two or three years have established organisations for real-estate transactions. Business has been very brisk. Every city and town in the country has property to sell – totalling some 15 billion square metres and worth more than 100 billion yuan.

13 August *The People's Daily* reports that Shanghai, in establishing nine limited companies, has broken through the old mould of public ownership, and revealed an interest in composite ownership with a new kind of public majority interest.

15–17 August The Political Bureau of the Central Committee of the CPC calls its tenth plenary meeting at Beidaihe to discuss and approve in principle 'Preliminary Plan on the Reform of Prices and Wages', which will be presented to the Central Working Conference in September and to the third plenary session of the Thirteenth Central Committee meeting for consideration.

18 August With the approval of the State Council, the People's Bank of China will raise the interest rate of deposits and loans from 1 September.

22–27 August The State Commission for Restructuring the Economic System, the World Bank and the United Nations Development Programme jointly call a seminar to consult on the management of fixed-asset investment.

29 August The third meeting of the Standing Committee of the Seventh National People's Congress made some proposals after hearing the report made by deputy premier Yao Yilin regarding the primary plan for price and wage reforms.

30 August The regular meeting of the State Council resolved to exercise proper control of prices in order to stabilize the markets, following its analysis of the current situation. The meeting also decided that price reform in the coming year would be introduced more gradually than this year, and that the raising of retail commodity prices would be done more slowly than this year. The meeting instructed the banks to offer guaranteed-value deposits, the interest rate of which would, over a three-year period be high enough to protect against the effects of price rises.

The State Council issues an urgent notice on the proper handling of price changes and the need for stable markets.

2 September The Political Bureau of the Central Committee of the CPC holds a plenary meeting which approves the strengthening of ideological and political work in the enterprises.

3 September   The People's Bank of China issues an announcement that from 10 September, the banks will offer guaranteed deposits of Ren Min Bi for a period of three to eight years.

8 September   The People's Bank of China announces for the first time the subsidised rate for guaranteed-value deposits for the fourth quarter of 1988; the annual subsidised rate for deposits over three years will be 7.28 per cent.

12–24 September   The Chinese Society for Enterprise Management and the American Society of Asset Evaluation jointly conducted a 'Seminar on Enterprises Asset Evaluation'.

13–17 September   The Central Committee of the CPC calls an open consultative conference and a forum for economic specialists, to seek opinion on the draft plans for price and wage reforms. Participants of both meetings put forward concrete suggestions on improving the economic environment and furthering the process of reform.

15 September   With the approval of the State Council, the short-term restructuring plan for investment management is defined. The plan includes instituting an improved self-regulating investment mechanism, management of the construction programme by a Board of Directors or management commission, and the system of contracted responsibility to cover investment risk.

15–17 September   The State Commission for Restructuring the Economic System calls a forum in Beijing to discuss the merging of enterprises and the making up of deficits and the increasing of surpluses as contained in the document 'Some Proposals on Advancing the Merging of Enterprises'.

15–21 September   A central working conference is held in Beijing. The conference discusses the problems involved in improving the general economic environment, adjusting the economic order and extending reform, and makes a number of significant policy proposals.

16 September   While meeting Japanese visitors, Deng Xiaoping described the development of the past ten years as gratifying. He said it was time to take stock of the experience; only then can progress be made.

17–20 September   The third seminar on Structural Reform in the smaller northern cities is held in Shijiazhuang. The Seminar participants exchange experience of structural reform in their economies and the measures adopted to invigorate the enterprises. They put forward proposals for improving the work of restructuring the economy.

20 September   Shanghai has selected eighteen large and medium-scale enterprises to begin a trial in operation.

22 September   Premier Li Peng signs and issues State Council Orders No. 15 and 16 promulgating 'Interim Regulations Governing the Construction of Guest Houses, Restaurants and Hotels', and 'Interim Regulations Regarding the Taxing on Banquets' respectively.

23 September   While meeting Japanese visitors from the economic circle, Premier Li Peng confirms that China would not change the direction of its reforms.
    Deputy Premier Yao Yilin meets the Soviet Price Investigation Group, and confirms that at the present moment we are not preparing to deregulate the prices of agricultural products including grain and edible oils, or of means of production; nor are there plans to reinstate those commodity prices that we have already deregulated.

25 September   The State Council issues a notice on the examination of taxation, finance and prices.

26–30 September   The third plenary session of the Thirteenth Central Committee meeting of the CPC is held in Beijing. The session approves the policy and projections proposed by the Political Bureau for improving the general economic environment, and the extending reform. It agrees in principle 'The Primary Plan for the Reform of Prices and Wages', and the 'Notice Issued by the Central Committee of the CPC on Intensifying and Improving Ideological and Political Work in the Enterprises'.

27 September   The State Council resolves to impose further controls on currency and to stabilize finance.
    Premier Li Peng signs and issues State Council Order No. 17 promulgating 'Interim Provisions on Royalties Levied on City and Town Land'.

28 September   Xinhua News Agency reports that Xinjiang and Inner Mongolia are starting a trial system of auctioning wool.
    The State Council issues a resolution regarding the use of specialised chemical fertilizers, agricultural chemicals and sprays, which will take effect on 1 January 1989.

30 September   Premier Li Peng, at the National Day Reception, stresses that one of the most pressing needs of the reform and construction is to unify action nationally and to adhere strictly to instructions.

2 October   Xinhua News Agency reports that during the first half of 1988, 70 000 urban and rural trade markets were held, surpassing the 1956 total – hitherto the highest number in the country's history. The volume of business transacted in these markets in 1987 amounted to 115.7 billion yuan, an eight-fold increase on the figure for 1978.

3 October   The State Council gives approval to Shenzhen City to operate its own plan, and the city was granted the power of economic management at the provincial level. We now have eleven such cities.

The general office of the Central Committee of the CPC, and the general office of the State Council draw up regulations governing those who retire from Party posts and government departments engaged in trade and open-door enterprises.

While meeting with the former premier of Federal Germany, Premier Li Peng states that the direction of reform would not change, but regulations maybe issued to adjust certain measures.

The Central Committee of the Party and the State Council issue a resolution on the screening and reorganisation of companies. They request that proposals be submitted to resolve the lack of distinction between government administration and enterprise management, and between official departments and commercial dealers, as well as offering a solution to the problem of profiteering from government supplies.

5–9 October   An All-China Economic Restructuring Seminar is jointly organized in Beijing by the propaganda department of the Central Committee, the State Commission for Restructuring the Economic System, and the Chinese Academy of Social Sciences was held. The seminar reflected on the theoretical gains and breakthroughs achieved over the past decade, and advanced a number of new questions for study and discussion. The leading comrades of the Central Committee and government interview participants on 8 October.

8 October   Deputy Premier Tian Jiyun gives a talk at the Working Conference for the All-China Planning of Foreign Trade. He stresses that improving the economic environment would not affect the open-door policy.

9 October   *The People's Daily* reports that China's economy has developed steadily. By the end of June, there were 14.13 million individual entrepreneurs and merchants, employing 22.24 million workers, and producing 27.1 billion yuan.

11 October The reform of Bengbu's housing system is developing steadily. From January to September of 1988 a total of 1126 houses were sold or about to be sold. Private loans for purchasing houses require that both principal and interest be repaid within ten years.

The Party's Central Committee holds a forum for non-party members. The leaders of the Central Committee and members of the democratic parties and non-affiliated individuals engage in open discussion of national affairs. The Party leaders listen to the suggestions made to improve the economy and further the process of reform.

15 October The general office of the State Council give notice that the State Council has decided to establish a Guiding Commission for Enterprise Reform to take charge and coordinate the implementation of the Law of Enterprises, and to study the major problems arising from enterprise reform with the intention of guiding the enterprises in transforming and improving their ways of working and strengthening management. The director of the Commission is Zhang Yanning.

19–20 October The representatives of sixteen cities engaged in restructuring trials meets in Anyang City to discuss political restructuring and how to extend the experiment in structural reform to medium-sized cities. Members of the central departments concerned are invited to attend the meeting.

22–28 October The Eleventh Congress of the All-China Federation of Trade Unions is held in Beijing. The meeting proposes reforming the unions and coordinating hundreds of millions of staff members and workers to play the leading role in the course of deepening the reforms.

24 October The State Council issues a notice resolving to strengthen price management and to strictly control price rises, and establishes a nine-point charter.

26 October The Organization Department of the Central Committee and the Ministry of Personnel jointly hold an international meeting to study the civil service and the proper use of human resources.

27 October *The Economic Daily* reports that Xinjiang, Inner Mongolia and Nanjing have each recently held wool auctions. They have also established wool markets; these have been welcomed by the people. This represents a new attempt to improve the circulation of means of production.

29 October The Political Bureau of the Central Committee of the CPC holds the thirteenth plenary meeting to discuss deepening rural reform and accelerating the development of agriculture. The meeting requests that the contracted responsibility system be improved.

31 October Xinhua News Agency reports that a forum to discuss the introduction of banks in factories was held in Xiangfan City. According to data presented to the meeting, by the end of September 1988 16 per cent of industrial enterprises with budgets had set up factory banks, which were playing a significant role.

1 November Xinhua News Agency reports that, in 1989, the Ministry of Commerce will undertake four new reforms to improve the market environment: integration of meat production and marketing, the establishment of optional markets in wheat and coarse cereals, the setting up of an inter-regional wholesale trade company, and experiments with urban consumer cooperatives.

2–7 November The Party's Central Committee and the State Council call a rural working conference to stress the need for deepening rural reforms, developing agriculture and working for a bumper harvest in 1989.

3–4 November The third Sino-Japanese economic symposium is held at Beijing. The Chinese participants summarise the major achievements of our ten-year reform of the economic system.

5 November Recently, the Ministry of Personnel called a seminar in Shenyang to study and discuss reform of the personnel system in enterprises and institutions. A proposal was made to engage cadres.

7 November The International Symposium called to review China's ten-year economic reform and future prospects is held in Shenzhen. Specialists from fifteen countries and regions attend the seven-day meeting. The meeting stresses that inflation will be overcome by furthering the reform process.

8 November The fourth meeting of the Standing Committee of the Seventh National People's Congress demands that organisations at all levels work to strengthen the democratic legal system so as to ensure the smooth progress of reform and construction. The full text of the 'Administrative Procedure Law (Draft)' is promulgated and submissions are requested.

9 November The State Science and Technology Commission and the

Ministry of Finance jointly draw up regulations to govern the accounting systems of publicly owned scientific and technological units.

Xinhua News Agency reports that China's real-estate market has overseen 170 000 transactions in the past three years. These represent a total of 10 million square metres. At present, there are 275 outlets throughout the country.

10 November The symposium to discuss the restructuring of the materials system closes in Beijing. The meeting concludes that regulation of the economy is beneficial to the growth of a market in means of production.

11 November The State Council issues a resolution on the strengthening of management in the steel-product industry. Production of cold-rolled steel sheets, cold-rolled silicon steel sheets, tin-plated steel sheets, and zinc-plated steel sheets will be specially managed.

12 November Xinhua News Agency reports that the ten-year reform has brought about a tremendous and beneficial change to our countryside. A rural economy based on self-sufficiency has gradually replaced the planned commodity economy. The value of non-agricultural output now exceeds the value of agricultural output. The rate of commodity production in the agro-industrial and agricultural sectors had increased 69 per cent by 1987.

23 November *The People's Daily* reports that 3 000 enterprises in Jiling Province practise the mortgage contract system for all staff members.

24 November Shanghai Wanguo Bond Company Ltd is founded in Shanghai. The company is licensed to issue special trading bonds and conducts a financial enterprise business totally independent of the banks.

28 November–5 December An All-China Restructuring of the Economic System and All-China Planning Meeting is held in Beijing. In accordance with the spirit of the third plenary session of the Thirteenth Central Committee meeting of the CPC, the meeting discusses and maps out the 1989 plan and reform programme. Premier Li Peng talks in the closing meeting, and stresses the need to combine deepening reform and the open-door policy with improvement in the economic environment.

30 November Premier Li Peng signs and issues State Council Order No. 24 promulgating 'Provisions on Auditing', which will come into effect on 1 January 1989.

5 December   The State Taxation Bureau decides to practise a system of personal tax declarations. Individuals must declare the amount of the income earned in a given tax period. The system will start on an experimental basis in Haidian District, Beijing.

6–8 December   Five units, including the Chinese Society of Enterprise Management, jointly call a meeting in Beijing to study ways of improving the contract system.

9 December   Xinhua News Agency publishes in full 'The Notice issued by the Central Committee of the CPC regarding the Strengthening of Ideological and Political work in the Enterprises'.

The Minister of Labour Luo Gan tells the Meeting of the Directors of the Labour Bureaus that contracted workers in the state-owned enterprises now number 8.05 million. A total of 9.6 million regular workers in 26 000 state-owned enterprises are optimally deployed.

18–22 December   The commemorative meeting for the tenth anniversary of the third plenary session of the Eleventh Central Committee meeting of the CPC is held today in Beijing. Thirty proposals theses out of 191 shortlisted by the meeting are recommended by the restructuring units.

20–24 December   The 1988 annual meeting of the Chinese Society for Study into the Restructuring of the Economic System is held in Zhengzhou. The meeting discusses the current reform situation and possible ways forward. The meeting also summarizes and maps out the future work of the Society.

21–23 December   The State Commission for Restructuring the Economic System convenes a training conference at Chengdu for enterprise cadres. The conference exchanges experience of training work, and puts forward suggestions to strengthen the training of cadres.

24 December   The Political Bureau of the Central Committee holds its fourteenth meeting to discuss the international situation and foreign-relations work. The conference stresses that we can achieve lasting success internationally in the long term, and therefore must concentrate our efforts toward reform and realisation of the four modernisations.

Xinhua News Agency reports that house cooperatives have sprung up in Shanghai, Wuhan, Shenyang, Kunming and a dozen other cities. There are now twenty such cooperatives, accounting for a total of 160 000 square metres.

25 December The book '*China's Ten-Year Restructuring of Its Economic System*', edited by the State Commission for Restructuring the Economic System is published.

27 December It is reported that in order to improve the enterprise contract system, the Ministry of Finance will extend the experimental separation of taxes and profits in 1989.

29 December The fifth meeting of the Standing Committee of the Seventh National People's Congress passes the 'Law on International Standardisation', which will come into effect on 1 April 1989. The conference also passes the revised 'Law of Land Management'.

30 December The State Council calls the fourth plenary meeting to review the work of the State Council and maps out the programme for 1989. Premier Li Peng states that the current round of new regulations is to ensure a smoother process of reform and opening to the outside world.

31 December Xinhua News Agency reports that China's economic strength in 1988 has increased. The gross national product exceeded 1300 billion yuan, an increase of 11 per cent in a year. The total volume of trade should reach US$100 billion, a 21 per cent increase in a year.

Index

243